A Hindu Theology of Liberation

SUNY series in Religious Studies

Harold Coward, editor

A Hindu Theology of Liberation

Not-Two Is Not One

ANANTANAND RAMBACHAN

SUNY PRESS

Published by State University of New York Press, Albany

Printed in the United States of America

For information, contact State University of New York Press, Albany, NY
www.sunypress.edu

Production, Diane Ganeles
Marketing, Anne M. Valentine

Library of Congress Cataloging-in-Publication Data

Rambachan, Anantanand, author.
A Hindu theology of liberation : not-two is not one / Anantanand Rambachan.
pages cm. — (SUNY series in religious studies)
Includes bibliographical references and index.
ISBN 978-1-4384-5455-9 (hardcover : alk. paper)
ISBN 978-1-4384-5456-6 (pbk. : alk. paper)
ISBN 978-1-4384-5457-3 (ebook)
1. Advaita. 2. Hinduism—Social aspects. 3. Liberation theology. I. Title.

B132.A3R362 2015
294.5'17—dc23 2014007246

10 9 8 7 6 5 4 3 2 1

For my beloved teacher
Pujya Swami Dayananda Saraswati
at whose feet I studied Advaita
as a pramāṇa
for knowing myself

Contents

Abbreviations

AU	Aitareya Upaniṣad
BG	Bhagavadgītā
BU	Bṛhadāraṇyaka Upaniṣad
BS	Brahmasūtra
CU	Chāndogya Upaniṣad
ĪU	Īśa Upaniṣad
KaU	Kaṭha Upaniṣad
KeU	Kena Upaniṣad
MāU	Māṇḍūkya Upaniṣad
MU	Muṇḍaka Upaniṣad
PU	Praśna Upaniṣad
ŚvU	Śvetāśvatara Upaniṣad
TU	Taittirīya Upaniṣad
US	Upadeśasāhasrī

The letters Bh added to the abbreviations of any text (as BSBh) indicate the commentary (*bhāṣya*) of Śaṅkara. I have also included the page numbers for ease of location.

Introduction

What Is Advaita?

Advaita (lit. not-two) is the name of one of several Hindu theological traditions that are rooted in the understanding of the four Vedas (Ṛg, Sāma, Yajur, Atharva) as revealed sources of authoritative teachings. More specifically, these traditions, and especially Advaita, look to the dialogues in the last sections of the Vedas, the Upaniṣads, as the repository of the highest teachings in the scripture. For this reason, the name "Vedānta" (literally, "end of the Veda") is usually appended to Advaita. Although regarding the Upaniṣads as the primary source for its teachings, Advaita looks also to the Brahmasūtra, an aphoristic (*sūtra*) summary of the contents of the Upaniṣads attributed to Bādarāyaṇa (ca. second century BCE) and to the Bhagavadgītā.[1] These are referred to in the tradition as the three pillars or the threefold foundation (*prasthānatrayī*).

Advaita is an exegetical tradition and looks to a line of distinguished teachers for the interpretation and transmission of the tradition. These teachers constitute the historical lineage (*sampradāya*), by which this tradition is preserved and transmitted. Among these are Bādarāyaṇa, author of the Brahmasūtra; Guaḍapādācārya (ca. sixth century CE), author of a commentary in verse (*kārikā*) on the Māṇḍūkya Upaniṣad; and Śaṅkarācārya, author of commentaries (*bhāṣya*) on the Brahmasūtra, the Upaniṣads (Īśa, Kena, Kaṭha, Praśna, Māṇḍukya and *Kārikā*, Muṇḍaka, Aitareya, Bṛhadāraṇyaka, Chāndogya, and Taittirīya), and the Bhagavadgītā. Śaṅkara is regarded as the principal historical systematizer and exponent of the Advaita tradition. He developed his teaching as an interpreter of the principal Upaniṣads and wrote elaborate and influential commentaries on these texts. He regards himself as offering an exposition of the tradition according to the lineage of teachers who preceded him.

Is Advaita a Theological Tradition?

Sarvepalli Radhakrishnan (1888–1975), perhaps the most celebrated Indian philosopher of the last century, wrote of Śaṅkara, the classical systematizer and exponent of the Advaita Vedānta (Nondual) in the following words:

> The Advaitism of Śaṁkara is a system of great speculative daring and logical subtlety. Its austere intellectualism, its remorseless logic, which marches on indifferent to the hopes and beliefs, its relative freedom from theological obsessions, make it a great example of a purely philosophical scheme.[2]

Radhakrishnan adds that the philosophy of Śaṅkara "stands forth complete, needing neither a *before* nor an after. It has a self-justifying wholeness characteristic of works of art. It expounds its own presuppositions, is ruled by its own end, and holds all its elements in a stable, reasoned equipoise."[3]

Radhakrishnan's introduction to Śaṅkara is eloquent and elegant. He is the foremost among a group of distinguished Indian scholars who intentionally choose to describe Śaṅkara as a philosopher, not a theologian, and Advaita as philosophy and not theology. The reasons for this choice are many, and a detailed treatment is beyond the scope of this presentation. It reflects the influence on India, in the late nineteenth and early twentieth centuries, of the natural sciences and of the combative debates between Christianity and science. Indian scholars and religious teachers were concerned to demonstrate that the religious traditions of India, unlike the Christian tradition, were closer to the natural sciences in the content of their teachings and method. They read backward into Śaṅkara and spoke of him as having, in the words of Swami Prabhavananda, an "undogmatic, experimental approach to truth."[4] Their preference for "philosophy" over "theology" was connected also with a specific understanding of the theological method and its identity with the Christian tradition. Theology was connected with the distinctive modus operandi of Christianity. In Radhakrishnan's view, the theologian is one who takes his stand on a particular denominational basis. He is identified with a specific religious tradition, and his purpose is to systematize, expand, and defend the doctrines of that tradition. The philosopher, on the other hand, is not bound by any particular religious tradition considered to be true. Religion, in general, is the field of inquiry.

Classifying Śaṅkara as a philosopher and Advaita as "a purely philosophical scheme" was not without challenges for writers such as Radhakrishnan. There was the "small" problem of Śaṅkara's reliance on the Upaniṣads (the final section of the Vedas) and his labors to interpret and defend the teachings of these texts. Whatever else one may say about Śaṅkara, one cannot deny that he devoted himself to expounding systematically the non-dual teaching of the Upaniṣads. Why would the constructor of a "purely philosophical scheme" devote his life to exegesis of this kind? Various ingenious and creative explanations were forthcoming. Śaṅkara, according to one commentator, relied on the Upaniṣads only to show his agreement with orthodox authority.[5] Another spoke of Śaṇkara as citing scriptures only to support conclusions reached independently of the scriptures.[6] Most important of all, we see the development of a novel interpretation of the origin and nature of the scripture. The Upaniṣads are presented as the fruits of spiritual experiments into the super-physical realm that yielded the same result.[7] Even as researchers in the empirical sciences cannot afford to ignore the findings of earlier investigators, the teachings of the Upaniṣads are there to guide us, but the experiments must be repeated in order that the conclusions be tested and verified by us.[8] The culmination of these experiments is personal experience (*anubhava*), presented as a form of perception that is self-certifying.[9]

Those who are familiar with my writings know that one of the principal concerns of my work is to refute this interpretation of the significance of the scripture for Śaṅkara and to establish its centrality in his methodology of Vedānta. Śaṅkara does not understand the Upaniṣads, the final section of the Vedas, to be the fruits of experiments conducted by the ancient sages of India.

Although it made interpreters like Radhakrishnan uncomfortable, Śaṅkara clearly understood the Vedas to be a revelation from *brahman*. Radhakrishnan's view that it is difficult to find support in the writings of Śaṅkara for the view that inquiry into the Vedas is the only means to the knowledge of *brahman* is, to say the least, bewildering. There is no dearth of evidence in the commentaries of Śaṅkara to establish that he saw the Vedas as the only source of this knowledge.[10]

The distinctiveness of the Vedas as a revealed *pramāṇa* is that it consists of words. The intended meanings of these words, direct and implied, must be properly understood. In addition, these meanings must be defended against alternative interpretations originating from traditions that accept the Veda as a valid source of knowledge but read its words differently and against those who contest the meaning of the Vedas on the basis of alternative *pramāṇas*. One of the central purposes of theology and the theological method, traditionally understood, is the ascertainment and defense of the meaning of revelation. Theology aimed to resolve internal inconsistencies in the revealed source of knowledge and to demonstrate that it does not contradict knowledge derived from other *pramāṇas*. If at the heart of the theological method is a rational understanding and exposition of the meaning of revelation (*pramāṇa vicāra*), then Śaṅkara stands solidly in this tradition, and his work is theological.[11] This is a succinct justification of describing my work as a Hindu theology of liberation. My characterizations of Advaita as a theological tradition and of the method of Śaṅkara as theological do not imply identity with the methods of Christian theology. The understanding of the Vedas as a valid source of knowledge, with the requirements of having a unique subject matter (*anadhigata*) and being free from contradictions with other valid sources (*abhādita*), give a distinct character to the meaning of theology and the theological method in Advaita. These terms cannot be employed uncritically.

The Need for an Advaita Theology of Liberation

Although this work is rooted firmly in the theological resources of the Advaita tradition, it is informed also by my dialogue with and learning from other traditions where there is a longer history of reflection on liberation theology. Such opportunities for interreligious learning are a precious gift and opportunity of our times.

Liberation theology, described by one author as "the major Christian theological achievement of the twentieth century," was inspired significantly by the deliberations of the Second Vatican Council (1962–65) and especially by a summons to eliminate economic inequalities.[12] Consistent with the prophetic tradition of Judaism, the distinguishing tenet of liberation theology is "a preferential option for the poor," expressed passionately in a religiously motivated commitment to liberate the oppressed from injustice and suffering. This commitment is articulated in a comprehensive understanding of the meaning of liberation/salvation that shifts the emphasis from postmortem existence to the quality of existence in this life. Liberation is no longer narrowly construed as emancipation from suffering in a future life. Its meaning is centered also on freedom from poverty, powerlessness, and injustice in this life and world.

In contrast to the traditional emphasis on the personal and individual nature of evil, liberation theologians call attention to evil as a social phenomenon. Although recognizing the significance of personal choice and responsibility, the focus is on "systemic evil," that is, the suffering that human beings inflict on each other by unjust economic, social, and political systems. Liberation theologians call attention to the social character of human existence and to the ways in which injustice is embedded in the conventional structures of society. The implication of this emphasis is that genuine change will be achieved only through the change and transformation of such systems. The reform of individual lives will not, by itself, result in the comprehensive liberation from structural oppression.

For the liberation theologian, religion and justice are inseparable. The practice of justice in human relationships is the highest expression of the religious life. The interior life of holiness and piety must find outward expression in a passion for justice. These two dimensions of authentic spirituality mutually nourish and are incomplete without each other. Without the concern for justice, personal piety becomes obsessively self-centered. At the same time, attentiveness to and cultivation of the interior spiritual life nourish and provide the motivation for the work of justice. Justice cannot be equated with charity. The latter seeks to offer relief and care to those who are the victims of injustice. Justice seeks to change and transform the structures that cause suffering. "Charity means helping the victims. Justice asks, 'Why are there so many victims?' and then seeks to change the causes of victimization, that is, the way the system is structured."[13] One of the distinguishing marks of liberation theology is that its commitment to economic, political, and social freedom is rooted in a religious worldview in which the understanding of what it means to be human is derived from a vision of the nature of God.[14] I have benefited from the insights of discussion and my dialogue with many of its exponents.

For various reasons, some of which are considered in the main body of this work, liberation theology has received little attention from contemporary Advaita commentators and thinkers, and there is a clear need for the articulation of a comprehensive understanding of liberation rooted in this tradition.[15] The necessity for this task arises from the fact that, as in other religious traditions, there are issues of injustice that need to be addressed. Prominent among these are caste and patriarchy. It is unfortunate that in both of these areas, the argument and struggle for justice are too often disconnected from the Hindu tradition. In the case of caste oppression, many seek liberation not through engagement with Hinduism, but by conversion to other religions or even by the rejection of religion. It is instructive that the largest number of converts in India from Hindu traditions to Buddhism and Christianity come from the so-called untouchable castes, popularly referred to as the Dalits. The most famous convert, Dr. B. R. Ambedkar, felt hopeless about the possibility of social liberation through Hinduism, publicly renounced the tradition, and, with almost 3 million followers, embraced Buddhism. He was convinced that caste injustice and oppression were intrinsic to Hinduism. It is urgent therefore that we ask whether Advaita offers a justification for concern about injustice in the world and resources for addressing these.

Not-Two Is Not One

One fundamental reason for the insufficient attention among Advaita commentators to the necessity for responding to injustice in the world is the interpretation of the meaning of Advaita (not-two) as requiring a negation of the world and indifference to it. In affirming the nature of the infinite (*brahman*), for example, some Advaita interpreters minimize the significance of the world by suggesting that the knowledge of *brahman* requires and results in the disappearance of the many. The world is likened to a sense-illusion that we conjure and experience because of our ignorance. Not-two is understood, in other words, to mean the negation of the many into one. "The world," as T. M. P. Mahadevan puts it, "is but an illusory appearance in *Brahman*, even as the snake is in the rope."[16] The implication here is that when the rope is properly known, the illusory snake will no longer exist. In addition, the disappearance of the snake is a condition for truly knowing the rope. Similarly, when *brahman* is known, the world ceases to be, and *brahman* cannot be known as long as the world is experienced. After the reality of the world is denied, it is easy to deny meaning and value for its concerns. When the reality of the world is denied in this manner, it is not consistent for one to be affected by events within it. To respond to the world is to grant reality to the world; it is to treat as real that which does not, in reality, exist. Interpretations like these provide justification for world-renunciation rather than world-affirmation and have been most strongly and clearly articulated in many of the monastic and ascetic strands of the tradition. Taken to their extremes, these interpretations make it difficult to take the world seriously.

In *The Advaita Worldview: God, World and Humanity*, I contest this interpretation of Advaita.[17] I argue that too much energy has been expended in Hinduism in establishing the so-called unreality of the world and too little on seeing the world as a celebrative expression of *brahman*'s fullness, an overflow of *brahman*'s limitlessness. Its value is derived from the fact that it partakes of the nature of *brahman* even though, as a finite process, it can never fully express or limit *brahman*. Instead of focusing on interpretative strategies that seek to disconnect *brahman* from the world and thus devalue it, the tradition, I argue, should return to the meaning of those texts that emphasize *brahman*'s deliberation and intentionality before and during the process of creating. If the world can be seen positively as the outcome of the intentional creativity of *brahman*, expressing and sharing *brahman*'s nature, it does not have to be rejected, negated, or argued away. It is not necessary, I contend, to deny the reality and value of the many to affirm the infinity of the one. Not-two (*advaita*) is not to be construed simplistically as one.

In the current work, I deepen some of these arguments (Chapter 3). This theological foundation enables me to articulate an understanding of the liberated life in the world (Chapter 4) and to show that the Advaita tradition offers a holistic liberation that has implications for our economic, political, and social relationships. I do this by selecting five issues of contemporary significance (patriararchy, homophobia, anthropocentrism, childism, and caste). In each case, I try to show how the core teachings of Advaita provide a critique as well as the theological vision and normative values for their overcoming.

Structure of Text

My work is divided into two parts. Part One offers an interpretative analysis and discussion of Advaita theology. This is essential for two important reasons. First, it identifies and expounds the interpretation of the tradition to which I am committed. There are alternative understandings of the tradition, and some of these are contested in the course of my discussion. Second, this theological discussion is the ground for my effort to develop an Advaita response to the issues identified in Part Two of this work. This work of applying Advaita to the analysis of these challenges becomes meaningful in the light of the normative discussion done here. The issues treated in Part Two are not exhaustive, and others may be added easily.

I have commented on some of these issues, treated in Part Two, in earlier publications. My purpose here is to bring these discussions together in a unified discussion where I can establish the normative theological and ethical perspectives of Advaita and use these as the basis for my analysis. The Advaita resources that I bring to the analysis of each issue will be obvious to the reader. Admittedly, there is some repetition of these normative arguments, but this also gives the reader the opportunity to focus on any issue of particular interest and to grasp the gist of the analysis. There are core arguments that cannot be avoided.

Advaita is a distinctive theological tradition (*sampradāya*) with its own corpus of texts, commentaries, and teaching lineage. As a Hindu tradition, it is not isolated but exists and thrives within the larger matrix of the family of Hindu traditions and cultures. Historically, it has influenced and absorbed the influence of these traditions. This makes it impossible, in a discussion like this one, to consider Advaita apart from this wider location and setting. This will become clear to the reader, especially in the chapters constituting Part Two of this work, where topics like caste, patriarchy, and the child are considered. Advaita has been and continues to be shaped by the cultural world of Hinduism. Advaitins must recognize this fact and have an obligation and responsibility to speak critically and constructively to the Hindu tradition. This is what I attempt to do in this work.

Although the evidence and examples that I employ in Part Two are drawn from the Hindu world, the issues treated are by no means exclusive to Hindus. Patriarchy, homophobia, anthropocentrism, and castelike structures are found across religious traditions and cultures. I also do not deny the progress made in India and elsewhere to address some of these issues. My concern is not only to identify these problematic issues but, even more important, to offer an alternative normative vision, drawn particularly from the Advaita tradition, that offers the ground for their challenge and refutation. My work is an attempt to identify an Advaita locus for reflection on matters of contemporary concern. It is essential, in my view, that scholars and practitioners of all traditions be ready and willing to acknowledge the reality of injustice, past and present, in our traditions. We need to be more self-critical and less defensive and to hold our traditions accountable to their highest teachings. The gulf between religious ideal and reality is an obvious one in every tradition. Citing the injustices of other traditions does not justify or excuse those within our own. There are many, in India and elsewhere, who address these issues from outside the Hindu tradition. I do so as a committed insider, as an engaged lover of my tradition. I invite my reader to see the critical but also, more importantly, the constructive dimensions of my work.

Chapter 1 outlines the Advaita understanding of suffering (*duḥkha*). Although sharing similarities with the Buddhist tradition, Advaita gives emphasis to suffering as the expression of a profound sense of self-inadequacy, described variously by Ernest Becker as "the struggle for self-esteem" or for "limitless self-extension." Greed is a symptom rather than a cause of this condition. The sense of insignificance is centered on oneself and is not overcome by extrinsic gains of anything finite. Advaita identifies the desire for self-adequacy as the longing for the infinite (*brahman*). This desire is ultimately rooted in ignorance because *brahman* is identical with the self (*ātmā*). The enduring solution to self-inadequacy is correct understanding of one's nature.

Advaita is an exegetical theological tradition that derives it teachings from the Vedas and especially from the last sections of these texts, the Upaniṣads. It regards the Vedas as a source of valid knowledge about *brahman* and offers a reading of the meaning of these texts, along with appropriate methods for enabling the committed student to see the truth of its teachings. This clarification about the nature of the tradition is important. Without it, the significance of the texts and exegetical work that I undertake here will not be understood. Chapter 2 therefore offers a discussion of Advaita as a teaching tradition that looks to scripture as a source of knowledge, the role of the teacher, and the necessity for faith in religious inquiry.

In Chapter 3, we turn to the fundamental teachings of Advaita about human selfhood and the traditional methods of instructing about it. Advaita teaches that the human self, at its most fundamental level, is not different from the limitless *brahman* and is present identically in every being. I also argue here that interpreters of Advaita must be careful not to describe the tradition in ways that suggest a radical *brahman*-world dualism. This disconnecting of the world from *brahman* leads to its devaluation. Chapter 3 concludes with suggestion that the Upaniṣads offer us a teaching that enables us to see the world as the overflow of divine fullness and celebration and not as the outcome of ignorance (*avidyā*).

In Chapter 4, building on the theological movements in the earlier chapters, I discuss the nature of the liberated life. Advaita must be careful not to problematize the world. The tradition does not invite world-rejection, but the correction of a false understanding of self and consequently a false view of self-world relationship. The possibility of liberation in life (*jīvanmukti*) underlines this important point. Liberation is compatible with a life of engagement in the world. Liberation frees us from greed, helps us to overcome the notion of separate selfhood, and enables us to see ourselves in all beings. The liberated life is expressed in relationships infused with compassion, generosity, and self-control.

Chapter 5 discusses the phenomenon of patriarchy in the Hindu tradition. Its defining characteristic is that women are accorded status only in relation to men. It is manifested in the preference for sons, in dowry demands, in the abortion of female fetuses, and in the treatment of widows. I argue here that, from the perspective of Advaita, women have value not in instrumental relationships with men, but because they equally and identically embody *brahman*. The Advaita teaching about the unity of existence in *brahman* is the foundation of the ethical principle of non-injury (*ahiṁsā*). The oppressive practices associated with patriarchy violate this central ethical norm.

Chapter 6 offers an Advaita response to homophobia. It refutes the claim that homosexuality is a modern Western import into Hinduism by looking at ancient sources that identify three sexes. There is no evidence in these sources of hateful persecution of third-sex persons, and the language is free from hate and denigration. The worth of the human person, in Advaita, is not located in his or her sexual identity, but proceeds from the identity of the self with the infinite. Unlike other traditions, sexual identity does not debar a person from liberation (*mokṣa*), that is, life's highest goal. The path is the same for heterosexual or homosexual persons.

Chapter 7 considers Advaita resources for overcoming anthropocentrism and for fostering a more harmonious relationship between human beings and nature. Although admitting the existence of such resources, I argue here that these have not always been a prominent part of the tradition because of the predominance of interpretations that devalue nature. I return in this chapter to a reading of Advaita sources that do not require negation of the world, but a celebration of its diversity and its ontological nonduality with *brahman*. Liberation does not isolate from the world of nature, but allows for its embrace. It invites us to see the interdependent nature of existence and the necessity of mutual obligations.

Chapter 8 discusses the value of the child in Advaita. The birth of every child repeats the cosmic creative process whereby the infinite creates and enters into the created. Sacred texts describing *brahman*'s immanence make specific mention of the child, female and male. The value of the child also is obvious in the condemnation of feticide, in life-cycle rituals that promote the prenatal and postnatal well-being of the child, and in the adoration of God as child. There is no religious justification in Advaita for a preference for sons. The value of children must find expression in the provision of fundamental needs and in practices that support their flourishing.

Chapter 8 treats the subject of caste oppression. In spite of legislation that prohibits caste discrimination, and although there are progress and change, the phenomenon of untouchability persists, and many Hindus continue to define the meaning of Hindu identity over and against those who are deemed impure and unequal. We must acknowledge the injustice and oppression of caste and the ways that religion is used for its legitimatization. Advaita stands opposed to a hierarchical social system that assigns different values to human beings on the basis of exclusive notions of purity and impurity. It stands for the equal worth and dignity of every human being as embodying *brahman.*

Chapter 9, the final chapter, offers a summary of the principal conclusions and insights of this work. There is an essential theological teaching in Advaita that affirms, without compromise or exception, the identity and unity of the infinite as the self of all beings and of the universe. *Brahman* is the single ontological truth of everything, allowing us to see the world as its celebrative multiplication. Advaita refutes all assumptions of human inequality that are the basis for oppressive social institutions such as patriarchy, caste, and homophobia. It is on the side of justice.

My aims in this work are modest. Although the reader may discern the policy implications of this discussion, this is not a work about policy. It is first and foremost a work of theology that has a twofold aim. First, to offer an interpretation of the Advaita that does not trivialize the world, but establishes its value and meaning in relation to *brahman.* Second, to retrieve from this interpretation the core guiding values that we must bring to our understanding of and response to issues of contemporary concern. I am not aware of a similar systematic effort coming specifically from the Advaita tradition.

The focus on Advaita is not meant to suggest that other Hindu traditions lack resources for speaking normatively to issues of contemporary concern. These traditions have distinctive arguments to offer. I have chosen to speak from the location of Advaita because it is the place of my personal commitment and primary scholarship. I hope that other Hindu non-dual and dualistic traditions will undertake similar theological investigations and that this will stimulate a rich intra-religious conversation. In addition, I hope that this work contributes to the larger ongoing conversation on the resources of religious traditions for justice and the overcoming of oppressive structures. Hindu traditions can learn from and have much to contribute to this dialogue.

Swami Vivekananda, one of the outstanding teachers in the lineage of Advaita Vedānta, was born on January 12, 1863. His 150th birth anniversary is marked with ongoing celebrations around the world. To honor his legacy and memory, I commence each of the chapters in Part Two of this work with a brief quotation drawn from his lectures and writings.

I am grateful to Saint Olaf College for granting me leave from my teaching to complete this work. My wife, Geeta, read my manuscript with characteristic diligence and offered invaluable suggestions. Her support is a special blessing in my life.

Part One

1

The Quest for Fullness

Human Problem as Suffering

Although the description of the human problem as *duḥkha* (suffering) is prominently associated with the Buddhist tradition, this description is not unique. The characterization of the unliberated human condition as one of *duḥkha* is not unusual in the Hindu tradition. It is also an assumption of the Hindu tradition that the condition of *duḥkha* is undesirable, even unnatural, and can be overcome. One well-known Hindu prayer used often to conclude temple and home worship expresses the desirability and hope for freedom from suffering for all beings.

> *Sarve bhavantu sukhinaḥ / Sarve santu nirāmayaḥ*
> *Sarve bhadrāni paśyantu / Mā kaścit duḥkha bhāgbhavet*
>
> *May all be happy. May all be free from disease.*
> *May all know that which is good. May no one suffer.*[1]

In the famous Chāndogya Upaniṣad (Chapter 7) dialogue between the student, Nārada, and his teacher, Sanatkumāra, Nārada approached his teacher with the confession that he is in a condition of suffering (*śoka*) and requests a teaching that will take him beyond his suffering (*śokasya pāram tārayatu*).

The liberated state is represented consistently as one of freedom from *duḥkha*. Bhagavadgītā (6:23) characterizes the purpose and end of the religious life as "disassociation from association with sorrow."[2] The heaviest of sorrows, according to Bhagavadgītā (6:22), does not overwhelm the liberated person (*duḥkhena guruṇāpi vicālyate*). The liberated is strikingly described as resting happily (*sukhaṁ*) in the body, having gained a happiness that does not decay (*sukhaṁ akṣayam aśnute*).[3] This is a joy grasped by the intellect and not born of contact between the senses and their objects. It is an unending joy that has its source in the recognition of the infinite (*brahman*).[4] Knowledge of one's identity with the limitless *brahman* constitutes liberation (*mokṣa*), and the Upaniṣads repeatedly use the word *ānandam* (bliss) to describe the nature of *brahman*.[5] The teacher Yājñavalkya in the Bṛhadāraṇyaka Upaniṣad (4.3.32) speaks of *brahman* as supreme bliss and of all beings as living on a particle of this bliss. According to Nārada, in Chāndogya Upaniṣad (7.1.3), the infinite alone is bliss; there is no bliss in the finite. It is clear therefore that the Hindu tradition understands suffering to be characteristic of the unliberated human condition. It is overcome in knowing *brahman* as one's self (*ātmā*). The state of liberation is the very opposite of suffering (*duḥkha*) and is spoken of as one of unending joy (*ānandam*).

The Universal Desire for Happiness

This desire to attain happiness and to avoid suffering is universal and intrinsic to human beings. The Dalai Lama describes it as having no boundaries and as needing no justification because it is "validated by the simple fact that we naturally and correctly want this . . ."[6] Although the specific objects of desire may vary at different moments in the life of a single individual, the desire to be happy is constant. Similarly, there may be national or cultural variations regarding desirable objects and methods employed for attaining happiness. What is common in the various stages of a single life, across generations, cultures, and nationalities, is the urge to gain happiness (*sukha*) and to avoid suffering (*duḥkha*).

Swami Dayananda Saraswati, a contemporary teacher of the Advaita Vedānta tradition, distinguishes between cultivated and uncultivated desires and characterizes the desire for happiness as uncultivated or embedded in human nature.

> Thus, we find that in addition to the basic urge to survive, there seems to be another basic urge that manifests in

> the mind. It can be expressed by saying, "I want to be full, complete, adequate, fulfilled, happy, self-possessed," and so on. However one says it, it means the same thing. Unlike all cultivated desires for a specific end that one picks up in time, this one seems to come along with birth. No one has to be told that being full, happy, etc. is desirable.[7]

This uncultivated desire for fullness is the source of all transitory and culturally determined desires. The fact of it being intrinsic to human nature means also that it cannot, like transitory and cultivated desires, be given up. It will simply find expression in another form or guise. *Duḥkha,* in the Hindu tradition, is the expression of the frustration that arises from what the Dalai Lama speaks of as a natural and universal desire to be happy and our failure to fulfill this desire in a satisfactory and lasting manner. It is the consequence of not resolving the fundamental human want.

Suffering as Mortality Anxiety

Duḥkha expresses itself existentially in a number of discernible ways. One of the ways that finds repeated mention in Hindu sacred texts is anxiety over the fact of human mortality. Anxiety over mortality is a fear that is unique to a self-conscious being able to reflect on the fact of finitude. No other animal, as far as we know, is endowed with the critical self-awareness that enables contemplation of the event of death before it occurs or that allows it to ponder the meaning of life in the face of its finitude. Anxiety about death was, for cultural anthropologist Ernest Becker, the fundamental human problem. The human predicament, in his words, is "that man wants to persevere as does any animal or primitive organism; he is driven by the same craving to consume, to convert energy, and to enjoy continued existence. But man is cursed with a burden no animal has to bear: he is conscious that his own end is inevitable, that his stomach will die."[8] The tragedy of our existence is our finitude, our fear of death and our "deepest need is to be free of the anxiety of death and annihilation."[9] Drawing on the work of the Danish philosopher Soren Kierkegaard, Becker identifies the underlying human anxiety as one that results from a consciousness of our animal limits. We are self-conscious animals.

> What does it mean to be a *self-conscious* animal? The idea is ludicrous, if it is not monstrous. It means to know that one is food for worms. This is the terror: to have emerged from nothing, to have a name, consciousness of self, deep inner feelings, an excruciating inner yearning for life and self-expression—and with all this yet to die.[10]

It is possible to disagree with Becker's characterization of anxiety about death as constituting the human predicament by arguing for the priority of the desire to be happy and the fact that happiness seems to be thwarted by the reality of mortality. In other words, the threat of nonexistence adversely affects our ability to be happy. Death threatens to end and separate us from all that we associate with happiness.

Anxiety about death is at the heart of the question of Naciketas to his teacher Yama in Kaṭha Upaniṣad (1.1.20). Naciketas speaks of the doubt and uncertainty existing among human beings about existence or nonexistence after death and pleads for instruction about the truth of death. "Tell us," he asks, "of that thing about which people entertain doubt in the context of the next world and whose knowledge leads to a great result" (1.1.29).[11] Maitreyī, in the Bṛhadāraṇkaya Upaniṣad 2.4.1, turns down the offer of ample wealth in favor of an instruction for the attainment of immortality. "If indeed," Maitreyī asks her teacher and husband, Yājñavalkya, "this whole earth full of wealth be mine, shall I be immortal through that . . . What shall I do with that which will not make me immortal? Tell me, sir, of that alone which you know (to be the only means of immortality)."[12] Accumulating wealth does not resolve human anxiety about death and leaves us, as Naciketas observes in Kaṭha Upaniṣad 1.1.27, unsatisfied.

The Bhagavadgītā 13:8 speaks of death (*mṛtyu*) as suffering in a list that includes birth, death, aging, and disease. The text invites the student to see repeatedly the defect (*doṣa*) of suffering (*duḥkha*) present in all four conditions and describes such seeing or understanding as constituting wisdom. This verse requires careful exegesis because it may be read as suggesting that existence itself is suffering and that freedom from suffering necessitates freedom from existence itself. Such an interpretation, however, is questionable in a tradition like Advaita, which affirms the possibility and primacy of liberation in life (*jīvanmukti*) and not at the end of existence in the world. Liberation does not free us from existence in the world or from aging, illness, and physical death. It promises to free from the mental and emotional suffering that these conditions may occasion. As we will see more clearly later, the Advaita tradition understands ignorance (*avidyā*) to be the root of human suffering and not birth itself. *Duḥkha* is properly understood to be a characteristic of the unliberated life and not of life itself. The Hindu emphasis in the analysis of suffering is on our emotional and psychological reactions to phenomena such as aging, illness, and death and not on identifying these with suffering. We should read the reference to birth as suffering in this verse and other similar ones as typical of the pairing that we find in Hindu texts. Death presupposes birth, and birth inevitably ends in death. Freedom from death implies freedom from birth. Bhagavadgītā 2:27 stated this insight earlier: "For that which is born, death is certain, and for that which is dead, birth is certain."[13]

Suffering and the Transient Nature of Experiences

Another significant expression of *duḥkha* may be found in the transient quality of all pleasurable experiences. This is a particularly poignant manifestation of *duḥkha* because the search for pleasurable experiences is one of our primary modes of fulfilling the natural desire to be happy. Yet each experience of pleasure grants a transient satisfaction and fails us in our search for fullness and adequacy of self. The Bhagavadgītā (5:22) cautions, "Because those enjoyments that are born of contact (between the sense organs and desirable objects) are the sources of pain alone (*duḥkhayonaya*), and have a beginning and an end, Arjuna, the wise person does not revel in them."[14] Although more extensive in meaning and calling attention to the impermanence, flux, and change that characterize all reality, the Buddhist teaching on *anicca* (Sanksrit: *anitya*) certainly includes the fleeting nature of all pleasures. In the second noble truth, the Buddha associates *duḥkha* with "union with the unpleasing and separation from the pleasing." Naciketas observes in Kaṭha Upaniṣad 1.1.27 that all pleasures are ephemeral, and unrestrained indulgence wears down the senses and leaves us dissatisfied.

Krishna's teaching in the Bhagavadgītā about the transient nature of pleasure follows logically from his statement that experiences with a beginning inevitably come to an end. As a subjective experience, pleasure is associated with our own classifications of objects and persons as desirable, undesirable, or neutral and the consequent development of likes (*rāga*) and dislikes (*dveṣa)* that condition our responses. In the gain of that which we regard as desirable and which conforms to our likes, we experience pleasure. The opposite occurs in the case of the undesirable object or person. Likes and dislikes are constantly shifting, objects and persons change, and, as Naciketas observed, the instruments of enjoyment decline and wane. Pleasures turn out to be capricious, leaving us wanting and incomplete. Understanding the fickle nature of pleasures leads to the state of informed detachment, quite different from a self-denial that is based on fear or the rejection of pleasures. It is described in Bhagavadgītā 2:64 as a state of freedom and tranquility that results from not coating objects in the world with subjective values based on likes (*rāga*) and dislikes (*dveṣa*) and thinking that such values are intrinsic to these objects. "One whose mind is controlled, moving in the world of objects, with sense organs that are under his or her control, free from likes and dislikes, attains tranquility."[15]

Suffering as the Experience of Inadequacy

Anxieties about the hovering presence of death and the fleeting nature of pleasure are well-recognized forms of *duḥkha*. Less tangible, but no less real, is what Becker refers to as the "ache of cosmic specialness."[16] Describing it also as "the struggle for self-esteem" and for "limitless self-extension," Becker notes its presence from earliest childhood and its reflection of the basic human condition. "[I]t is not that that children are vicious, selfish or domineering. It is that they so openly express man's tragic destiny: he must desperately justify himself as an object of primary value; he must stand out, be a hero, make the biggest possible contribution to world life, show that he *counts* more than anything or anyone else."[17]

It is a yearning to stand out, to be "an object of primary value," the "one in creation." It is at heart a desire for meaning, a need to believe that what we do is "truly heroic, timeless, and supremely meaningful." We may argue that what Becker characterizes as the struggle for self-esteem or as the desire to enjoy primary value reveals a fundamental experience of self-lack, self-insufficiency, or inadequacy. It is the nagging consciousness of oneself as an incomplete being and the inner turmoil this generates. Positively, the feeling of insecurity manifests in a continuous seeking for security through the pursuit of different ends.

There are encounters in the Upaniṣads that exemplify the anxieties about death and the transiency of pleasure.[18] Perhaps the one that most eloquently describes the experience of *duḥkha* as the absence of meaning involves Nārada in the Chāndogya Upaniṣad (Chapter 7). Nārada wanted instruction from his teacher Sanatkumāra, but the teacher requested that he first describe the various intellectual disciplines that he had studied and mastered. Nārada provided an exhaustive list that included sacred texts, grammar, ritual, mathematics, logic, ethics, war, science, astronomy, and the arts! At the end of it all, Nārada confessed, "Here I am sir, a man full of sorrow. Please, sir, take me across to the other side of sorrow."[19] Nārada's sorrow, in Becker's terms, was the "failure to find a meaning for his life, some kind of larger scheme into which he fits. . . . It is the expression of the will to live, the burning desire of the creature to count, to make a difference on the planet because he has lived, has emerged on it, and has worked, suffered and died."[20]

Inadequacy and the Multiplication of Desires

The urge to overcome the gnawing sense of self-inadequacy and to achieve fullness of being finds expression in multifarious desires. Among the prominent of these are the desires for wealth, fame, and power. The insatiable quest for wealth, beyond the decent satisfaction of one's needs, is explicable by the fact that wealth acquisition is a culturally acceptable way of seeking to add self-value and to overcome the sense of lack in oneself. Material acquisitions enable us to entertain thoughts of fullness of self and, in Becker's terms, "cosmic specialness." The same is true of our modern preoccupation with the gain of fame. The gain of fame, however momentary, is one of the widely accepted aspirations of contemporary culture. Modern technologies of communicating and receiving information offer new possibilities for pursuing this goal. Anonymity seems to be equated today with insignificance and lack of self-worth. The pursuit of wealth, already mentioned, often has fame as its objective, based on the assumption that persons of wealth are admired and that most of us aspire to become like them. The thought of being admired by others allows the wealthy or famous person to own him- or herself as a being of value. Wealth or fame itself does not confer adequacy or add tangibly to one's significance. Because these are culturally approved and valued pursuits, their gain enables a human being to entertain a thought of self-worth and to overcome, however temporarily, a sense of insignificance and to become acceptable to oneself. It is, in other words, the thought that matters. Bṛhadāraṇkaya Upaniṣad 2.4.5 states this truth beautifully in its famous dictum "All things become dear for one's own sake (*ātmanastu kāmāya sarvam priyam bhavati*)." Fame is sought for the purpose of self-acceptance. One confers value upon oneself indirectly through the approval of others.

What has been said of wealth and fame may also be said of the thirst for power. When it is not sought or used for the purpose of alleviating suffering, it becomes what Becker understands as another element in the cultural hero system to make us believe that we have ultimate worth. The Bhagavadgītā 16:13–15 describes well the attitude of searching for security of self through wealth, fame, and power and the thought process involved.

> Today, this is gained by me. I will gain this (also) which is pleasing to the mind. This (much) wealth I have; this wealth also I will have later.
>
> This enemy is destroyed by me and I will destroy others also; I am the ruler; I am the enjoyer; I am successful, powerful, and happy.

> Those who are totally deluded due to lack of discrimination say, "I have wealth. I was born in a very good family. Who else is equal to me? I will perform rituals. I will give. I will enjoy."[21]

What the Bhagavadgītā offers us here is a composite picture of the thought process of one who searches to overcome his sense of limitation by the acquisition of wealth, fame, and power and who is driven by the need to stand out from everyone else ("Who else is equal to me?"). It is the search for self-importance that is pursued by favorably comparing oneself to others who are regarded as inadequate. "And it is only by contrasting and comparing himself to *like* organisms, to his fellow men, that he can judge if he has some extra claim to importance. Obviously, it is not very convincing about one's ultimate worth to be better than a lobster, or even a fox; but to outshine 'that fellow sitting over there, the one with the black eyes'—now that is something that carries the conviction of ultimacy."[22]

The Persistence of Inadequacy

The tragic nature of the quest for self-acceptance and self-value through pursuits such as pleasure, wealth, fame, and power, as attested in the experiences of human beings across cultures and times, is that such gains consistently fail to satisfy and leave us wanting. There are many reasons for this. First, the problem of inadequacy is a notional one centered on oneself. It does not arise because of any gain or any loss and is not resolved, therefore, as a consequence of any gain or loss such as wealth, fame, or power. One is in search of self-adequacy and not in any of these as ends in themselves. Because the problem of self-inadequacy is not caused by the loss of wealth, fame, or power, the addition of these cannot be the solution. Huston Smith made this argument in different words when he wrote, "While it is not true to say that men cannot get enough money, fame and power, it is true to say that men cannot get enough of these things when they want them greedily, when they make them the supreme forces of their lives.

These are not the things men really want, and man can never get enough of what he does not really want."[23] Our intrinsic existential problem of inner lack will not be resolved by the addition of anything extrinsic to the self.

Second, as noted by Becker, we strive for self-value by comparing and contrasting ourselves with others. What this implies, of course, is that any value attributed to oneself though gains such as wealth, fame, and power is dependent on others enjoying less or on the unequal distribution of these goods. When these things are sought for one's fullness of being, one can never have enough because the value of what one gains is always relative to others' accomplishments. One lives in perpetual anxiety of losing self-value because of the gains of another. We become participants in a race without a finish and without any hope of fullness and enter into a relationship of psychic competition with others. The consequence is the ubiquitousness of envy, described by Becker as "the signal of danger that the organism sends to itself when a shadow is being cast over it, when it is threatened with being diminished."[24] Although the transient worth of these gains is certainly connected with their relative character, it also is the outcome of the wider truth of change that affects everything finite. All gains originating in time are subject to time and hence change and uncertainty.

The fundamental human predicament, as understood in Advaita, is that of a self-conscious being experiencing a profound sense of inner lack and insignificance and discovering that culturally approved gains such as pleasure, wealth, fame, and power do not resolve this emptiness. Wanting persists in spite of all gains. Every finite gain provides a momentary satisfaction, fleetingly removing our sense of want but leaving it to return with nagging insistence. Want is the ever-active incubator and source of multifarious desires. Some of these desires are focused on gaining ends not already possessed (*pravṛtti*), and others take the form of striving to eliminate what one perceives to be the sources of unhappiness (*nivṛtti*). Both kinds of desires and the appropriate actions for their achievement do not liberate from persisting want. Not recognizing this predicament and hoping that the next desire will lead to lasting freedom from want, we become victims of greed, an insatiable condition of always wanting more. Swami Dayananda summarizes the human predicament succinctly:

> Any gain from change also always involves a loss. When one gains something, there may be an initial release from a sense of inadequacy, but one then finds that the original problem still remains. By gaining or disposing of one thing or another, the problem of inadequacy is not solved. Adequacy, freedom from being incomplete, is the end I seek behind all my forced pursuit of security, *artha*; but no gain or disposal accomplishes that end.[25]

If we understand *duḥkha* (suffering) to fundamentally be this condition of want and dissatisfaction with ourselves, then we should think of greed as a symptom rather than a cause of the problem.[26] Greed, whatever its object, is a response to the condition of inadequacy and not its cause. This is a very important point to which we return at various points in our discussion. Without a resolution to the problem of lack, the source of desires, greed goes untreated. Greed is acknowledged in the Hindu tradition as a cause of actions that inflict pain on others (Bhagavadgītā 3:36–37) and on oneself (Bhagavadgītā 16:21). It is often paired with anger (*krodha*) as a source of suffering. It is, however, symptomatic and not fundamental.

Overcoming the Problem of Inadequacy: The Limits of Action

Understanding this fundamental human predicament is an important first step toward its eventual resolution. Such understanding is the consequence of mature reflection on the nature of one's search and on the limits of various gains to overcome our need for adequacy. Muṇḍaka Upaniṣad (1.2.12) describes well this process of examining and reflecting on one's experiences. "Having analyzed the worldly experiences achieved through effort, a mature person gains dispassion, discerns that the uncreated (limitlessness) cannot be produced by action."[27]

What the thoughtful person understands is that all finite gains accomplished by action do not lead to freedom from the state of want. Freedom from want does not seem to be a product that follows from actions performed. These may at best produce a temporary release from want, but the condition of wanting soon reappears.

Conviction about the limits of finite gains to dispel the suffering of inadequacy leads to an attitude of dispassion or detachment (*nirvedam*). It is an appreciation of the fact that while finite actions can generate results necessary for satisfying legitimate human needs, it is illusory to think that these will overcome entirely our deep-rooted sense of want. Śaṅkara, in his commentary on the Brahma-sūtra 1.1.4, identifies four possibilities for action. Through actions, we can create an effect (like a pot from clay), modify or transform an existing effect (milk into yogurt), reach somewhere (like traveling from one destination to another), or cleanse and purify something (like removing dust from a mirror). Such limited actions are useful for accomplishing specific finite ends but do not seem to overcome inadequacy. It is important also to note that any adequacy that is the effect of a finite action will itself be finite and transient. A created fullness, the Muṇḍaka Upaniṣad text suggests, will be a limited one. The attitude of detachment spoken of in this verse should not be construed as implying an attitude of fear or disgust toward the finite. It is a mature understanding of the limits of the finite to solve the fundamental human problem. The Bhagavadgītā 2:59 cautions that it is only such wisdom and not the suppression of sense activity that liberates from unhealthy attachment and greed toward finite gains. An active life, infused with healthy detachment, is superior, according to Bhagavadgītā (3:6–7), to an inactive one in which one still harbors misconceptions about sense objects and finite gains. "The one who, controlling the organs of action, sits with the mind remembering those sense objects is deluded and is called a person of false conduct. Whereas, Arjuna! the one who, controlling the sense organs with the mind, remaining unattached, takes to the *yoga* of action with organs of actions, is far superior."[28]

Understanding the human problem is a necessary step toward any search for its resolution. Suffering (*duḥkha*) properly describes this problem, even though its expressions are many and include the anxiety over mortality that Becker emphasizes, the transience of pleasure, the wish for significance, and the persistence of inadequacy. The sense of insignificance and inadequacy is centered on oneself and on notions that one has about oneself and is not overcome by extrinsic gains such as wealth, fame, power, or pleasure. We feverishly, and often recklessly, pursue finite ends hoping through these to overcome self-lack and to attain the fullness of being that we truly want. Citing the work of Kierkegaard, Becker addresses the fact of our non-awareness of our motives in action. "We seek stress, we push our own limits, but we do it with our *screen against despair* and not with despair itself. We do it with the stock market, with sports cars, with atomic missiles, with the success ladder in the corporation or the competition in the university."[29]

It is significant that Naciketas, in the Kaṭha Upaniṣad 1.1.26, in his encounter with Death, also rejects all the rewards offered, such as wealth, power, long life, social status, and sense-pleasure. Naciketas turns down the offerings of Death with the observation that these are finite and leave human beings wanting and discontented. Naciketas sees through the "screen of despair" described by Becker. "Ephemeral are these, and they waste away the vigor of all the organs that a man has. All life, without exception, is short indeed. Let the vehicles be yours alone; let the dances and songs be yours."[30]

In Becker, awakening to the predicament of our illusory quest for significance leads to despair. There is not much to be offered when we confront the reality of an existence that seems meaningless. Becker articulates this rhetorically.

> When you get a person to emerge into life, away from his dependencies, his automatic safety in the cloak of someone's power, what joy can you promise him with the burden of his aloneness? When you get a person to look at the sun as it bakes down on the daily carnage taking place on the earth, the ridiculous accidents, the utter fragility of life, the powerlessness of those he thought most powerful—what comfort can you give him from a psychotherapeutic point of view?[31]

Although few contemporary thinkers have articulated and described the human problem as powerfully as Becker, his solution does not take us out of the realm of the illusory. Becker's solution to existential despair is the release of one's creative powers in work. Through work, "he satisfies nature which asks that he live and act objectively as a vital animal plunging into the world; but he also satisfies his own distinctive human nature because he plunges in on his own *symbolic* terms and not as a reflex of the world as a given to mere physical sense experience. He takes in the world, makes a total problem out of it, and then gives out a fashioned, human answer to that problem."[32] Although this "humanly created meaning" is also illusory, it is a necessary illusion, argues Becker, because it provides the heroic justification and meaning for life.

Despair as Opportunity

Despair is also a painful reality in the Advaita tradition. Vedāntasāra (1.30) describes the student as "scorched with the fire of the endless round of birth and death" and as going to a teacher as a person "with his head on fire rushes to a lake."[33] In similar language, Vivekacudamani (36) characterizes him as afflicted by an "unquenchable fire," "shaken violently," and "terrified." This sorrow of despair is also a moment of opportunity. The Muṇḍaka Upaniṣad (1.2.12) text cited above advises the despairing human being in the following words: "To know That, he should go, with twigs in his hand, to a teacher who is learned in the scriptures and who is steadfast in the knowledge of himself." The same text also advises the teacher on her response to the student. "To that student who has approached properly, who has a resolved mind, who has mastery over mind, that wise person should teach that *brahmavidyā* by which one knows the imperishable, the limitless truth as it is."

We had earlier highlighted Becker's identification of the human longing for "limitless self-extension," "cosmic significance," the urge "to be the *one* in creation." The Advaita tradition, following the Upaniṣads, names and identifies this desire as the intrinsic desire for *brahman* (the infinite), where alone there is freedom from suffering (*duḥkha*). The infinite is, according to the Advaita tradition, what human beings really want, as opposed to the unending finite ends that we pursue. The coincidence of terminology between Becker and the Upaniṣads is, to say the least, fascinating. Chāndogya Upaniṣad (7.23.1) speaks of the ultimate object of human longing in these famous words. "That which is infinite, is alone happiness. There is no happiness in anything finite. The infinite alone is happiness. But one must desire to understand the infinite."[34]

Later in the Chāndogya Upaniṣad (8.7.1), students go to their teacher, Prajāpati, after hearing that it is the knowledge of the infinite alone that culminates in the fulfillment of all desires. Bṛhadāraṇyaka Upaniṣad (2.4.5) is even more specific and offers a list of objects of desire that are sought not for their own sake but in pursuit of the infinite. These include husbands, wives, children, wealth, other worlds, and deities. The teacher advises that after understanding that the infinite is the object of human search, we should hear about, reflect on, and contemplate its nature.

Identifying the one end of human longing to be the infinite (*brahman*) is important for several reasons. We gain clarity about the human predicament that helps to end the frenzy of greed that is fueled by the illusion that gains of wealth, fame, or power will confer self-adequacy. It leads, as we have noted earlier, to a state of healthy detachment that is a consequence of understanding the possibilities and limits of finite gains. As important, the understanding of the human problem to be the quest for the infinite helps us also to think about the appropriate methods that may be employed for gaining this end.

The Uncreated Infinite

Muṇḍaka Upaniṣad (1.2.12), cited earlier, mentions that the fruit of reflection on the nature of action is the understanding that the infinite, literally the uncreated, is not the created effect of an action. All actions, physical and mental, originate in time and can only be performed for a limited duration. The effects of any such actions will necessarily be finite and subject to change and loss. It is a contradiction to understand or to think it possible to bring the infinite into existence through finite actions. "A limited being," writes Swami Dayananda, "through limited action gains a limited result. A series of limited results do not add up to limitlessness. A limited being plus a limited result, plus limited results, endlessly, still equals a limited being. By a process of becoming, the inadequate and limited being will never become limitless. Any changes one brings about, within or without, will not change the limited into the limitless."[35] We also are reminded here of the admonition in the Buddhist tradition that Nirvana should not be thought of an effect of anything. Walpola Rahula argues this point forcefully.

> Nirvana is not the result of anything. If it would be a result, then it would be an effect produced by a cause. It would be *samkhata* "produced" and "conditioned." Nirvana is neither cause nor effect. It is beyond cause and effect. Truth is not a result nor an effect. It is not produced like a mystic, spiritual, mental state, such as *dhyana* or *Samadhi*. TRUTH IS. NIRVANA IS.[36]

This claim about the nature of action, it must be emphasized, includes, from the Advaita perspective, actions that may be regarded as religious in character. The Advaita tradition accepts the possibility of the existence of worlds of pleasure (*svargaloka*) or worlds of pain (*narakaloka*) attained after death. These are attained through the performance of virtuous action (*puṇya*) or, in the case of unhappy worlds, non-ethical ones (*pāpa*). Because the attainment of these worlds is the consequence of finite actions, commended or proscribed, the gain is impermanent (*anityā*), and there is always return to the world of birth and death (*saṁsāra*). If heavenly worlds are impermanent, so also are hellish ones.

Our failure to attain fullness of self, according to the Advaita tradition, is the consequence of not discerning the true object of our search and our employment of inappropriate methods. The creation of finite effects thorough the employment of finite means is referred to in Advaita as the method of *aprāptasya prāpti* or the gain of that which not yet gained. The proper method for such an end is action (*karma*). The quest for fullness through the acquisition of wealth, fame, power, or pleasure, or by the performance of good works (*puṇya*), religious or ethical, is illustrative of this method and, Advaita claims, does not lead to a resolution of the human problem. The desire for fullness cannot be ignored and is not satisfied by finite gains.

The Human Problem as Ignorance (Avidyā)

Advaita does not stop with an identification of the human problem and skepticism about its resolution. The gain of that which is not yet gained is not the only model for the human problem and its solution. Advaita understands the Upaniṣads to propose the model of gaining that which is already gained (*prāptasya prāpti*). The issue, according to Advaita, is that we do not interrogate the problem of inadequacy itself. In other words, we assume inadequacy and then go about seeking a resolution through finite gains. The gain of that which is already gained seems paradoxical, but it is quite clear that this is exactly what Advaita proposes. The infinite (*brahman*), the object of human seeking, constitutes the nature of the seeking self. It is a fundamental error to think otherwise and to search for the infinite as though it is an object separate and different from oneself. The reality and availability of the infinite is at the heart of Advaita's resolution to the human problem, and is not unlike the often-quoted teaching and assurance of the Buddha that echoes so well the nature of the infinite in the Upanisads.

> Monks, there is the unborn, unoriginated, unmade, and unconditioned. Were there not the unborn, unoriginated, unmade and unconditioned, there will be no escape for the born, originated, made, and conditioned. Since there is the unborn, unoriginated, unmade, unconditioned, there is escape for the born, originated, made, conditioned . . . this indeed is the end of suffering.[37]

Although paradoxical, the method of gaining the gained is common in human experience. The story of the tenth person has become a classic parable in Advaita as an illustration of this method. It tells of ten disciples who were on their way to a pilgrimage site when they came upon a swollen river. In the absence of a boatman, they decided to swim across. On reaching the opposite shore, the student-leader took a count to ensure that everyone was safe. To her dismay, one was missing. Every member did likewise, but ended with the same conclusion that the tenth person was lost. A passerby, attracted by their lamentations, inquired about their problem. After listening patiently, he assured them that the tenth person was not lost and requested that the leader do another count. When she stopped at nine, the passerby said with a smile, "You are the tenth person!" Everyone immediately understood the nature of the error and rejoiced in the "gain" of their fellow disciple.

The model of gaining that which is already gained obtains when the problem is one of ignorance, and its resolution is through knowledge. In the case of the parable above, the loss of the tenth person was entirely notional. The tenth person was always present and available. In fact, the tenth person could not be any closer because the seeker of the tenth person was the tenth person, and there was no spatial or temporal separation between the seeker and the sought. What needed to be interrogated, as done by the passerby, was the very assumption that the tenth person was lost. In a similar way, contends Advaita, although the problem of self-inadequacy and want is a common human one, we need to turn the searchlight of inquiry on it and examine its validity. It should not be an unexamined assumption about oneself that then becomes the primary motivation behind what Buddhism speaks of as *tanha* (craving or thirst).

The Advaita resolution of the human predicament is the teaching that, like the tenth person searching for herself, one is the full and adequate being that one wishes to become. The problem is ignorance of the truth of oneself, and this is dispelled by knowledge. If liberation (*mokṣa*) from the human problem is accomplished through knowledge, and if this knowledge is to be regarded as valid, then knowledge must have a source regarded as valid. It is to the question of liberating knowledge and its source that we turn next.

2

The Validity of Non-Duality

Vedas: The Source of Liberating Knowledge

The Advaita tradition, as discussed in Chapter 1, understands the fundamental human problem and its resolution on the model of gaining that which is already gained or accomplishing the accomplished. In this model, the root of the human problem is traced back to ignorance and is to be resolved by knowledge. The consequence of ignorance is the conclusion that one is incomplete and inadequate and the resulting search to become full and complete. The fundamental Advaita claim is that one is the limitless being that one struggles, in futility, to become. Like the tenth person discovering herself to be the tenth person through instruction, and gaining freedom from the sorrow and fear of thinking that the tenth person is lost, the knowledge of one's identity with the limitless (*brahman*) frees from the suffering of self-lack.

This understanding of the human predicament clarifies the Advaita emphasis on knowledge as the direct means to freedom (*mokṣa*) and its argument for the limits of action in the attainment of liberation. Actions, however, that are performed worshipfully as an offering to God facilitate and are conducive to the gain in knowledge. Such actions are commended in Advaita. Action is not opposed to ignorance, and, in this case, actions that are motivated by the hope of achieving fullness of self spring from ignorance and will not eliminate it. When one is already what one seeks to become, no amount of searching outside oneself resolves the problem. Such a search becomes a part of the problem. The primary ignorance on the basis of which one engages in a search for fullness has to be dispelled by knowledge. It is for this specific reason that Muṇḍaka Upaniṣad 1.2.12 advises the student, who has grasped the human problem of wanting to be full and the frustration of failing to gain it, to go to a teacher who is learned in the scriptures (*śrotriya*) and who is steadfast in knowledge (*brahmaniṣṭham*). The scriptures referred to in the Mundaka Upanisad 1.2.12 are the four Vedas (*Ṛg*, *Sāma*, *Yajur*, and *Atharva*), and the Advaita tradition looks to the teachings of the Vedas as the authoritative source for its understanding of the nature of the self and its identity with the limitless. Advaita regards the four Vedas as a source of valid knowledge (*pramāṇa*) and understands the teachings of the Vedas as satisfying the criteria for valid knowledge. The understanding of the Vedas as a *pramāṇa* is a neglected subject in the contemporary study of the Hindu tradition, although this approach may lend a fresh perspective to the meaning and significance of scriptures and a unique way of understanding their authority. Although this chapter speaks of the Vedas as "scripture" or "sacred text," these meanings are secondary. Primarily, "Veda" connotes a teaching or body of knowledge.

The Threefold Criteria for Valid Knowledge

Valid knowledge (*pramā*), according to Advaita, is knowledge that conforms to the nature of the object that one seeks to know. Such knowledge is generated only by the application of a valid and appropriate means of knowledge (*pramāṇa*) and has three principal characteristics. First, valid knowledge must not be contradicted by knowledge derived from another valid source. Non-contradictedness (*abādhita*) is a crucial quality of valid knowledge for Advaita. An invalid statement or erroneous experience, such as mistaking a rope for a snake, is negated on the basis of being contradicted. Second, knowledge gained through a valid source discloses information that is not attainable through another source (*anadhigata*). Each valid source is unique in the kind of knowledge it provides. A valid source of knowledge becomes redundant if the information it provides is obtainable otherwise. With respect to perception, for example, the eyes are unique in the knowledge provided of forms and color. *Anadhigata* is the affirmation of the special relationship that exists between the object to be known and the particular means employed. The means employed is dependent on the object that one desires to know. Along with uniqueness and non-contradictedness as characteristics of valid knowledge, Śaṅkara occasionally adds the quality of fruitfulness. The teachings of the scriptures, Advaita claims, fruitfully remove the deep-rooted sense of inadequacy born of self-ignorance. The lives of liberated persons are a powerful testimony that the teachings of the Vedas work. On the basis of these criteria, Advaita recognizes six valid sources of knowledge: perception, inference, comparison, postulation, non-cognition, and the Vedas.[1]

The Subject Matter of the Vedas

The justification in Advaita for a special means of knowledge, like the Vedas, is that it provides the knowledge of those things that cannot be known through any of the available sources of knowledge; this knowledge is fruitful (*phalavat arthabodhaka*) and is not contradicted by the revelations of another valid source.

According to Advaita, the two categories of knowledge that cannot be gained through any other valid source and are available only through the Vedas are *dharma* and *brahman*. *Dharma*, in this context, refers to scripturally approved ethical and ritual actions. Advaita does not disagree with the argument that the knowledge of human ethics is not dependent solely on scriptural revelation and may be inferred from what is necessary for the proper functioning of human communities. Ethics may also be derived from mutual interpersonal expectations and the obligation to treat others as one wishes to be treated. The special revelation of the Veda is that commended actions, ethical and ritual, produce desirable subtle results, referred to as *puṇya*, that give rise to pleasant or pleasurable experiences in the future. Similarly, disapproved actions generate undesirable subtle results (*pāpa*) that create unhappy or painful future experiences. This connection is not known from any other source, such as perception or inference. Under the subject matter of *dharma*, we may also include the teaching about a future life in a heavenly world (*svarga*), because meritorious actions, ethical and ritual, are often performed with the hope of gaining life in such a world. In addition to the attainment of heaven, the Vedas also mention various other ends that may be achieved through the performance of prescribed ritual action. These include, for example, rituals to generate rainfall or to have children. All of these depend on actions aimed at producing an outcome that is not already in existence. Ritual and ethical injunctions are followed, and these generate the desired results. Because all actions are finite, the results produced are also transient. The claims for the validity of the Vedas as a source for the knowledge of *dharma* require faith (*śraddhā*) in these teachings, because the connection between a particular action and its result is not a matter of perception.

Advaita looks upon the Vedas as consisting broadly of two sections. *Dharma*, as described above, is the authoritative concern of the first three sections of the Vedas (*saṁhitā*, *brāhmana*, and *āraṇyaka*), referred to as the *karmakāṇḍa* (action-section). These sections, in general, provide scripturally approved methods for pursuing and attaining goals such as wealth, power, fame, pleasure, and, as noted above, heavenly worlds of pleasure. The tradition does not condemn those who pursue such finite ends, religious or secular, once this is done with attentiveness to ethical norms and especially the concern to avoid causing harm and suffering to others. It recognizes that many, in all religions, look to their traditions to support and enhance their attainment of such goals. The Advaita contention is that the revelation of the action-section of the Vedas does not resolve the fundamental human problem of self-inadequacy. It does not address the matter of self-ignorance that is at the heart of this problem, and, as long as this persists, one will continue to search in frustration for fullness through finite gains. The highest purpose of religion, according to Advaita, is to resolve the human problem at its most fundamental level.

When one comes, thorough the analysis of experience, to understand the nature of the human predicament and the fact that fullness seems elusive and cannot be an action-generated end, the Vedas, as we see in the Muṇḍaka text (1.2.12), direct one to a teacher and to their wisdom-section (*jñānakāṇḍa*). The wisdom-section is the final and fourth section of the Vedas, referred to as the Vedānta (lit. end of the Vedas). It comprises the Upaniṣads.[2] The Upaniṣads are structured in the form of dialogues between students and their teachers. There are more than one hundred such dialogues in the four Vedas, but a dozen or so, selected by the earliest commentators, have gained special significance. The different titles used for the Upaniṣads are often indicative of the focus of the text or even of its beginning. Kena Upaniṣad, for example, starts with the word "*kena*" meaning "by what," while Praśna Upaniṣad consists of a series of six questions (*praśna*).

The Action and Knowledge Sections of the Vedas

Although Advaita considers the Vedas in their entirety to be a valid source of knowledge, it distinguishes between the action-section and the wisdom-section in important ways. The same revelation is explicitly understood to offer methods for attaining different but legitimate human ends and to address different human needs. The two sections are distinguished in at least four important ways:

1. Subject matter: The action-section, as we noted already, is concerned with the revelation of *dharma* and finite goals such as wealth (*artha*) and pleasure (*kāma*), here and in the hereafter, attainable through approved ritual and ethical actions. The subject matter of the wisdom-section is the limitless (*brahman*).

2. Student: The qualified student or aspirant for the action-section is someone who has not yet understood the limits of finite gains created by action. She has not yet grasped the fundamental human problem. The student of the wisdom-section has grasped the limits of such ends and understands that her search is for the limitless.

3. Result: The action-section has prosperity in this or other worlds as its result. The result of the wisdom-section is liberation (*mokṣa*) from self-inadequacy.

4. Connection: The teaching revealed in the action-section informs us of various ends that do not yet exist and that are to be actualized through appropriate human action. Knowledge, in itself, is not the end. The wisdom-

> section, on the other hand, reveals an already existing reality (*brahman*), and knowledge here is an end in itself. Knowing one's identity with *brahman* liberates just as the tenth person is liberated by the words of the passerby. These words revealed that the tenth person was always present and available but erroneously thought to be missing.

The two sections of the revelation are not antagonistic to each other and do not undermine each other's authority. Each exercises authority in its own sphere and subject matter and in relation to particular goals and aspirants.

Relationship between the Means of Knowledge and Object

Why do we need a distinctive source of knowledge, consisting of words, to know the limitless *brahman*? Why is *brahman* not knowable, like other objects, through other well-known sources of valid knowledge such as perception or inference? According to Advaita, the means of knowledge that one employs must be appropriate to the object that one seeks to know. The nature of the object, in other words, determines the choice of the means of knowledge. There is a logical interdependence between the nature of the object to be known and the means of knowledge utilized (*pramāṇa prameya sambandha*). The color of an object, for example, may be known uniquely through the eyes, while its odor is apprehended through the organ of smell. The cornerstone of the Advaita case for the words of the Upaniṣads as the appropriate valid source for knowing *brahman* is grounded in an argument about the nature of *brahman*. This case consists of arguments about the limits of other ways of knowledge as well as for the appropriateness and effectiveness of a teaching through words.

Let us begin with arguments about the limits of other ways of knowledge. Each sense organ, for example, is naturally capable of revealing a quality that is appropriate to its own nature. Sound, sensation, form, taste, and scent are their respective spheres of functioning. *Brahman*, however, remains unapproachable thorough any of these because it is without form, sound, touch, smell, or taste. *Brahman* is limitless, and to be an object of sense knowledge is to be finite and limited, to be one object among many objects. A sense-apprehended *brahman* is a contradiction.

In addition to the inherent limitation and specificity of the sense organs, there is the impossibility of objectifying *brahman*. Knowledge, in general, involves a distinction between a knowing subject and an object of knowledge. We know things by making these objects of our awareness, and, in this manner, they become available for scrutiny and analysis. Knowledge involves objectification. Kena Upaniṣad 1.2 describes *brahman* as the "ear of the ear, the mind of the mind, the speech of speech, the breath of the breath and the eye of the eye." The same Upaniṣad later describes *brahman* as that which speech, the mind, the eye, the ear, and the breath cannot objectify, but by which these are all known and objectified. As the Bṛhadāraṇyaka Upanisad (2.4.14) asks rhetorically, "Therefore through what instrument should one know the knower owing to which this universe is known and who else should know it?" The subject matter of the Upaniṣads is *brahman*, identical with the self (*ātmā*) and not known through objectification or, therefore, through any means of knowledge employing the method of objectification. Perception as a way of knowledge is valid only with reference to realities, internal and external, that can be objectified. *Brahman* is the self, the subject that is never available for objectification.

The limits of perception as a mode of knowing *brahman* mean also that all other ways of knowledge (inference, comparison, postulation, and non-cognition), dependent as these are on perception, are inapplicable to *brahman*. Valid inferential knowledge is based on the invariable relation between the thing inferred and the ground from which the inference is made. The standard example of inference, "where there is smoke, there is fire," is based on the invariable co-presence between smoke and fire. This invariable co-presence is dependent on the data of perception that establish that there is never smoke without fire. *Brahman* has no perceptually discernible quality that may be used to establish a valid inference about its nature.

The limits of perception and inferential-based ways of knowledge support the Advaita position that reasoning, apart from the revelation of the Upanisads, is incapable of informing us conclusively about the limitless. This is the position of Śaṅkara, Advaita's principal systematizer and exponent. In his Brahmasūtra commentary (2.1.11), he comments on the inconclusiveness of reason with regard to knowing *brahman*.

> Although reasoning may be noticed to have finality in some contexts, still in the present context it cannot possibly get immunity from the charge of being inconclusive; for this extremely sublime subject matter, concerned with the reality of the cause of the universe and leading to the goal of liberation, cannot even be guessed without the help of the *Vedas*. And we said that It cannot be known either through perception, being devoid of form, etc., or through inference, etc., being devoid of grounds of inference. (322)

A comment like the one above should not be read to mean that the Advaita tradition rejects all forms of reasoning in relation to knowing *brahman*. Advaita vigorously endorses the use of arguments that are ancillary to the Upaniṣad *pramāṇa* and that demonstrate the reasonableness of the teachings of the texts and their noncontradiction by other valid ways of knowing. This is Śaṅkara's point in his commentary on Brahmasūtra 1.1.2.

> The realization of *Brahman* results from the firm conviction arising from the deliberation of the (Vedic) texts and their meanings, but not from other means of knowledge like inference, etc. When, however, there are Upaniṣadic texts speaking of the origin, etc. of the world, then even inference, not running counter to the Upaniṣadic texts, is not ruled out, in so far as it is adopted as a valid means of knowledge reinforcing these texts; for the Upaniṣads themselves accept reasoning as a help. (15)

The meaning and claims of the texts should be examined in the light of reason and argument. The primary role of reason is to demonstrate the tenability of and to support the teachings of the Vedas. Reason is not an independent means to knowing *brahman* or an alternative to the scripture. The revelation of *brahman* is not accessible thorough independent reason, but this revelation cannot be unreasonable and in conflict with the disclosures of other valid ways of knowledge.

The Liberating Power of Words

Having sketched the Advaita arguments for the limits of conventional ways of knowing, let us turn to some of its central arguments for the words of the Upaniṣads as the single appropriate *pramāṇa*. We may begin by noting that in the traditional Advaita self-understanding, the teaching about the nature of *brahman* constituting a valid source of knowledge is a revelation from *brahman*. The Vedas themselves are the source for the claim that the knowledge of *brahman* originates from *brahman*. Bṛhadāraṇyaka Upaniṣad (2.4.10), for example, notes, "Those that are called Ṛg Veda (Yajur Veda, etc.) are but the exhalation of this great Being." From its origin in *brahman*, this wisdom is transmitted from teacher to student and is preserved and enriched though such succession. This tradition of the continuous transmission of knowledge from teacher to student is known in Sanskrit as *guru śiṣya paramparā*. It gives rise to a distinctive lineage, in this case of Advaita, known as a *sampradāya* (flow of teaching). Bhagavadgītā (4:1–2) speaks of the origin of knowledge in God and the transmission through a teaching tradition. "I taught this imperishable *yoga* to Vivasvān, Vivasvān taught it to Manu, (and) Manu taught it to Ikṣvāku. Handed down from generation to generation in this way, the kings who were sages knew it. (But) with the long lapse of time, Arjuna, this *yoga* has declined in the world."[3]

Although the Advaita tradition has not expended significant effort considering the actual method by which the teachings of the Upaniṣads are received originally from *brahman*, the emphasis is on the fact that those (*ṛṣis*) to whom the teachings were given originally are recipients and not "creators" of knowledge. They are described as perceivers of verses of the Vedas (*mantra draṣṭaraḥ*) and not creators (*mantra kartā*s). A deliberate process, wherein words become the primary vehicles, then transmits the teachings. This original structure is embedded in each Upaniṣad, which consists of a dialogue between teacher (*guru*) and student (*śiṣya*) about the nature of *brahman*. It is in the process of this teaching itself that liberation is discovered. Students exclaim, as they do at the end of the Praśna Upaniṣad (6:8) dialogue after a meaningful exposure to the teacher's instruction, "You indeed are our father who have ferried us across ignorance to the other shore. Salutations to the great seers (*ṛṣis*)! Salutations to the great seers!"

We discussed earlier the Advaita understanding of a valid source of knowledge (*pramāṇa*) as providing a unique knowledge that is not derived from other sources, that is fruitful and not refuted by other sources. We also considered Advaita arguments for the inappropriateness of other ways of knowing (perception, inference, etc.) in relation to *brahman* (e.g., the absence of perceptible qualities in *brahman* and its status as a non-object). How is it possible for the words of the Upaniṣads to function as a direct and valid source of knowledge? Words can provide valid knowledge when the object of knowledge is readily and immediately available, not separate from the knower by a gap of time or space, and does not have to be created or brought into existence. The words in the action-section of the Vedas (*karmakāṇḍa*) do not fulfill themselves merely through proper understanding of their meanings. These words provide directions for action, ritual and ethical, that must be subsequently implemented in performance to produce a desirable result. Knowledge is indirect. In the case of the story of the tenth person, on the other hand, the words "You are the tenth person" fulfill their intention and purpose when rightly comprehended because the tenth person is immediately available and lost only in ignorance. The words in the wisdom-section of the Vedas (the Upaniṣads) function like the words addressed to the tenth person. For a person coming to a teacher of Advaita with a calm mind and control over her senses (Muṇḍaka Upaniṣad 1.2.13), the words of the teacher can result in the immediate "gain" of the limitless.

In his commentary on Brahmasūtra 1.1.1, Śaṅkara responds to an objector asking whether the limitless (*brahman*) is known or unknown. The point of the question is that if the limitless is known, there is no need for an inquiry or dialogue about it. If, on the other hand, the limitless is entirely unknown, it cannot become the object of a desire to know. Śaṅkara's response is to explain that the limitless is not unknown. "Besides," says Sankara, "the existence of *brahman* is well known from the fact of Its being the Self of all; for everyone feels that his Self exists, and he never feels, 'I do not exist.' Had there been no general recognition of the existence of the Self, everyone would have felt, 'I do not exist.' And the Self is *brahman* (12)." As awareness, the fundamental content of the I-notion, or I-sense, the limitless is self-luminous; it does not require the aid of anything else to reveal itself. The impossibility of denying one's existence testifies, according to Advaita, to the self-revealing character of *brahman*. The operation of the senses and the mind in acts of knowing depends on the presence and availability of the self as awareness. Sankara's comment on Brahmasūtra (2.3.7), is pertinent here: "Any idea of the possibility of denying the existence of the Self is illogical, just because it is the Self. For the Self of any one does not require to be revealed to any one with the help of any other means. For such means of knowledge as perception etc., that are taken up for proving the existence of other things that remain unknown, belong to this very Self" (455).

The words of the Upaniṣads, therefore, do not instruct the student about a remote or unavailable self, but about one that is always available. Such words, then, like those spoken to the tenth person, are capable of conveying direct knowledge.

If the limitless is always available in this way as the content of the I-notion and as the ground of all cognitive processes, what is the need for the Upaniṣads as a means of knowledge? Like the tenth person erroneously thinking of himself as lost, the limitless, though ever luminous as one's own self, is erroneously identified with the finitude of body and mind and is thought of as an object, limited by time and space. It is the negation of this ignorance that is the specific purpose of the Upaniṣad instruction. The Upaniṣads, or any other means of knowing, cannot create the limitless. The teaching seeks only to identify it as immediately present and to remove false notions about its nature. This is accomplished through a deliberate teaching process that is characteristic of the Advaita tradition and the end result of which is freedom (*mokṣa*) from self-lack.

One of the important reasons for emphasizing the immediate availability of the limitless, and clarifying the nature of the ignorance pertaining to it, is that it establishes the possibility of the words of the Upaniṣads, giving rise to direct and immediate knowledge. Knowledge derived from words is not direct and immediate when the object concerned is to be brought into existence or not immediately available. If an object is available but not properly recognized, knowledge derived from words can be sufficient. This is the basis for the important distinction in the Advaita tradition between action and knowledge in relation to liberation. Action is a right and appropriate solution when the problem involved is gaining something not yet gained. Knowledge, on the other hand, is adequate for gaining that which is already gained. Advaita, as noted earlier, understands the human problem and its resolution to be of the latter kind. There is a fundamental interrelationship between the nature of *brahman* and the means through which it can be known, as well as between the ignorance as the fundamental problem and knowledge as the resolution. The words of the Upaniṣads are thus understood to be both logical and adequate.

The Value of a Teacher

The Muṇḍaka Upaniṣad text (1.2.12), cited throughout our discussion, advises the student to seek knowledge from a teacher and describes the qualified teacher as one who is well versed in the scripture (*śrotriyam*) and established in the limitless (*brahmaniṣṭham*). The necessity and importance of the teacher are reiterated throughout the Upaniṣads. Chāndogya Upaniṣad 6.14.2 informs us that the person who has a teacher knows, while Bhagavadgītā 4:34 instructs that knowledge is to be sought by respectfully questioning and serving one's teacher. Why this emphasis on the role of the teacher? If the Upaniṣads are the source of valid knowledge, why is there a necessity for a teacher? The word *śrotriya*, derived from a Sanskrit root meaning "to hear," signifies a person who knows the scripture. The Vedas are referred to, in Sanskrit, as *śruti* (that which is heard), pointing to the oral preservation and transmission of the teachings and giving importance to knowledge and not text. Traditionally, one heard the words of the Vedas from one's teacher. A *śrotriya*, therefore, is a person who knows the content of the Vedas and, in this particular context, the teachings of the Upaniṣads.

It also implies a process of learning within the specific tradition (*sampradāya*) of Advaita. There is a distinctive Advaita exegesis and interpretation of the meaning of the Upaniṣads, expressed in the conviction that the central aim of the Upanisads is to reveal the identity of the self (*ātmā*) and the limitless (*brahman*). This teaching, according to Advaita, is most directly and concisely articulated in great sentences (*mahavākyas*) such as "That Thou Art" (*tat tvam asi*), Chāndogya Upaniṣad 6.8.7; "This self is limitless" (*ayam ātmā brahma*), Maṇḍukya Upaniṣad 2; "Awareness is limitless" (*prajñānaṁ brahma*), Aitareya Upaniṣad 5.3; and "I am the limitless" (*ahaṁ brahmāsmi*), Bṛhadāraṇyaka Upaniṣad 1.4.10.[4] Systematic study within the Advaita *sampradāya* grants familiarity with the very specific methods that have been developed to transmit the meaning of the Upaniṣads. Some of the common methods employed, to be discussed subsequently, include the cause and effect method, the analysis of the three states of experience method, the analysis of the five sheaths method, and the distinction between seer and seen method. We have already noted that the limitless is not an object of the mind or the senses. Most of the pedagogical methods with which we are familiar and which are employed in instruction have been developed to impart knowledge of things that can be objectified. In the case of *brahman*, however, the special challenge is to instruct about a non-object. Unusual methods, with which a teacher must be familiar, are a necessity, and these are received through immersion in a tradition. Being limitless, instruction about *brahman* requires a very special use of words because it cannot be directly indicated by finite words. Words have to be skillfully and deliberately wielded to successfully impart knowledge.[5]

Why does the Upanisad describe the ideal teacher as a *śrotriya* (one who knows the Vedas) and a *brahmaniṣṭham* (established in *brahman*)? The Upaniṣads assume that the qualified teacher is one who has experienced intensely the human problem, approached a teacher herself, and discovered her identity with the limitless. Such a teacher, who knows the suffering that is synonymous with the human predicament and also its overcoming, is capable of teaching with a directness and conviction. One who is just a *śrotriya* can communicate only an indirect teaching; she can teach what she has heard, but not what she *is*. Such a teacher cannot instruct about *brahman* with the immediacy and power of personal example that will be liberating for her student. The full potential of the Upaniṣad as a *pramāṇa* that enables one to see oneself clearly will remain undisclosed. In a similar way, one may be a *brahmaniṣṭha* who knows the truth of her identity with the limitless but without the depth of learning in the scriptures and pedagogical methods that are necessary for effective teaching. Such a person represents an inspiring ideal and presence, but it is the integration of traditional learning and life-centeredness in *brahman* that characterizes the ideal teacher. Advaita is essentially a teaching tradition that seeks to communicate a direct knowledge about oneself, and the teacher who embodies this wisdom is the best instructor for the communication of this teaching.

The Necessity of Faith (Śraddhā)

The centrality of the Upaniṣad as a valid source of knowledge and the pivotal role of the teacher in the transmission of this teaching highlight the necessity for faith (*śraddhā*) as a requisite for inquiry. Unlike other Hindu traditions that seem quite deliberate in efforts to downplay the necessity for faith, Advaita makes no such claim. The importance of faith is implicit in the claim that the Upaniṣads are the valid source for our knowledge of *brahman*. This means that there is no alternative method but the teaching that is communicated through words. This may not be as anachronistic as it first sounds. The validity or invalidity of a source of knowledge may be established only by its actual employment. It is irrational to dismiss a priori the claim of the Advaita tradition that the Upaniṣads are a valid source of knowledge. The ability of the eyes to convey valid knowledge of forms and colors can only be established by the actual use of the eyes. Swami Dayananda Saraswati uses a very interesting illustration to make this point.

> Let us suppose that a man who was born blind undergoes a new surgical procedure that will enable him to see. The surgery is considered to be a success and the doctors are convinced that the man will see. After removing the bandages, the doctor says, "Please open your eyes." But, keeping his eyes tightly closed, the man says, "Doctor,

> I will only open my eyes when you prove that I can see." What can the doctor do now? He is being asked to prove that the man's eyes are a means of knowledge and that they are capable of sight. But how can he do that? He can only say: "I think you will be able to see. The surgery went very well and there is no reason why your eyes should not see." Even if the doctor forces the man's eyes open, the only proof that he will be able to see is the sight registered by the eyes themselves.[6]

This understanding of the functioning of the *pramāṇa* does not imply an uncritical acceptance of its claims. We noted earlier that one of the essential characteristics of valid knowledge is that it should not be contradicted or refuted (*abādhita*). One of the significant arguments of Śaṅkara in his commentary on Brahmasūtra 1.1.2 is that the inquiry into the nature of *brahman* admits the use of other sources of valid knowledge because *brahman* is an immediately available and already existing reality. He contrasts this with the revelations concerning *dharma* (ritual and ethical actions and their results) that are the subject matter of the action-section of the Vedas. The claim that a specific ritual, if performed properly, will produce a desired result cannot be examined by employing other sources because the result is yet to be produced. Although Advaita proposes that the teachings of the Upaniṣads constitute the valid source for our knowledge of *brahman,* it welcomes the examination of the validity of these claims from the perspective of other *pramāṇa*s. This is especially necessary when the revelations of the Upaniṣads seem to contradict truths established by other *pramāṇas*. A *pramāṇa* should not contradict itself, and it must not contradict the valid truths of another *pramāṇa.*

We may explore this a bit further by examining the criterion of novelty or uniqueness (*anadhigata*), discussed above, as a characteristic of a valid knowledge. The criterion means that the Upaniṣads have a prescribed sphere of authority. It is not authoritatively distinctive where it provides information that one may obtain or has obtained from another valid source. It is not the function of the scripture to disclose matters within the range of human experience ascertainable through our ordinary ways of knowledge. If it contradicts a well-established fact of our everyday experience, it cannot be considered authoritative because such a matter is outside its authority. Śaṅkara speaks directly on this issue in his commentary on Bhagavadgītā 18:66.

> *Śruti* [Veda] is an authority only in matters not perceived by means of ordinary instruments of knowledge such as perception—i.e., it is an authority as to the mutual relation of things as means to ends, but not in matters lying within the range of perception; indeed *śruti* is intended as an authority for knowing what lies beyond the range of human knowledge. . . . A hundred *śrutis* may declare that fire is cold or that it is dark; still they possess no authority in the matter. If *śruti* should at all declare that fire is cold or that it is dark, we should still suppose that it intends quite a different meaning from the apparent one; for its authority cannot otherwise be maintained: we should in no way attach to *śruti* a meaning which is opposed to other authorities or to its own declaration. (513)

If the Vedas did describe fire as being cold or dark, we would be obliged to construe its meaning figuratively, because the purpose of the scripture is not to create anything new or to reverse the nature of anything. The text is fundamentally revelatory in purpose. Elsewhere, in Bṛhadāraṇyaka Upaniṣad 2.1.20, Śaṅkara returns to this important point, contending that one "cannot prove that fire is cold, or that the sun does not shine, even by citing a hundred examples, for the facts would already be known to be otherwise through another means of knowledge. And one means of knowledge does not contradict another, for it only tells us about those things that cannot be known by another means" (209).

Advaita is very specific about some of the subjects that are not the concern of the Vedas. These include details about the creation that are ascertainable by the methods of observation and inference, or knowledge about human beings derived from physiology or psychology. The claim that each valid source of knowledge operates within its own defined sphere has helped the tradition avoid some of the conflicts between religion and the empirical sciences that often stand in the way of constructive dialogue between these disciplines. Religion ought not to claim authority in fields where its methods and sources are inappropriate, and the empirical sciences must realize also the limits and assumptions of the investigative tools that are employed.

In the Advaita tradition, therefore, faith (*śraddhā*) refers to the willingness, on the part of one who understands the human problem, to inquire with an open mind into the teachings of the Upanisad *pramāṇa*. As in the case of all other ways of knowing, one cannot make an informed judgment on its validity unless one is willing to employ it. Bhagavadgītā 4:39 emphasizes the necessity of faith as a requisite for knowledge. "One who has faith, who is committed to that (knowledge) and who is master of one's senses gains the knowledge. Having gained the knowledge, one immediately gains absolute peace."[7] The Advaita tradition transmits itself with the confidence that teachings of the Upaniṣads satisfy the criteria of valid knowledge (novelty and non-contradictedness) and fruitfully provide a meaningful solution to the human problem by teaching that each one is the full being that he or she aspires to become. Faith enables the student to approach the means of knowledge with an attitude of trust and sincerity of purpose. It does not demand the abandonment of critical faculties but an exposure to the *pramāṇa*. *Śraddhā* excludes cynicism, not critical inquiry.

A Teaching Tradition

Muṇḍaka Upaniṣad 1.2.12 directs a person not to the text, but to the teacher (*guru*). Commenting on this verse, Śaṅkara explains, "The emphasis in 'only to a teacher' implies that he should not seek for the knowledge of Brahman independently even though he is versed in the scriptures" (104). The Advaita tradition understands itself as an inquiry into the meaning of the Upaniṣads as a valid source of knowledge based on the application of certain established tools of exegesis.[8] It sees the teachings of the Upaniṣads as capable of liberating a person directly and immediately from the sorrow of the human condition and preserves, along with an interpretation of the meaning of the Upaniṣads, distinctive methods of teaching to facilitate self-understanding. It is the role of the Advaita teacher, one who knows the content of the Upanisads and is established in its vision, to communicate the meaning of the texts utilizing special pedagogical methods. The subject matter here is a non-object and cannot be taught by methods developed to instruct about things that can be objectified either by the senses or the mind. In addition to its character as a non-object, the limitless (*brahman*) cannot be directly signified by any word because of the finite meaning of words. The Upaniṣad *pramāṇa* is constituted of words, and, if these finite words are to shed finite references and reveal the infinite, they must be used dexterously in special ways. The skillful use of limited language to indicate the limitless is a function of a qualified teacher.

The Upaniṣads expect that the process of teaching will generate doubts about the claims of the Upaniṣads. Few students will come to teachers without firm convictions about themselves, especially deeply entrenched notions that one is an incomplete being, limited by time and space, subject to birth and death. The radical Upaniṣad teaching that the self is limitless stands diametrically opposed to such ways of thinking and leads to doubt and questioning. The teacher is the student's partner in this dialogue and interrogation of the teaching. The Bhagavadgītā 4:34 speaks of learning through the method of questioning (*paripraśnena*). A learned teacher (*śrotriya*), conversant with text and tradition (*sampradāya*) and who is herself free from doubts about her nature (*brahmaniṣṭham*), is the ideal person for this process of teaching. The importance of a teaching tradition is underlined by Śaṅkara in his commentary on Bhagavadgītā 13:2. He advises that a teacher who is not familiar with the traditional method of teaching (*sampradāya*) "is to be neglected as an ignorant man, though learned in all the scriptures" (*śāstras*) (330).

3

The Full Self

The Advaita tradition affirms that the fundamental human problem, expressed in a sense of want, inadequacy, and incompleteness, is resolved thorough a process of teaching that transmits the central insight of the Upaniṣads about the nature of the self (*ātmā*) and its identity with the limitless (*brahman*). The Advaita teacher utilizes pedagogical methods that aim to remove the misunderstanding that the self is limited by time and space and has characteristics that are specific to the body such as height, weight, and gender. The teacher's purpose is to explain the nature of the self as identical with the limitless (*brahman*) and as free and full. The teaching process is predicated on the assumption that, owing to ignorance (*avidyā*), the limitless seems to be limited; liberation is not a matter of becoming, but one of understanding. The logic of ignorance as the human problem explains the Advaita insistence that knowledge of the nature of the self is the only direct means to liberation. The tradition does not negate the role of religious disciplines and practices involving action, but understands the role of these as supplementary and indirect. These are most helpful when they facilitate the gain of knowledge, but can never be a substitute for teaching. Correct understanding alone negates ignorance, while action may be compatible still with ignorance.

Although the process of teaching in Advaita is an integral one, and distinct movements may be difficult to discern, we may, for the purpose of this discussion, identify three principal steps or phases in instruction. First, because the finite attributes of the body and mind are attributed wrongly to the self and the self is identified fully with these, it is necessary to distinguish the self from what it is not. Second, the nature of the self as free from all limits must be unfolded. The third movement in Advaita instruction is to clarify that the self that is identical with the limitless (*brahman*) is not one object in a universe of many objects. It constitutes the reality and the irreducible truth of all that exists. This is the gist of the Chāndogya Upaniṣad 3.14.1 text "All this indeed is *brahma*" (*sarvam khalvidam brahma*). We consider each movement in turn with the use of specific Upaniṣad texts and Advaita methods of instruction (*prakriyās*).

The Method of Distinguishing Knower and Known

To point out the self that is wrongly identified with the body and mind, Advaita teachers utilize the instructive method (*prakriyā*) of distinguishing between the knower and known or subject and object (*dṛg-drsya prakriyā*). It is based on the experience, in the act of knowing, of a distinction between a knowing subject and a known object of knowledge and on the difference between the two. Its aim is to show the body, senses, and mind as objects of knowledge and distinct from the knowing subject. Kena Upaniṣad begins typically with a question from student to teacher. "Willed and prompted by whom does the mind alight on objects? Led by whom does the breath of life flow in and out? Who prompts people here to speak these words? Which shining being leads the eyes and ears?"[1]

In the student's question, the mind includes all mental functions, the breath of life represents all physiological activities, speech stands for the organs of action, and the eyes and ears point to every sense organ. The student is not inquiring about the psychological or physiological functioning of the body-mind complex, because such knowledge is available through other ways of knowing, such as perception or inference. The instrumental nature of the body and mind leads the student to suspect that these are not self-explanatory and do not function independently. These all have a dependent character and serve the interests of some conscious other. In the second verse of the Kena Upaniṣad, the teacher confirms the intuition of his student about the instrumental and dependent nature of the body and mind composite. "It is indeed the Ear of the ear, the Mind of the mind, the Speech of speech, the Breath of breath and the Eye of the eye. The wise, freeing themselves from this world, become immortal."

Although speaking in his reply about what other Upaniṣad texts name as the *ātmā*, the Kena teacher does not provide any such label. If the teacher had responded to his student by saying that it is the *ātmā* because of which one hears, thinks, speaks, breathes, and sees, he would give his pupil a new word or name but not help her to understand anything about herself. Instead of a name, he responds with the intriguing and challenging expressions "Ear of the ear, Mind of the mind, Speech of speech, Breath of breath, and Eye of the eye." What does the teacher want to convey by such formulations? The "Ear of the ear" points clearly to that which enables the ear to function as an instrument of hearing and without which it will cease to do so. It makes all hearing, seeing, and thinking possible. What is that, therefore, upon which the mind and all senses depend and in whose absence there is no mental or sense processes? Let us take the example of seeing.

Seeing requires an (i) object of sight with form, such as a book or computer. It requires also (ii) an instrument of sight, the eyes; and (iii) an attentive mind with the correct thought form to recognize the book as book. If the appropriate thought form is not present, the object may be seen but not recognized or may be wrongly identified as something other than a book. There is a fourth factor, however, without which the eyes will not see and the act of seeing does not occur. When one says, "I see the book," the object is present, the instrument (eye) is present, the mind with the correct thought form is present, and awareness is present. In the absence of awareness, there is no seeing. Object, instrument, and mind may be available, but, in the vision of the Upaniṣads, there is no seeing in the absence of awareness. A different example may clarify this Upaniṣadic teaching. Let us imagine that one enters a room looking for one's pen. The pen sits on the desk, but both pen and desk are enveloped in total darkness. One will recognize the pen if it is seen, but the darkness obscures any seeing. A flick of the switch on the wall immediately illumines the room, table, and pen in rays of light, and the pen is located and recognized. In a similar way, it is awareness present in each sense organ and in the mind that makes the act of knowing and thinking possible. It is this awareness that the Upanisads speak of as *ātmā*.

What is true of the act of seeing obtains also for every other act of sense perception. Hearing (sound-ear-mind-awareness), touching (sensation-skin-mind-awareness), smelling (scent-nostril-mind-awareness), and tasting (taste-tongue-mind-awareness) occur only in the presence of awareness. Awareness is the necessary common factor for all perceptual processes. The Kena text describes this awareness as the "Mind of the mind" because it enables thinking to occur and makes thoughts known. When a book is seen with the eyes and recognized with the thought "This is a book," this thought is revealed because of the presence of awareness.

The Singularity of the Self

Is this awareness singular or is it plural? In other words, is there a distinct eye-awareness, ear-awareness, skin-awareness, mind-awareness, as different as the various objects of perception and experience? It is obvious from this Kena verse that the "Ear of the ear" is the "Mind of the mind" and the "Eye of the eye." Instruments of perception are many, but the awareness that enables perception is identical in each one. *Dakṣiṇāmūrti Stotra* (4), a hymn composition attributed to Śaṅkara, employs a visual example to illustrate the unity of *ātmā* in the midst of a multiplicity of sense organs. "All this world shines after Him alone shining in the consciousness 'I know,' after Him alone whose consciousness luminous like a light of a mighty lamp standing in the bosom of a many-holed pot, moves outwards through the sense-organs such as the eyes."[2]

If one places a lamp in a pot with several holes, beams of light will radiate from each aperture illumining objects within the range of each beam. Although the rays, to the undiscerning, appear to be manifold, the source is single and unbroken. In a similar way, a singular awareness radiates through all five senses and mind, revealing and illumining forms, sounds, smells, sensations, tastes, and thoughts.

One wonders about the status of this Advaita claim for the unitary nature of awareness in relation to the Buddhist teaching about the nature of consciousness, generally listed as the fifth of the five aggregates (*khandas*). In Buddhist analysis, consciousness is presented as a response to the stimulus of external phenomena and treated as being of six kinds. "Thus," in the words of Walpola Rahula, "like sensation, perception, and volition, consciousness also is of six kinds, in relation to six internal faculties and corresponding six external objects."[3] What is of significance here for discussion and clarification between both traditions is whether such an understanding is suggesting differences in the nature of consciousness itself (visual consciousness, hearing consciousness, and mental consciousness) or if the differences are in the realm of the faculties and the objects to which these relate. Of course, there is also the important Advaita teaching that awareness is not subject to arising because it is timeless and illumines everything that is subject to arising.

Awareness is free also from all gender constructions. Kena Upaniṣad (2) switches from the neuter (*yat*) to the masculine (*sah*) in speaking of the *ātmā*, making the point that it is free from every gender attribute. This verse is inclusive of the entire mind-body complex, making it clear that nothing is separate from the *ātmā*. It is immediately available and does not have to be sought in a different place or time. It is present in every act of thinking, speaking, seeing, hearing, tasting, touching, and smelling. Body and mental activity become the teaching means for pointing out the self.

The Immortality of the Self

After describing the *ātmā* as "Ear of the ear," the Kena teacher concludes the verse with the teaching "The wise, freeing themselves from this world, become immortal." What do the wise free themselves from? How does this freedom result in becoming immortal? The wise gain freedom from wrongly identifying and equating the *ātmā* with the instruments of perception and thinking. The *ātmā* is understood to be the Eye of the eye and not the eye, the Mind of the mind and not the mind. The wise person comprehends the difference between awareness and all its objects, especially the body, senses, and mind. The intimate association between awareness and its instruments makes it easy, and even natural, to identify these completely and to mutually attribute the nature of one upon the other. Bhagavadgītā 13:15 describes the *atma* as being within and outside all beings, the moving and unmoving, far and near and as unknown because of its subtlety.

A popular illustration used by Śaṅkara and other Advaita teachers clarifies the nature of this mutual confusion. Suppose one took a round iron ball and immersed it in a bonfire. When the iron ball gets red because of intense heat, it is removed and placed on the ground. Someone who was not a witness to the process may then describe it as "a round red ball of fire." In this statement, "roundness," an attribute of the ball, is imposed on the fire, and "redness," a quality of fire, is imposed on the ball. Both are mistakenly identified with each other because the ball is not intrinsically red and fire not round. Even though in close association, the distinct natures of ball and fire may be understood. In a similar way, the nature of awareness, associated with but intrinsically free from the attributes of body and mind, is understood by the wise.

Why is the wise person described as becoming immortal through this knowledge? The reason, according to Advaita, is that while objects of awareness are subject to change and time, awareness, the witness of everything, is unchanging and constant. As Bhagavadgītā 2:20 states:

> "This (self) is never born; nor does it die. It is not that, having been, it ceases to exist again. It is unborn, eternal, undergoes no change whatsoever, and is ever new. When the body is destroyed, the self is not destroyed."[4]

In all stages of life—childhood, youth, adulthood, and old age—there are changes, physically, mentally, and emotionally. Awareness illumines and makes all such changes known; time itself is an object in relation to awareness.

The Self as Free from the Limits of Time

One of the distinctive methods (*prakriyās*) employed in Advaita to teach about the timeless nature of awareness is the analysis of the three states of experience (*avasthā-traya-prakriyā*), based on the analysis of the Māṇḍūkya Upaniṣad. The essential argument here is that awareness is invariably present in the states of waking, dreaming, and sleep. It is the witness of all the events occurring in these states. In the waking state, awareness is present, along with the mind and body and the waking world. In the dream state, awareness continues, along with the mind, but the waking world and body give way to a dream world and body. In the sleep state, the waking and dream worlds, bodies, and mind give way to a condition of unknowing. Awareness still is, however, because the absence of knowing is known. In other words, "I am aware that I did not know anything." The analysis of the three states of experience aims at pointing to awareness as the invariable presence in all changing states of experience and in all stages of life.

The immortality that is described in the Kena text is not a process of transforming the mortal into something immortal. It is not the case also of attaining a state of immortality after the death of the body. *Ātmā* is, by nature, free from the limits of time, and mortality is attributed to it only when it is erroneously identified with the attributes of finitude belonging to body and mind. "This (self)," as Bhagavadgītā 2:24–25 puts it, "cannot be slain, burnt, drowned, or dried. It is changeless, all pervading, stable, immovable and eternal. This is said to be unmanifest, not an object of thought, and not subject to change. Therefore, knowing this, you ought not to grieve."[5] Fear of death is overcome here and now through understanding oneself to be the "Ear of the ear" and the "Mind of the mind."

The Unity of the Self

We considered, earlier, the Advaita teaching that though perceptual and mental processes differ, awareness in the body is not multiple. Does awareness differ, however, from one body to another? Are there distinctions between the awareness in one body and another? The entire purpose of Advaita instruction is to transmit the understanding that awareness is the substratum and content of the "I" notion or sense. Each student listening to the Kena teacher is meant to appreciate that she is the Ear of the ear and Mind of the mind. *Ātmā* is to be understood not as the unique Ear of a specific ear, but as the Ear of all ears and the Mind of all minds. Bhagavadgītā 13:13 and 13:33 use two striking visual

images to teach about the identity of awareness in all beings. The first describes *ātmā* as a cosmic person and all sense organs and organs of action as belonging to *ātmā*. "That has hands and feet on all sides, has eyes, heads and mouths on all sides, has ears on all sides; it stands in the world, pervading everything."
The second (13:33) likens the *ātmā* to the one sun that lights up our entire world. "Just as one sun illumines this entire world, so also the *kṣetrī* (one who exists in the field) illumines the entire *kṣetra* (field)."[6]

The Self as Free from Space Limits

What is clear from verses like these in the Bhagavadgītā and similar texts in the Upaniṣads is that awareness is not two. There is a single awareness knowing and objectifying all minds and all bodies. Liberating wisdom, in Advaita, finds expression always in the understanding of *ātmā* in all beings and all beings in *ātmā* (Bhagavadgītā 6:29).[7] The identity and unity of *ātmā* in all beings is generally presented in the Upaniṣads and Bhagavadgītā along with claims for its all-pervasiveness or transcendence of spatial limits. The analogy used most often by Advaita teachers to instruct about its transcendence of spatial limits is space (Bhagavadgītā 9:6; 13:32). Swami Dayananda explains the claim in this way:

> The moon is in awareness because I am aware of the moon. Between awareness, you and the moon in awareness, what is the distance? There is no distance. Between I the awareness and the moon in awareness, if there is any distance, what should it be? Space. And the space is where? In awareness. Between awareness and space there cannot be any distance. Therefore, in awareness is the space, in space is the moon, in space is the sun, in space are the stars, in space are all the planets. All of them, the whole physical universe is in space and space is in awareness. Therefore between awareness and any object in the world what is the distance? There is no distance between awareness and this physical world.[8]

The teacher's answer to the student's question in the Kena Upaniṣad about the enabling ground of mental and sense functioning is awareness. It is the *ātmā* as awareness that enlivens all physical and mental activity. It objectifies everything without itself ever becoming an object. Awareness cannot become an object to itself. Awareness is timeless and invariably present in all states of experience. As the unitary, indivisible self of all, *ātmā* is not limited by space. It is the all-pervasive reality in which the objectified universe exists.

If this is the entirety of the Advaita teaching, the tradition will culminate in proposing a panentheistic but ultimately dualistic view consisting of awareness and a world of distinct objects that exists in awareness. Awareness may be all-pervasive, but the radical difference between awareness as subject and the world of objects is not overcome. Awareness is still subject to the limits of being a specific object, even an all-pervasive one, in the midst of other objects. The principal teaching technique employed by Advaita teachers to explain the non-duality between subject and object and to clarify that awareness is not one object in a world of many objects but constitutes the nature of all objects is the cause and effect pedagogy (*kāraṇa-kārya prakriyā*).

The Relationship between Cause and Effect

Although there are examples of this method of instruction throughout the Upanisads, the one most commonly cited and employed by Advaita teachers occurs in the Chāndogya Upaniṣad (6). The dialogue here is between the teacher, Āruni, and his son, Śvetaketu. Śvetaketu was sent away by his father for twelve years to study the Vedas, because he wanted his son to become a learned person in accomplishments. When Śvetaketu returned home after his long years as a Vedic student, Āruni discovered that he was "conceited, regarding himself as a great scholar, and arrogant." To burst the bubble of his son's haughtiness and to show the continuing incompleteness of his knowledge, Āruni asked if he had inquired about "That through which the unheard becomes heard, the unthought of becomes thought of and the unknown becomes known?"[9] In response to Śvetaketu's request for an explanation of this teaching, Áruni provides three analogies (6:4–6) dealing with cause and effect relationships.

> Just as through a lump of clay, everything that is made of clay becomes known; modifications of clay are due to words, mere names; clay alone is real.
>
> Just as through a single ingot of gold, everything that is made of gold becomes known; modifications of gold are due to words, mere names; gold alone is real.
>
> Just as thorough a single nail-clipper, all that is made of iron become known; modifications of iron are due to words, mere names; iron alone is real.

Following his son's request for further instruction (6:7), Āruni connects his analogies with the emergence of the universe as the self-multiplication of the infinite.

> In the beginning, my dear, that was Being only, one, without a second. Some say that, in the beginning, this was Non-being, only one without a second. From that Non-being sprang Being.
>
> "But how could it be so, my dear?" said he. "How could Being be born from Non-Being? in fact, this was Being only, in the beginning, one, without a second.
>
> It thought, "May I become many; may I grow forth."[10]

If we keep in mind the limits of all finite analogies, useful only as teaching devices, the intent of Āruni's instructive analogies is clear. In the case of clay, gold, and iron and their multiplication into various products, new ontological realities are not created. A clay pot has no existence apart from clay, and so its creation may appropriately be described as word- or name-created (*vācārambhaṇaṁ vikāro nāmadheyaṁ*). This is obvious from the fact that when the clay pot exists, clay also exists. If the clay pot is not, clay still is. If clay is not, however, the clay pot is not. The existence of the clay pot as effect is inseparable from that of its cause, clay, and entirely dependent on it. It has no being apart from clay. It is this fact that leads the teacher to affirm that clay alone is real (*satyam*). In relation to its cause (*kāraṇa*), the clay pot as effect (*kārya*) cannot be described as existent or nonexistent.[11] It is not independently existent, because its existence is entirely dependent on clay. It is not to be described also as nonexistent because, unlike a dog's horns, its existence is established by perception, a valid source of knowledge. It has pragmatic value and can be used for transporting and storing water, even though it does not have its own independent ontological reality. The relationship between clay and a clay pot, as cause and effect, is asymmetrical. The clay pot is clay, but clay is not a clay pot. If we insist that clay is a clay pot, then it is necessary to establish that wherever there is clay, there is also a clay pot, and the untruth of such a claim is obvious. Clay has the potential to assume multiple forms.

The relationship between cause and effect in an example such as that between clay and a clay pot may be described as not-two (*advaita*). To describe it as one negates the existence of the clay pot; to describe it as two ignores the fact that the clay pot has no substantial existence apart from the clay. If clay is real (*satyam*), we may describe the clay pot as unreal (*mithyā*) once it clear that the clay pot is not illusory or, as noted earlier, nonexistent. *Mithyā* describes anything that is substantially dependent on its cause or substratum for existence.

Moving from this finite analogy to describing the relationship between *brahman* and the universe, the Taittrīya Upaniṣad (3.1.1) describes *brahman* as that from which all beings are born, that by which they live after birth, and that into which they all return.[12] The texts also demonstrate a concern to teach the singleness and non-dual nature of *brahman* (*ekamevādvitīyam*) (Chāndogya Upanisad 6.2.1).[13] The non-dual nature of *brahman* should be understood to mean that it is free from distinctions of every kind. Because *brahman* alone exists prior to the emergence of the universe, there is nothing else different from it (*vijātīya*) or similar to it (*sajātīya*) from which it may be distinguished. Being without parts, there also are no internal distinctions (*svagata bheda*) that characterize the simplicity of its nature. From this whole and indivisible infinite, the universe emerges as an intentional act of self-multiplication. The sentence used most frequently in the Upanisads is "Let me become many (*bahusyāma*).[14] It is here that the limits of the clay–clay pot example become obvious, because the Upaniṣads do not present the self-multiplication of the infinite as a pantheistic transformation. Change is a process occurring in time and space, and the infinite source of time and space does not become subject to these created elements. The infinite is not depleted or lost by the act of creating but remains single and non-dual (*ekamevādvitīyam*). The Upaniṣads, in the interpretation of the Advaita tradition, want to communicate a distinctive cause and effect relationship (*kāraṇa-kārya sambandha*) in which the infinite, without being subject to time, loss of nature, or limitation of any kind, generates effects. Its relationship with such effects can only be described as not-two (*advaita*), because the existence of the effects cannot be denied, even though the substance of their existence is the infinite. A multiplicity of effects does not compromise the truth of non-duality or the Upaniṣad teaching that "[v]erily, all this universe is *brahman*. From Him do all things originate, into Him do they dissolve and by Him are they sustained" (Chandogya Upaniṣad 3.14.1).[15]

Returning to the text of the Kena Upaniṣad, the heart of the teacher's instruction is that it is *ātmā* as awareness that sustains all life-functions. *Ātmā* is identical in all beings, transcending time and space limits. The discussion of the special cause and effect relationship between *brahman* and the universe clarifies that *brahman* is free also from the limits of being one object (*vastu*) among other objects, because multiplicity is in form and name alone, and the infinite constitutes the substantial being of all that exists. In the Kena Upanishad, this identity between the awareness ("the Eye of the eye") and the infinite *brahman* is affirmed in a series of almost identical poetic verses (1.5–1.9).

> That which is not revealed by speech, but by which speech is revealed, know that alone to be *brahman* and not this that is worshipped here.
>
> That which the mind does not objectify, but by which the mind is known, know that alone to be *brahman* and not this that is worshipped here.[16]

For the first time in the Kena Upaniṣad, a name, *brahman,* is used for that which the teacher has been describing as the Ear of the ear and Mind of the mind. The naming of this as *brahman* is understood by the Advaita tradition as an unequivocal affirmation of the identity of *ātmā* and *brahman,* the infinite. Sentences in the Upaniṣads that propound this teaching are referred to in Advaita as *mahāvākyas* (great sentences). Traditionally, there are four such sentences identified in the Upaniṣads, one from each of the four Vedas.[17] These verses in the Kena Upaniṣad, although not listed as great sentences, enunciate the same teaching, identifying the infinite as the awareness that enables and objectifies all sense, physiological, and mental functions. The infinite is not a specific object in the world, however sacred such an object may be regarded.

The Kena Upaniṣad text started with an identification of awareness as the ultimate factor in the human personality. The revelation that this awareness is *brahman,* the infinite self of all, is at the heart of the liberating teaching of Advaita. It is this teaching that liberates from the human predicament of suffering caused by a sense of want and inadequacy. The comprehension of this teaching overcomes the problem of ignorance that is synonymous with wrongly identifying oneself with specific limited objects of knowledge.

Overcoming the Brahman-World Dualism

We explore further, in the next chapter, the meaning and implications of liberation for our life in the world and for our relationships. Here, we should note that understanding one's identity with the infinite *brahman* should not result in an attitude of hostility or fear toward the finite. Advaita claims about the nature of reality ought to engender an appreciation of the limits of the finite, but not disgust toward anything that is, by nature, bound by space and time. Unfortunately, the necessary Advaita method of instruction, and especially the method of distinguishing between the knower and known, subject and object, are not always properly complemented by instruction emphasizing the special non-difference of cause and effect. This leads to a devaluation of the world and its disconnection from the infinite. Although a non-dualistic tradition,

Advaita often seems in theory and practice to advocate a dualism that negativizes and condemns the world while commending the value of the infinite. This understanding of the meaning of Advaita must be refuted by emphasizing that it is improper to dualistically distinguish the existence and reality of the world from the infinite. Returning to our Upaniṣad analogy of the relationship between clay and clay pots, it is correct, as we noted above, to say that the clay pot is clay, but not that clay is a clay pot. In a similar way, we may say that the world is *brahman*, but not that *brahman* is the world. If Advaita does not proclaim the world to be *brahman*, then we are left with two problematic options. First, we may deny the reality of the world, likening it, as so many Advaita interpreters do, to an illusion. This option, however, betrays the knowledge and experience of the world through valid sources of knowledge such as perception and inference. The existence of the world is *pramāṇa-siddha*, that is, established by a valid source of knowledge. This option denies also the Advaita argument that the world does exist independently of the human mind (BSBh 2.2.28). It is not a subjective human error or projection. The non-duality of Advaita does not require a denial of the reality of the world. Second, one may admit the reality of the world but attribute its origin and reality to some insentient source other than *brahman*, such as *māyā*.[18] This explanation of the world, however, compromises fundamentally the teaching of non-duality that all is *brahman* and that the world originates from, is sustained by, and returns to the infinite. Advaita is not opposed to the existence of diversity, but it certainly excludes the claim that there are ontological realities other than *brahman*. To describe the world as *brahman* expresses, as we shall see in the next chapter, value for the world while at the same time affirming the limitless nature of *brahman*.

Following this mode of characterizing the *brahman*-world relationship, the liberated person, understanding her identity with *brahman* and the limits of her body and mind, does not disown or reject these. She owns the body and mind as herself while at the same time not identifying herself entirely with these. It is appropriate to say that the body and the mind is *ātmā*; it is not appropriate to say that *ātmā* is the body or the mind, because such a statement implies its loss through transformation into something finite and identifies it completely with particular objects. The consequence is a denial of the limitless nature of the *ātmā*. Owning the body as one of the forms of the infinite rightfully ensures that the physical is not denounced as that which is sinister and suspect and disconnected from the reality of the infinite. Advaita does not justify any radical spirit-matter dualism that assigns these realities to distinct ontological categories, disassociating the latter from the former and condemning it as the realm of evil. Liberation implies the freedom from wrongly identifying the self with the limits of the mind-body complex. It does not confer on the liberated the qualities of omnipotence and omniscience. What it does mean is that these limits are no longer sources of anxiety because the liberated person no longer confines her identity to the body and mind. The body and mind, at the most fundamental level, are one's own self, like the clay pot is clay. Any object, however, does not limit the self.

Although the Advaita tradition is concerned centrally with explicating the nature of the relationship between the infinite and the world (*kāraṇa-kārya prakriyā*) and, as we noted above, utilizes various Upaniṣadic analogies to clarify this relationship, the tradition is not interested in matters related to details and order of the creation of the world. Such matters come under the purview of other valid sources of knowledge, such as perception and inference, and are not the authoritative concern of the Upanisads as a *pramāṇa*. The teachings in the Upaniṣads center on liberation (*mokṣa*), and information about the details of creation are not understood by Advaita as central to this purpose. In the Advaita perspective, passages in the Upaniṣads that describe the sequence of creation are meant for instruction about *brahman* and do not have any independent significance. The analogy of clay and clay pots is meant to teach that all things originate from, are sustained by, and return to *brahman* and the non-difference of cause (*brahman*) and effect (world).

The Purpose of Creation in Advaita

It is true also that the Upaniṣads and the Advaita tradition do not focus much on a purpose for creation. This is not to imply that we should not concern ourselves with this matter. While admitting the limits of all language in relation to the infinite, including the language of purpose, it is useful, as I hope this study will make clearer in later chapters, to consider a possible purpose for creation. Advaita is uncompromising in its claim that the universe has its origins in *brahman* and in no other source, sentient or insentient. It refutes also the possibility of spontaneous creation. As Śaṅkara states in his commentary on Brahmasūtra 1.1.2, "The universe cannot possibly be thought of as having its origin from any other factor, e.g., *pradhāna* (primordial nature) which is insentient, or from atoms, or non-existence, or some soul under worldly conditions (viz., *hiraṇyagarbha*). Nor can it originate spontaneously; for in this universe people (desirous of products) have to depend on specific, space, time and causation" (14). Śaṅkara also negates the possibility that *brahman* may be irrational in motivation. Such arguments refuting a spontaneous creation and irrationality in *brahman* open the possibility for us to speculate meaningfully about a possible purpose for *brahman* in creating.

Two of the creation passages in the Upaniṣads (Taittirīya Upaniṣad 2.6.1 and Chandogya Upanisad 6.2.1–6.2.4) use the identical sentences "Let me become many; let me be born." In the Taittirīya text, the desire of *brahman* to become many is followed by a text emphasizing deliberation and intentionality in the act of self-multiplication (*sa tapotapyata sa tapastaptvā*). How may we construe this wish on the part of *brahman* to become many? I concur with Advaitins who argue that we cannot understand such a desire as signifying any lack or insufficiency in the infinite. *Brahman* is the unique and single source of everything; there is nothing with *brahman* and nothing beyond *brahman.* The all in all cannot lack anything because nothing exists that it is not and that may be an object of its desire. It seems odd to propose that *brahman* may create something and then pursue it as an object of desire. Any act of *brahman,* if we may describe the limitless as "acting," can only proceed from the limitless nature of *brahman.*

I find support for this viewpoint in the Taittirīya Upaniṣad (3.6.1), dialogue between the teacher, Varuṇa, and his son, Bhṛgu. Bhṛgu approaches his father for instruction about *brahman,* and Varuṇa defines the infinite as "that from which all beings are born, that by which they live after birth and that into which they all return." Applying this definition, Bhṛgu then contemplates *brahman* serially as food, life-breath, and mind. On each occasion, he shares his contemplation with his teacher and is advised to ponder further. Finally, Bhṛgu returns to this teacher, having contemplated *brahman* as fullness (*ānanda*). "He knew fullness as *brahman*. From fullness all these beings are born; by fullness they live after birth and into fullness they return."[19] Bhṛgu is not requested by his teacher to inquire further. This important text suggests powerfully that we must think of creation as expressing the limitlessness of the infinite, an overflow of divine fullness and a celebration of what the infinite is.[20]

Celebrative self-expression, if I may so characterize the Upaniṣadic suggestion of *brahman*'s motive in creation, may be thought of as a purpose with one important proviso. Because it does not spring from any want, it does not have a self-directed character, and the infinite does not seek a private end from creation. "Love" is the word that is used often to describe actions that are performed without selfish intent and without expectation of personal reward. May we use it to describe the unconditional expression of *brahman*'s fullness in creation? The Taittīriya Upaniṣad 3.6.1, cited above, speaks of *brahman* as continuously sustaining that which is created (*ānandena jātāni jīvanti*). The pouring of divine fullness is continuous. May we speak also of this sustaining activity as loving?

Creation as celebration and as proceeding from the fullness of the infinite confers value to the world and becomes, very importantly, a model for human action. These are matters to which we return in subsequent chapters.

4

The Liberated Life

Suffering and Ignorance

Although there are differences in emphasis and description, the traditions of Buddhism and Advaita Vedānta share an understanding of the human problem as suffering (*duḥkha*). Suffering expresses itself in anxiety about mortality and in fears about the transient character of pleasurable experiences. Most importantly, for Advaita, suffering is present in the insistent sense of self-lack, self-insufficiency, and incompleteness. It is experienced as a fundamental sense of insecurity of self. The desire to overcome this uncomfortable sense of uncertainty about the value of oneself is often the propelling drive behind the insatiable acquisition of wealth, power, and fame. Such pursuits become, too often, futile efforts to add value to oneself. Because the problem of lack, according to Advaita, is centered on notions of self, the solution will not be found outside oneself. Wealth, power, or fame does not intrinsically add to or alter the nature of self; through such acquisitions, we may come to hold different notions about the value of the self, but such notions are always relative to the gains of rivals and will never overcome the suffering that is rooted in our self-insecurity. Finite efforts, as all efforts must by nature be, will never eliminate want in the self or bring about its completeness.

When the Advaita tradition looks to the immediate cause of the suffering that is associated with our sense of self-lack, it identifies it as self-ignorance (*avidyā*). Inadequacy of self is the consequence of erroneous notions that assume the self to be an individualized entity, limited by time and space, and different and distinct from other individualized selves and objects in the universe. To overcome these presumed limits, one engages in actions of various kinds that have the fundamental purpose of engendering fullness of self. As noted in Chapter 3, Advaita proceeds by interrogating these widely held notions about self and instructing a radically different understanding that refutes claims about its isolation and limitedness. The heart of the Advaita teaching is that the self that we erroneously assume to be finite is in fact identical to the infinite *brahman,* which constitutes the ground, truth, and fundamental nature of all that exists. The self is not a "thing" among other "things," sentient and insentient, but, as in the analogy of clay and clay pots, the self is the essential reality of all that exists.

Knowledge and Liberation

Although Advaita speaks of suffering as caused by ignorance, we should be very careful that we do not characterize ignorance in ways that appear to grant it any metaphysical substantiality.[1] Advaita locates suffering in *avidyā,* but ignorance implies only a specific way of thinking about the nature of reality and, in particular, about the nature of self. Ignorance is thinking that the self is an isolated, limited entity, distinct and different from every other self. Similarly, liberation is knowing that the self is without limits, free and identical in all beings. What the Advaita tradition speaks of as *avidyā* and *mokṣa* (liberation) are mutually exclusive ways of understanding the nature of the self. Knowledge and ignorance are conditions of the mind; the infinite self remains unaffected by whatever thoughts one may have about its nature. Appropriate thought forms that correspond to the nature of the self as free from limits displace ignorance, which is of the nature of erroneous notions about self. The fact that *avidyā* is notional only establishes the possibility of its negation. If, on the other had, it has a substantial reality, its removal becomes impossible and some form of escape from this world becomes necessary for liberation. It is the notional nature of *avidyā* that makes possible also what Advaita regards as the state of living liberation (*jīvanmukti*). This is the understanding that liberation is a particular state of being in this life and world and not a place to be reached after the death of the body. *Avidyā,* we cannot emphasize enough, is not identical with the world, but with a certain way of being in the world. Liberation is a different way of being here and now that follows the right understanding of the nature of oneself. Kena Upaniṣad 2.5, speaking of the knowledge of the infinite, puts the emphasis rightfully on the present and on life in this world. "If one knows here, there is truth; if one does not know here, there is great destruction."[2]

The Meaning of Saṁsāra

What has been said above about *avidyā* may also be said of *saṁsāra.* The latter term is used often negatively, in Advaita and in the wider Hindu tradition, to be synonymous with ignorance and also with the world and life within it. This uncritical equation of the world and existence in it with *saṁsāra* ignores fundamental Advaita teachings. First, by negatively characterizing the world as *saṁsāra,* we ignore the most basic of Advaita insights that the world is *brahman.* Advaitins must exercise philosophical vigilance to avoid attributing independent existence to world or admitting a world-*brahman* dualism. It is easier to do this when the world as world is negativized. Advaita (not-two) describes the special relationship between world and *brahman*; the world is *brahman*; *brahman* is not the world. Advaita does not intrinsically denigrate the world. Second, the negativization of the world as *saṁsāra* overlooks the fact that the world as world is not the human problem. At the heart of the problem is a false notion of self and consequently a false understanding of self-world and self-other relationships. Advaita does not call on us to reject the world, but offers a new understanding of self that leads to a transformed view of the world. This understanding finds confirmation in the Advaita affirmation of living-liberation, the possibility of attaining liberation in this world. This is a clear attestation of the compatibility of liberation with life in the world. Liberation is not equated with escape from the world.

If we attempted to summarize the worldview of Advaita in terms of diagnosis, etiology, prognosis, and therapy, structurally similar to the four noble truths of the Buddhist tradition, the following will be a likely expression:

1. Diagnosis: Suffering (*duḥkha*), expressing primarily in a sense of self-lack and inadequacy.
2. Etiology: The primary cause of suffering is ignorance (*avidyā*), which is the false notion that the self is an individualized and separate entity, limited by time and space and distinct from the world and other selves.
3. Prognosis: Liberation (*mokṣa*) is possible here and now and is attained by the negation of *avidyā*.
4. Therapy: Knowledge of oneself (*ātmājñāna*) is the effective antidote to ignorance, and this knowledge is gained by inquiry into a valid source (*pramāṇa*) with the aid of a qualified teacher (*guru*). The Upaniṣads constitute the valid source of knowledge of the self.[3]

Liberation (*mokṣa*) is awakening through knowledge to the truth of the self. The Upaniṣad *pramāṇa* and teacher do not bring into existence a new self or change the existing self into something different. Liberation is the correct understanding of the self that is always present but mistakenly identified to be what it is not. It is a discovery of what has always been true about ourselves through the compassionate instruction of a teacher who has made this discovery and embodies its meaning. The self, which is always free, but regarded as bound, is now known to be free. Because the self is without limits, self-knowledge transforms our understanding of our relationship with others and the universe.

Ignorance and Its Consequences

Although we may speak of ignorance and knowledge as mental states, one contrary to the nature of the self and the other corresponding to it, the differences could not be greater. To understand better the implications of liberation for life in the world, we should first consider the consequences of ignorance. Muṇḍaka Upaniṣad (2.2.8) speaks of the loosening of the "knots of the heart (*hṛdayagranthi*)" as a consequence of the knowledge of *brahman*. The expression is repeated in Kaṭha Upaniṣad 2.3.15: "When all the knots of the heart are destroyed, even while a person is alive, then a mortal becomes immortal. This much is the instruction (of all the Upaniṣads)."[4]

The knots of the heart are traditionally identified as threefold—ignorance (*avidyā*), greed (*kāma*), and *karma* (greedful actions). These are spoken of as knots because of their nature as binding agents. They constrict and limit our understanding of self, depriving us of the freedom to live with fullness and contentment. The primary knot is ignorance. This takes the form of a fundamental misconstruing of the self, considering it to be individual, distinct from other selves and from the world. In the place of the unconstructed self, constituting the ground and nature of all that exists, we identify and cling to a constructed ego-self, fashioned from prevailing cultural and social norms and thought to be different from other constructed selves. Such a constructed ego-self is necessarily limited and experiences the anxiety, inadequacy, and insecurity of its limitedness. Because such a sense of self-lack and insignificance is uncomfortable and unacceptable, one develops desires for objects and for more intangible gains, such as fame, hoping thereby to overcome the haunting lack and emptiness. For various reasons, discussed in Chapter 1, such gains do not fill the lack experienced by the constructed self, and the fundamental human problem remains unresolved. Instead of interrogating our assumptions about the nature of self or reflecting on the limits of finite gains, we multiply desires and become victims of an insatiable greed. We competitively rival others for "more" wealth, fame, power, and success. Greed finds expression in greedful actions, the kinds of actions that more likely to be socially destructive and indifferent to the well-being of others.

Although the discussion of the three knots (ignorance-greed-greedful actions) in the Advaita tradition and, more broadly, in Hinduism has focused on the individual nature and effects of these knots, it is clear that the knots of the heart have social and institutional expressions. Our search for self-value by asserting our superior worth over others finds social expression in group identities, often formed on the basis of nation, ethnicity, religion, tribe, or caste, that profess exclusive value over other groups. The demeaning of the other, when it is a group phenomenon, seems, unfortunately, to offer a measure of legitimacy and shelter from critical scrutiny. In a somewhat similar way, individual greed, born out of a sense of inner lack, generates and provides support for corporations and institutions whose single motive is the maximization of profits and that are more than willing, as we have witnessed in the near collapse of our financial system, to employ measures that are reckless and detrimental to the public good. What we too often fail to discern is the manner in which such institutionalized greed expresses and mirrors our own insatiable needs, born of self-lack. A better understanding of the relationship between the individual and institutional or structural expressions of ignorance and greed will help the Hindu tradition more realistically address social problems that arise from persistent oppressive and unjust structures.

The glimpse given to us in Bhagavadgītā 16:13–15 into the thinking process of a person who is bound by the knots of the heart may be applied easily to a corporation or institution.

> Today, this is gained by me. I will gain this (also) which pleases me. This wealth I have; this wealth also I will have later.
>
> This enemy is destroyed by me and I will destroy others also; I am the ruler; I am the enjoyer; I am successful, powerful and happy.
>
> Those who are totally deluded due to lack of discrimination say, "I have wealth. I was born in a very good family. Who else is there who is equal to me? I will perform rituals. I will give. I will enjoy."[5]

Untying the Knots of the Heart (Ignorance-Greed-Greedful Actions)

If the first knot of the heart is ignorance, followed by greed and greedful actions, it follows logically that it must be also the first to be untied.[6] This knot is untied by overcoming false notions of a separate self, limited to the body. The liberated understands the self to be the limitless (*brahman*) that is the reality-ground of all that exists. The nature of the self as constituting the whole of existence means that it is full and complete, without lack or insufficiency. The fullness of the self, conveyed in the famous Taittirīya Upaniṣad 2.1.1 text, *satyam jñānam anantam brahma* (*brahman* is truth, knowledge and infinite), is what is expressed in the word *ānanda*. *Ānanda* points to the nature of the self as free from want, insecurity, and insignificance, and this is synonymous with the fact of self as infinite (*ananta*). That self-lack is overcome by self-knowledge is indicated clearly in Chāndogya Upaniṣad 8.7.1, where students approach their teacher for the knowledge of *ātmā* that results in attaining all desires and all worlds. The idea here is that the fullness sought through desires for objects in the world is attained through knowing the full self.

The loosening of the knot of self-ignorance, resulting in a radically new understanding of self in all, leads to an untying of the knot of greed (*kāma*). Although most translators render *kāma* as desire and speak consequently of liberation as resulting in freedom from desire, I prefer to render *kāma*, in this context, as greed. The reason is that liberation is not incompatible with desire and especially desires for the well-being of others. Liberation is incompatible with greed, which is a condition of insatiable lack and want. The connection between understanding the fullness of self and freedom from greed is made clear in Krishna's teaching to Arjuna in Bhagavadgītā 2:55, describing the nature of a liberated person: "When all greedful desires in the mind are given up, and one is pleased in the self by the self, one is said to be a person of steady wisdom."[7]

It is the discovery of the fullness of the self that makes release from the knot of greed possible. The Bhagavadgītā (2:59) cautions us that greed will not be overcome through any effort to forcibly restrain sense-indulgence. The longing for objects of enjoyment is not thereby transcended. It is only understanding of the nature of the self that brings freedom from greedful longing. The ideal is a freedom in the world that is gained by insight into the fullness of self.

Ignorance is the root of greed that, in turn, finds outward expression in greedful or selfish actions, resulting in suffering to oneself and to others. Freedom from greed unties the knot of greedful actions, but does not diminish our capacity to act. This is an important distinction that is not always made with clarity. Even as we must distinguish between desires and greedful desires, we should not identify actions with selfish actions. Generally speaking, the use of the terms, *kāma* and *karma* in texts like the Upaniṣads and Bhagavadgītā refers to greedful desires and action that originate from the condition of ignorance. This should not be construed, however, to mean that the condition of liberation is synonymous with freedom from all desires and inaction. Close reading of these texts reveals that liberated persons are capable of desiring and engaging in action. The desires and actions of the liberated are qualitatively different. The Upaniṣads and the Bhagavadgītā, speaking out of respect for the freedom of the liberated, do not make prescriptive declarations that are directed toward her. Bhagadavadgītā 3:17 is a typical example: "Whereas, for the person who delights in the self, who is pleased with the self and who is contented in the self alone, there is nothing to be done."[8]

The expression "there is nothing to be done" (*tasya kāryaṁ na vidyate*) should not be read as meaning "nothing *can* be done" or as "nothing *should* be done." It emphasizes the freedom in action granted to the liberated. There is no action necessary to be undertaken for the attainment of fullness of self. *Moksa* means freedom from ignorance, but also freedom in action.

Freedom from ignorance and greedful desires liberates our motivations and energizes us to desire and work for the well-being of others. This is Krishna's teaching in Bhagavadgītā 3:25, where he states that the liberated person acts as energetically as the unliberated, but does so for the good of the world (*lokasaṅgraham*). The Advaita commentator Śaṅkara concurs and paraphrases Krishna's meaning in the following words: "For Me (Krishna) or for any other person who, knowing the Self, thus seeks the welfare of the world, there is nothing to do except it be with a view to that welfare of the world at large." What is of significance here is the possibility of a way of being in the world, free from the knots of the heart and not characterized by greedful desires and selfish action.

The Social Implications of Liberation

Our focus, so far, has been on the meaning of liberation as freeing us *from* the knots of the heart. This is a direct consequence of the overcoming of ignorance about the nature of self. The emphasis in traditional Advaita teaching has been on the identity between self and the infinite *brahman* and its freedom from the limited characteristics of body and mind. There are, however, other significant social implications of the meaning of liberation. These meanings have received less attention from Advaita commentators. It is to some of these that we now turn.

Identity with All Beings as Love

To know the self as *brahman* is to know oneself as the self of all because the self is not-two. Hindu sacred texts return to this insight again and again. The liberated, according to Bhagavadgītā 6:29, sees the self as abiding in all beings and all beings in the self (*sarvabhūtastham ātmānaṁ sarvabhūtāni cātmani*). In the Īśa Upaniṣad (6–7), such seeing frees from hate, delusion, and sorrow. "One who sees all beings in the self alone and the self in all beings, feels no hatred by virtue of that understanding. For the seer of oneness, who knows all beings to be the self, where is delusion (*mohaḥ*) and sorrow (*śokaḥ*)?"

The overcoming of hate is the direct consequence of this awakening to the truth of the other as one's own self. To hate, reject, or be hostile to another is to hate, reject, and be hostile to oneself. Understanding the self's indivisibility is the deepest identity that one can have with another. Seeing another *as* oneself is different from the affinity that may be forged with another on the basis of shared religious faith, cultural traits, ethnicity, or nationality. It is closer to what it means to recognize another as a member of one's species (human beings), but all of these affinities still have the character of exclusivity on the basis of religion, culture, ethnicity, nationalism, and species. The Advaita teaching invites us to see ourselves in *all;* it is not constricted by an anthropocentrism. Although the term is not directly employed in the Upaniṣads, such seeing may be appropriately described as loving.

The delusion (*mohaḥ*) that is overcome is synonymous with ignorance or with the false notion of separate selfhood that must, by the fact of separateness, be limited and inadequate. Because the notion of separate selfhood is a fundamental source of suffering, its overcoming liberates from sorrow (*śokaḥ*). Seeing oneself in others means that one's self-worth is not diminished by another's gain, because that gain also can be owned as one's own. The implication, of course, is that the other's loss and suffering are also one's own; we learn to embrace and identify with the other both in joy and in sorrow. Bhagavadgītā 6:32 praises the best *yogī* as one who knows the pain and joy of others as her own.

Compassion

Another way of speaking about this identity with others in joy and suffering is compassion (*karuṇa* or *dayā*). In Bhagavadgītā 12:13, Krishna describes as dear to him the person who has no hatred toward any being, who is friendly and compassionate (*karuṇa*), who is non-possessive, non–ego-centered, tranquil in pleasure and pain, and forgiving. The expression of friendliness (*maitraḥ*) is compassion (*karuṇa*). Later (16:2), compassion toward all (*dayā bhūteṣu*) is listed as a quality of a person enjoying a divine disposition.

Compassion, as expressing the unity and oneness of self, the seeing of oneself in another, is clearly implied as an outcome of the liberated life. In the Advaita tradition, desirable conduct follows as an expression of the nature of reality that is not-two. For this reason, right ethics, in the highest sense, is not presented generally in the Upaniṣads in the language of injunctions or prescriptions. Ethics is presented in the context of descriptive references to the conduct of the liberated person in the world. We have noted above, for example, that the Īśa Upaniṣad (6–7) text speaks of the liberated as free from hate. The Bhagavadgītā (5:25 and 12:4) describes the liberated as delighting in the welfare of all. The emphasis in the Upaniṣads is on ontological teaching, describing the truth of reality, and less on ethical injunctions, because the fundamental human problem is characterized as ignorance of the nature of reality (*atma* as *brahman* and constituting the nature of all existence). If ignorance is the source of greed and selfish actions, liberation, the overcoming of ignorance, frees from greed and ego-aggrandizing actions.

The Advaita assumption appears to be that this transformation from greed (*kāma*) to compassion (*karuṇa*) occurs spontaneously. It is also true that the tradition assumes that a person who comes to a teacher (*guru*) in the quest for liberation has lived a life of virtue, following the general dictates of ethics (*sādhāraṇa dharma*) meant for all human beings. These include virtues such as non-violence, truth, non-stealing, and generosity. The cultivation of virtue is understood in Advaita as a necessity for the gain of knowledge of *brahman*. A virtuous life is a means to self-knowledge and an expression of this knowledge.[9]

I want to suggest, however, that the transformation from greed to compassion is not always as spontaneous as we may hope, and the Advaita tradition can learn in this regard and benefit from dialogue with the Buddhist tradition, especially its Mahayana expressions. The Mahayana tradition has emphasized the inseparability of wisdom and compassion and, in the ideal of the Bodhisattva, made compassion integral to our understanding of what the liberated life means when lived out in the world. In addition to articulating a fundamental relationship between wisdom and compassion, Mahayana has emphasized our need for disciplined practices to awaken and deepen our understanding of compassion as a way of being. The Advaita ideal of the living liberated (*jīvanmukta*) is consistent with the ideal of the Bodhisattva, but needs the latter to more fully realize the meaning of the liberated life.

Generosity

The active expression of compassion is giving (*dānaṁ*), and this is commended highly as a virtue throughout the Hindu tradition. Taittirīya Upaniṣad 1.11.1–4 records an ancient commencement address in which the teacher gently commends giving to his graduating class, and does so by qualifying carefully what constitutes appropriate giving. Giving should be done with faith (*śraddhayā deyam*). Faith here signifies an understanding of the unity of existence, the truth that we exist indivisibly in each other, and giving is the overflow of this truth in relationships. Giving with such faith ensures that our giving is not a calculated "giving," that is, motivated by an obsession with personal rewards and benefits. Giving should be done according to one's means (*śriyā deyam*) to emphasize the cultivation of generosity. It should be done with humility (*hriyā deyam*) and friendliness (*saṁvidā deyam*) that reflects a value for and an attitude of respect and reverence for those who receive. The Taittirīya Upaniṣad also recommends giving with fear (*bhiyā deyam*) to impress upon us the seriousness of giving and the concern that it is done in the right manner and with appropriate states of mind and heart. Kaṭha Upaniṣad opens with a story about a son's fears for his father who was not giving according to his means because of miserliness. The son was concerned about the dire consequences of such an improper attitude in giving.

The Bhagavadgītā 17:20–22 follows the Taittirīya Upaniṣad in emphasizing the importance of proper motive in giving and specifies five features of inappropriate giving. First, giving that is motivated by a desire to receive something in return either from the recipient or anyone else. Second, giving that is done reluctantly or grudgingly. Third, giving at an improper time and or place. Fourth, giving to undeserving persons. Gifts should not be given to those who would misuse these gifts or use the resources for inflicting suffering on others. Fifth, giving that is done disrespectfully and with contempt for the receiver, expressed in words of insult, ridicule, or threats. The Bhagavadgītā commends giving to deserving persons, without expectation of return, at the right time and in the right place. The highest motive for giving is compassion (*dayā*) because this expresses, more than any other way of being, the truth of life's unity. Such giving puts the emphasis on the fact that the value of the action is primarily in its compassionate character. The Bhagavadgītā 17:20 articulates this beautifully in the expression "*dātavyam iti*," meaning "it is to be given," or, in other words, giving is good.

Interdependent Existence

The deepest ground, in the Hindu tradition, for compassion and giving is the identity of self in all. These values express the deepest truth about the nature of reality. The tradition, however, does not ignore the empirical or pragmatic (*vyavahārika*) truth that everything exists interdependently. Every facet of the whole that shares the nature of *brahman* exists in an interdependent relationship. The ontological identity that underlies diversity is compatible with interdependent existence. The truth is articulated powerfully in Bhagavadgītā 3:12, which defines a thief as someone who enjoys the gifts of others without offering anything in return. The Bhagavadgītā, in chapter 3, visualizes the universe as an interdependent functioning whole, the thriving and prosperity of which requires the mutual fulfillment of obligations. Failure to fulfill our obligations by following the natural wheel of interdependence is described as sinful and wasteful (3:16).

Krishna (3:13) uses an eloquent analogy to speak of interdependence and accompanying obligations. "Good persons who eat the remnants of sacrifice are freed from all impurities; unrighteous persons who cook only for themselves eat sin."[10] In this verse, Krishna uses the image and example of the ancient fire ritual to speak about interdependence. In this ritual, a special fire altar is constructed, and worshippers sit around the fire making offerings and reciting sacred verses from the Vedas. At the end of the ritual, food, some of which would have been offered into the fire, is distributed among participants. Food is received, but only after it is worshipfully offered. In the structure of all Hindu worship, giving always precedes receiving. This idea of giving and receiving is lifted up by Krishna as a model for human life in the world, characterized by generosity and sharing with others. As we make offerings into the sacred fire, we offer our service to the world, before or while receiving that which we require for our own sustenance and well-being. Because our lives are nourished by the giving of so many (teachers, ancestors, other human beings, and the elements), we express gratitude by generosity. If we are receivers only and not givers, the resources of the word are soon depleted, and we are, as Krishna notes, thieves.

Interdependent living is what the Bhagavdgītā speaks of as *yajña,* characterized by giving and receiving. A community practicing the *yajña* mode of being prospers. This, according to the Bhagavadgītā 3:10, is the way prescribed by the creator for the prosperity of the world: "In the beginning, the Creator, having created beings together with *yajña* said, 'By this may you prosper; may this be your wish-fulfilling cow.' " The mythological cow (*kāmadhuk*) referred to in this verse has a woman's head, a cow's body, a bird's wing, and is believed to grant the wishes of the person who owns it. Our cow of plenty is our ability to live not only for ourselves and to cultivate the virtue of giving (*dānaṁ*). Our prosperity and well-being is linked with the prosperity and well-being of all other beings.

There is a wonderful ancient Hindu story that illustrates this truth. It is said that the creator of the world invited the divine and demonic beings to a grand dinner. The divine beings occupied one side of the banquet hall and the demonic the other side. They sat in rows facing each other. Foods of every imaginable kind were laid out in beautiful dishes before each guest, and everyone was anxious to begin the feast. The creator stood up, invited everyone to enjoy the meal, and then specified one condition for eating. No elbows must be bent! The demonic beings were enraged and started hurling abuses at the creator. They stood up as a group and walked out. The divine beings, on the other hand, found a way to enjoy the lavish meal without bending their elbows. Seated in rows facing each other, they stretched their hands across and fed one another.

One of the finest illustrations of the interdependence of all forms in the creation occurs in Chāndogya Upaniṣad (chapter 6). The discussion in this chapter begins with the teaching that the entire universe is the outcome of *brahman*'s self-multiplication ("May I become many; may I grow forth.") Although the Upaniṣads are not concerned with providing details of the sequence and order of the creation and are not regarded as a valid source of knowledge for this purpose, the Chāndogya Upaniṣad is an example of a text that does offer a suggestive account. *Brahman* is described as first creating fire. Fire then multiplies itself and creates water. Water, in turn, multiples itself and creates food. The text continues to describe a further process of the triplication of these three realities that involves combining with each other; each element enters into the other (Chāndogya, 6.4.1–2).

> In Fire, the red color is the color of Fire; that which is white belongs to water and the black color is that of Food (Earth); thus vanishes *Fire-ness* from Fire, being only a modification of words, a mere Name; and what is real is only that there are three colors.
>
> In the Sun, the red color is the color of Fire, —the white is that of Water, —and black that of Food (Earth); thus vanishes the *Sun-ness* from the Sun, being only a modification of words, a mere Name; and what is real is only that there are three colors.[11]

The text continues in a similar vein, speaking about other phenomena such as the moon and lightning. The idea, in general, is that the independent ontological identity of each element vanishes when one understands the other elements to be present. "Sun" or "Fire," the text suggests, are only labels that conceal the truth (*satyam*) of the element's nature, that is, its interdependent nature (fire, water, and earth). The Chāndogya Upaniṣad, of course, leads the student to the ultimate teaching that reality is non-dual and that the nature of everything existing is *brahman*. This teaching is not opposed to the fact that everything also exists interdependently. All forms are forms of *brahman*, and all exist interdependently.

What we have in the Upaniṣads is both an understanding of the interdependent character of all forms, sentient and insentient, as well as their ultimate non-dual nature. Human beings are part of a complex matrix that includes ancestors, teachers, other than human living beings, and the elements. Our dependence on this matrix for our well-being requires, as the Bhagavadgītā explains so eloquently, that we contribute to its sustenance through our generosity to others. This understanding of interdependence is deepened by the Advaita teaching that the self and world are not-two. This insight, not of a shared self, but of an identical self, is the ontological ground for relationships of compassion and giving. It is true that the Advaita tradition has placed more emphasis on ontology than on ethics, but there is no good reason why the ethical implications of its ontology should not be detailed. It is expected that those virtues that enhance the gain of liberating knowledge will express spontaneously in the life of the liberated.[12] We should not, however, take this for granted, and the ethics of Advaita, and especially the social implications of these, need to be elaborated and emphasized. This task becomes even more important when we are arguing for a socially engaged Advaita.

Control-Give-Have Compassion

Let me conclude this chapter with a narrative from the Bṛhadāraṇyaka Upaniṣad (chapter 5.2.1–3) that highlights the centrality of three virtues that are both the means to liberation and well as the expression of the meaning of liberation. The text tells of the teacher Prajāpati and his students, who are described as divine (*deva*), human (*manuṣya*), and demonic (*asura*). All three lived for many years with their teacher studying the Vedas. After completing their studies, the divine beings approached Prajāpati and requested a final instruction. He uttered the syllable "da" and asked if they had understood. They explained that he meant "control" (*dāmyata*), and he agreed. Next, the humans approached Prajāpati with the same request, and he repeated the syllable "da." They understood him to mean "give" (*datta*), and Prajāpati affirmed their understanding. Finally, the demonic beings requested instruction, and Prajapati uttered "da." They heard him to mean "be compassionate" (*dayadhvam*), and Prajāpati again concurred.

This dialogue is insightful because the teacher chooses, in his final instruction to his students, to speak of fundamental values—self-control, generosity, and compassion. Knowledge of the Vedas, the text suggests, results in a certain way of being in the world, and one has not really understood the text if these values are not central to one's way of living. These constitute the finest fruits of knowledge. Self-control is the unique human ability to modify our behavior when our ways of thinking and acting cause suffering to others. Because we lack the biological controls of other species, we need to exercise voluntary ethical restraint. Self-control may also be regarded as a necessary outcome of the interdependent character of our lives. Because it is possible to interpret self-control in limited and negative ways, it is important for the Upaniṣad to commend generosity. Self-control may be understood as abstention from actions that cause suffering to others; it may not always be seen as providing any motivation for vigorous engagement in actions that aim to overcome suffering. Self-control may be expressed in self-centeredness and selfishness. It is important that Advaita ethics has a positive component, and this is assured through the practice of generosity that is the active promotion of the well-being of others. Finally, the highest and most profound reason for the practice of generosity is compassion (*dayā*). Generosity that is motivated by compassion is rightly motivated, will value the dignity of the recipient, and liberates us from being obsessed with personal rewards or successful outcomes. There is a sense in which an action performed from compassion is its own end, and nurturing compassion as the fundamental motive for acting ensures the growth and transformation of the actor.

With this perspective on the Advaita understanding of the human problem, its resolution in liberation from self-ignorance, and our consideration of the principal implications of liberation, we turn our attention now to a consideration of the significance of the Advaita teachings for life in the world. In undertaking this analysis, it will be necessary to reinterpret the meaning of some of the central teachings of Advaita and, where needed, question certain interpretations. There are interpretations of the meaning of liberation that seem to negate and devalue the world and advocate indifference to suffering. Such interpretations are usually associated with a focus on the meaning of liberation where the emphasis is on personal freedom from self-ignorance that may be disconnected from engagement with social, economic, and political systems that inflict suffering.

Our discussion of Advaita ought to have made it clear that the root cause of suffering, both individual and as manifested in oppressive social, economic, and political structures, is ignorance of the nature of the self as identical in all. There is a need for individual transformation through a well-assimilated wisdom about the nature of self that liberates from greed. Without such transformation of ourselves, there is little hope of changing the social structures within which we exist. We will continue to perpetuate systems of oppression. Individual transformation, according to

Advaita, is necessary for meaningful and enduring social transformation. At the same time, many traditions, including Advaita, have in the past and present spoken of the need for individual cognitive and ethical transformation without attentiveness to the suffering that is inflicted by oppressive social and economic systems and of the need to identify and transform these. Our contention is that Advaita *should* concern itself with such systemic sources of suffering and *does* offer resources for addressing and overcoming such suffering.

Part Two

5

Liberation from Patriarchy

> *"It is very difficult to understand why in this country so much difference is made between men and women, whereas the Vedānta declares that one and the same conscious Self is present in all beings."*
>
> —CW 7, 214[1]

In any discussion of attitudes toward women and the treatment of women in Hindu society, one must be attentive to the fact of diversity. "Hinduism" is more appropriately thought of as a family name that encompasses an astounding variety of theological doctrines and practice. Regional customs and traditions differ, and there is no central institution or figure speaking authoritatively for all Hindus in matters of doctrine and practice.[2] It should not surprise us, therefore, to discover significant differences in the status and roles ascribed to women in Hindu society. Although these differences must be readily acknowledged, it is still possible to make certain meaningful generalizations and to discern prevalent attitudes toward women. My discussion in this chapter draws significantly from classical Sanskrit texts that are explicitly masculine in their orientation and focus on *brahmin* traditions, but these texts have and continue to enjoy prestige within the broad Hindu tradition.[3] Although there is increasing evidence to suggest that the non-brahminical traditions have accorded greater value and recognition to women, it is also true that caste subgroups (*jātīs*) seek to ascend the ladder of caste hierarchy by adopting the values and behavior of those at the top. This is the process known as Sanskritization or Brahmanization, which looks to the Hindu tradition presented in the classical Sanskrit texts as normative.[4] Once the process of Sanskritization continues and as long as the values of the Sanskrit texts are held to be normative, these texts cannot be ignored and will have to be engaged in critical dialogue.

In her study on women in Hinduism, Katherine K. Young draws attention to the disturbing trend in India where the economic growth in the rural areas has resulted in more conservative attitudes toward women and their withdrawal from the workforce. Young associates this trend with the continuing process of Sanskritization or the imitation of *brahmin* values. This new trend toward closeting women, argues Young, seems to involve both cultural and economic factors. It obviously keeps women out of the competitive job market, and it also harkens back to the idea that the status of a family increases if the women in a family are not educated and do not work outside the home.[5]

Such trends should not surprise us when prominent and influential Hindu teachers continue to advocate the position that a woman's place is only in the home. In a disturbing publication, a popular Hindu guru offers a ludicrous argument for closing the workplace to women. It is typical of such male arguments to claim that the intention is the well-being of the woman and to assume the prerogative of defining and speaking for women. Women, contends this writer, are more prone to tears and less capable of tolerating pain and scolding; thus, they are better off if they are kept in the safe seclusion of the home, protected by men who are brave and able to bear the cruelty of the outside world.[6]

Paradoxical Attitudes toward Women

Any survey of attitudes to women in Hinduism reveals glaring contrasts and ambiguities. One of the earliest examples of these ambiguities comes from the most famous work on Hindu law, the Manusmṛti (ca. 200 BCE–100 CE). The author of this work, Manu, comments on the duties and obligations of women.

> By a girl, by a young woman, or even by an aged one, nothing must be done independently, even in her own house.

> In childhood a female must be subject to her father, in youth to her husband, when her lord is dead to her sons; a woman must never be independent.
>
> Though destitute of virtue, or seeking pleasure (elsewhere), or devoid of good qualities, (yet) a husband must be constantly worshipped as a god by a faithful wife.
>
> No sacrifice, no vow, no fast must be performed by women apart (from their husbands); if a wife obeys her husband, she will for that (reason alone) be exalted in heaven.
>
> A faithful wife, who desires to dwell (after death) with her husband, must never do anything that might displease him who took her hand, whether he be alive or dead.[7]

Manu also requests that women be treated with honor.

> Women must be honoured and adorned by their fathers, brothers, husbands, and brothers-in-law, who desire (their own) welfare.
>
> Where women are honoured, there the gods are pleased; but where they are not honoured, no sacred rite yields.
>
> Where the female relations live in grief, the family soon wholly perishes; but that family where they are not unhappy ever prospers.[8]

If Manu appears too ancient and remote, it is important to note that his prescriptions for women continue to be influential. Hindu scholar Vasudha Narayanan cites extensively from a Tamil manual titled *Dirgha Sumangali Bhava* that was published in 1979. It is a manual for the married Hindu woman that echoes many of the traditional viewpoints articulated by Manu and preserves ancient stereotypes.[9]

If we turn to the Rāmacaritamānasa, of the sixteenth-century poet Tulasīdāsa, we encounter several examples of the negative stereotyping of women. Tulasīdāsa's work is a vernacular reworking of the ancient Sanskrit *Rāmāyaṇa* of Vālmīki and has been extremely influential. Gandhi described it as the greatest literature in the religious literature of the world, and a scholar described the *Rāmāyaṇa* as the Hindu's favorite book.[10]

In Tulasīdāsa's work, Daśaratha, the king of Ayodhyā, blames the banishment of his favorite son, Rāmā, on the fact that he (Daśaratha) trusted a woman. "What a thing to happen at a time such as this! I am undone by putting trust in a woman like an ascetic who is ruined by ignorance when he is about to win the fruit of his austerities."[11]

In addition to the suggestion that women ought not to be trusted, Daśaratha's outburst is also revealing because of the comparison that he chooses to make. He likens his own plight to that of an ascetic who is destroyed by ignorance when his spiritual endeavors are just about to bear fruit. This is a significant analogy because of the fact that women are also held to be responsible for the religious fall of men. In a conversation between the sage Nārada and Rāmā, in the same text, Nārada asks Rāmā to explain why he did not allow Nārada to get married. Rāmā offers a lengthy denunciation of women as obstacles to all that is noble and worthy in the life of men.

> Lust, wrath, greed, pride and all other violent passions form the sturdy army of infatuation; but among them all the most formidable and calamitous is woman, illusion incarnate.
>
> Listen sage, the Purāṇas and Vedas and the saints declare that woman is the vernal season to the forest of infatuation; like the heat of summer she dries up all the ponds and lakes of prayer and penance and devotional exercises.[12]

Later in the *Ayodhyākāṇḍa*, Bharata, Rāmā's younger brother, also vents his anger against all women. The following words are addressed to his mother, whom he blames for the banishment of Rāmā.

> How could the king trust you? Surely God must have robbed him of his senses in his last hour! Not even God can fathom the ways of a woman's heart, the repository of all deceit, sin, and vice.
>
> Being simple, amiable and pious, how could the king understand the nature of a woman?[13]

Bhārata pronounces many of the prevalent stereotypes. Women are difficult to understand, they are deceitful, sinful, and they exploit the simplicity and good nature of men. One of the most troubling statements in the Rāmacaritamānasa about women occurs in the *Sundarakāṇḍa* when women are lumped together with drums, rustics, animals, and members of the lowest caste, and all of these are described as objects that are fit to be beaten.

A passage like this may be read easily as a justification of violence and abuse toward women. Such views may encourage complacency toward domestic violence and lead women to feel that it is a deserved form of punishment. Swāmi Rāmsukhdās offers the following advice to an abused woman about an appropriate response.

> Question: What should the wife do if her husband beats her and troubles her?
>
> Answer: The wife should think that she is paying her debt of her previous life and thus her sins are being destroyed and she is becoming pure. When her parents come to know this, they can take her to their own house because they have not given their daughter to face this sort of bad behaviour.
>
> Question: What should she do if her parents don't take her to their own house?
>
> Answer: Under such circumstances what can the helpless wife do? She should reap the fruit of her past actions. She should patiently bear the beatings of her husband

> with patience. By bearing them she will be free from her sins and it is possible that her husband may start loving her.[14]

The Significance of Women in Relation to Men

What emerges clearly from these texts is that women are accorded significance and status only in relation to men. They are regarded with the highest esteem in their roles as wives and mothers. For a woman, marriage and the service of her husband become the purpose of her life and the means to her liberation. She is to look upon her husband as her lord, and, through the service of her husband, she accomplishes what an ascetic might attain after many years of arduous discipline.

Hindu texts are generally one-sided in emphasizing the obligations of women to men in marriage. In the following quotation from the Rāmacaritamānasa, Anasūyā, wife of the sage, Atri, instructs Sītā about the obligations of a Hindu wife.

> Listen, O princess; mother, father and brother are all friendly helpers to a limited degree; but a husband, Sitā, is an unlimited blessing; and vile is the woman who refuses to serve him.
>
> Fortitude, piety, a friend and a wife—these four are tested only in time of adversity. Though her lord be old, sick, dull-headed, indigent, blind, deaf, bad-tempered or utterly wretched, yet if his wife treats him with disrespect, she shall suffer all the torments of hell. To be devoted in thought and word and deed to her husband's feet is her only religious duty, her only guiding rule.[15]

The tragic consequence of perceiving the significance of women only in relation to men is seen most clearly in Hindu attitudes to widows. Widows, particularly those in the upper castes, were regarded as inauspicious. The widow not only mourned the loss of her husband, but also suffered the guilt of living longer than he had. It was felt in some circles that if she were pure and faithful, like Sāvitrī, she could save her husband from death itself.[16] She was required to shave her head and avoid all forms of personal adornment. With the death of her husband, she had lost the most important reasons for living and was debarred from the quest for the first three goals of Hindu life, *artha* (wealth), *kāma* (pleasure), and *dharma* (family religious ritual). From an early age, girls are instructed to pray for the longevity of their husbands-to-be in order to be spared the plight of widowhood. Boys are not required to pray or fast for the longevity of their wives. A married woman whose husband is alive enjoys an auspicious status (*sumangali*). A widow is inauspicious (*amangali*) and unfit for participation in festivals and ceremonies.[17]

While the status of the widow has been improving, the stigma of inauspiciousness continues to linger. Narayanan reports that while widows are no longer required to shave their heads, some South Indian communities do not permit them to be present before religious leaders, and they are not allowed to have the *sātari* (a symbol of God's grace) touch their heads.[18]

Dowry and the Devaluation of Women

The continuing practice of giving and receiving dowries is another custom that demeans women and makes a daughter less desirable than a son in many families. According to A. S. Altekar, the dowry system is based on the Hindu view of marriage as a *dāna* or gift. In the Hindu marriage ceremony, the girl (*kanyā*) is given as a sacred gift *(dāna)* by her father to the groom. Because a religious gift is usually accompanied by a gift of cash or gold, the bride is accompanied by a small gift of cash or ornaments.[19]

Whatever its historical roots may have been, today the dowry, in too many instances, is a condition for the performance of a marriage and a tool for the exploitation and degradation of Hindu women. While its practice was outlawed in India in 1961, its popularity has not declined, and rising consumerism feeds the flames of desire and demand. The bride is increasingly seen as the means to materialistic aspirations for conspicuous items such as cars, scooters, refrigerators, and televisions. Her husband and in-laws, to keep the supply of consumer items flowing, often put the young bride under unconscionable pain and pressure. Her hopeless predicament sometimes drives her to suicide. Where greed is untempered by compassion, her husband or his relatives may even murder her. The preferred method is to set her on fire and explain away her horrendous death as an accident in the kitchen. The bridegroom is now free to exploit another family. At least two women are killed each day in this manner in New Delhi.[20]

Statistics released by the government of India in 1987 show a steady rise in the numbers of dowry deaths. These rose from 999 in 1985 to 1,786 in 1987. In 1993, the figure was 5,582.[21] In 2010, according to statistics released by the National Crime Records Bureau, the figure climbed to 8,391. This means that a bride is burned every 90 minutes.[22] While these figures are extremely disturbing, the reality may be much worse because cases of domestic violence usually are not reported. Male education has resulted in increasing demand for dowries, because a college diploma enhances one's economic potential and allows the parents of the bridegroom to make higher demands. While the dowry was much more prevalent among members of the upper castes, the desire of the lower castes to imitate the higher ones has resulted in its widespread and increased popularity.[23] The Dowry Prohibition law, passed in 1961, has been largely ineffective in dealing with this tragic custom.

In this tragic and unjust context, the preference for sons in Hindu families does not come as a surprise. The increasing demands of the dowry system make daughters unwanted economic liabilities, and some Hindus are not averse to employing the most sophisticated technology to prevent their births. Abortion is legal in India, and medical procedures such as amniocentesis and ultrasound are commonly used to determine the gender of the unborn child and, if the fetus is female, to request a termination of the pregnancy. Figures for one New Delhi clinic in 1992–93 show that of a total of 13,400 abortions performed, 13,398 were of female fetuses. One study done in the state of Maharashtra revealed that of 8,000 fetuses aborted, 7,999 were female. The exception was a Jewish mother who desired a daughter.[24] It is estimated that between 4 million and 12 million girls were aborted in India between 1980 and 2012.[25] The practice of female abortion and female infanticide has lowered the ratio of men to women in India. In 1991, the ratio was 927 women for 1,000 men.[26] In 2011, this ratio dropped to 914. The decline was even higher in wealthier families with high educational attainment, suggesting easier access to illegal abortions.

Religious Rituals and the Preference for Sons

The preference for a son (*putra*) in Hindu families is also rooted in religious belief and practice. The eldest son in a Hindu family enjoys a special status because he has the privilege of offering the *piṇḍa* (rice ball) each year when the rites, called *śrāddha,* are performed for the departed parent. This ritual, it is believed, saves the parent from suffering in the afterlife. In the words of Manu, "Because a son delivers his father from the hell called *put,* he was therefore called *put-tra* (a deliverer from *put*) by the Self-existent himself."[27]

The role of the son in the performance of postmortem rituals causes preferential regard for male offspring, and families sometimes continue to have children until a son is born. Crawford calls for a reassessment of the beliefs surrounding *śrāddha* rituals and argues that Hindu ethics would be better served by emphasizing the doctrine of *karma* that teaches personal responsibility for our destinies.

There may be a very pragmatic reason why sons were given the responsibility of making annual offerings on behalf of departed ancestors. Traditionally, the married male child remained a part of the joint household, while the daughter left her home and took on a new identity as part of her husband's home. Her obligations were all centered on her husband and his family. Today, with the growth of nuclear families, both males and females are leaving the ancestral home and establishing households of their own. A married daughter may be closer geographically and may have time for and interest in the performance of family rituals. This change in family structure and pattern is an appropriate time to reconsider the eligibility of women to perform these rituals.

Hinduism also debars women from leadership and participation in religious rituals because of the belief that the female becomes polluted during the events of menstruation and childbirth.[28] Women have been ranked in the lower orders of the caste system and prohibited from study and recitation of the Vedas.[29] Female bodily fluids are thought of as polluting during two of the distinctive expressions of female sexuality, menstruation and childbirth. In some orthodox homes, the menstruating woman is not allowed to cook or to participate in a domestic religious ritual. Among the Havik *brahmins* of Mysore, for example, women must take special precautions to ensure that they do not pollute others during the period of menstruation. A Havik woman does not serve food to her family or eat with them during this time.[30]

Here again, it is necessary that Hindus adopt a rational view of normal female bodily functions rather than continue to hold to the beliefs of an era when the nature of such biological processes was not understood. The perception of uniquely female bodily processes as polluting is clearly a male-centered view that provides further justification for the exclusion of women from male-controlled spheres.

One of the promising developments in recent times has been the initiative taken by certain Hindu movements to train women as priestesses. In 1975, Shri Shankarrao Thatte of Pune began the training of women in priestly roles. Since his death in 1987, his wife, Mrs. Pushpabai Thatte, has continued this work under an organization named Shankar Seva Samiti, and it has spread to all parts of Maharashtra. While there has been opposition from orthodox circles, the initiation of priestesses "has been accepted by most educated people, (and) welcomed as a revolutionary step in Indian society."[31] In South Africa, the reformist Arya Samaj movement, founded by Swami Dayananda Saraswati in 1875, has been training priestesses, and a branch of the movement in Trinidad initiated its first priestess. While the training appears to be almost entirely focused on liturgy and religious ceremony, one hopes that it will develop an intellectual and scholarly dimension that will enable women to be creative interpreters and teachers of the Hindu tradition.

Karma and Violence to Women

The previous passage by Swami Rāmsukhdās points to a sinister interpretation and use of the Hindu doctrine of *karma* to condone resignation and fatalism on the part of women with regard to their abuse by and subjection to men. I have personally heard many accounts of abused Hindu women who were sent back by their parents or advised to return to the homes of their husbands because the suffering inflicted on them was a just reward for their actions in earlier lives. A woman who chooses to leave her husband also causes disgrace and embarrassment to her parents and elders.

The doctrine of *karma*, however, ought not to be perverted and misused to sanction oppression and injustice. While the teaching on *karma* underlines responsibility by emphasizing that human actions produce consequences for the doer, it does not propose that all experiences in life are the consequences of actions in past lives, and it certainly does not require silent and passive submission to injustice and violence, physical and psychological. Men who abuse women are choosing to do so, and the doctrine of *karma* must not ignore this fact by transferring blame and responsibility to the victim. Instead of advocating resignation to abuse, Hindu teachers must condemn gender injustice as a violation of fundamental Hindu values. If *karma* entrusts us with responsibility for the condition of our lives, Hindu leaders ought to be empowering women to be active agents of change rather than advising stoic acquiescence in suffering.

The Intrinsic Value of Women

The major problems faced by women in the Hindu tradition arise because of patriarchal and androcentric views that affirm the value and significance of women only in relation to men. In view of this fact, a major task for the Hindu tradition is to articulate a value for women that is not dependent on their subservient relationship to men. This would be a value that comes from the very fact of their being. The Advaita tradition offers us valuable resources for this task. The Advaita tradition teaches, as described earlier (Chapters 3 and 4), that the self (*ātmā*) is identical with the infinite (*brahman*). As the Bhagavadgītā 13:27 puts it: "The one who sees the Lord, as remaining the same in all beings, as the one who is not being destroyed, in the things that are perishing, he alone sees."[32]

When the implications for human relationships are enunciated in sacred texts, they are done in terms of a vision of equality, and there is no good reason why this equality should not also be construed in terms of gender.

> Wise people are indeed those who see the same (Brahman) in a *brāhmaṇa* who is endowed with knowledge and humility, in a cow, in an elephant, in a dog and (even) in a dog eater.
>
> The cycle of birth and death (*saṁsāra*) is won over here itself (in this life) by those whose mind is rooted in that which is the same in everything (that is Brahman). Since Brahman, that is free from any defect, is (always) the same, they (the wise people) abide in Brahman. (Bhagavadgītā 5:18–19)[33]

The *Śvetāśvatara Upaniṣad* (4:3–4) specifically identifies the divine with women (*strī*) and unmarried girls (*kumārī*) as well as with men and boys.

> You are a woman; you are a man; you are a boy or a girl.
> As an old man, you totter along with a walking-stick.
> As you are born, you turn your face in all directions.
>
> You are the dark blue bird, the green one with red eyes, the rain-cloud, the seasons, and the oceans. You live as one without a beginning because of your pervasiveness, you, from whom all beings are born.[34]

In the Hindu tradition, *brahman* is identified with that which is true or real (*sat*), and the real persists in all periods of time. As that which is absolutely real, *brahman* is understood to have the greatest value. Things that are subject to change, and are not existent in all time periods, do not lack value, but are not viewed as having ultimate value. The human form, though finite and perishable, is precious because it is the abode of the imperishable self, and it is the instrument for attaining liberation (*mokṣa*). If the human form derives its value from *brahman*'s immanence, then it is an expression of ignorance to despise and oppress women who, like men, embody *brahman*. The forms that embody that which we consider to be of ultimate value must also command our respect and reverence. The oppression of women also reflects an alienation resulting from our failure to see ourselves in them. To oppress another is to oppress oneself because of the indivisibility of the self.

Women have value and significance not because of their instrumental roles and relationships to us as wives and mothers, but because they, like us, equally embody *brahman*. Their worth is an intrinsic one and does not come indirectly through males. The great Advaita teacher Ramana Maharshi (1879–1950) affirmed this truth in a firm stand that he took after the death of his mother. His mother spent the last years of her life at his *āśram* and became his disciple. Upon her death, Ramana was convinced that she had attained liberation and was not subject to rebirth. It is customary for the body of a liberated person to be buried rather than cremated. Some disciples expressed doubt about whether the body of a liberated woman should be treated like that of a liberated man. Ramana's answer was unequivocal. "Since *jñāna* (Knowledge) and *mukti* (Deliverance) do not differ with the difference of sex, the body of a woman Saint also need not be burnt. Her body is also the abode of God."[35]

The Necessity to Connect Religious Teaching and Social Reality

Although this teaching about the identity of the self in all beings has been clearly enunciated in texts such as the Upaniṣads and the Bhagavadgītā, it has usually remained as a religious ideal and has not always been used as a reforming norm to question and critique social structures and unjust gender relationships. One reason is that this teaching is usually sought by the celibate renunciant (*sannyāsin*), who is ritually freed from social ties and obligations and who may not be interested in the nature of social reality. A religious ideal, however, that is disconnected from social reality and the life of the community becomes irrelevant quickly. The Hindu tradition has to ensure that its worldview does not become so compartmentalized that its highest teachings have no bearing on the condition of human existence in society. The doctrine of divine immanence, so deeply rooted in Hinduism, and especially in the Advaita tradition, must become a powerful searchlight to illuminate and heal the exploitative and oppressive structures of Hindu society.

Ahiṁsā: Its Significance for Women

The Advaita teaching about the identity and unity of existence through *brahman* and the value of all life that emerges from *brahman* is the foundation of the ethical principle of *ahiṁsā* (non-violence). Belief in the immanence and the identity of the self requires us to demonstrate reverence and consideration for life in all its forms, avoiding injury or suffering to others. Divine immanence is so central to the Hindu understanding of God that even a text like the *Rāmacaritamānasa* of Tulasīdāsa, cited before for some misogynistic verses, cannot avoid its implications. In often-recited verses from the *Bālakāṇḍa,* Tulasīdāsa reiterates the doctrine of divine pervasiveness and expresses his reverence for all beings and for the entire creation.

> Knowing that the whole universe, whether animate or inanimate, is pervaded by the spirit of Rāmā, I ever adore the feet of all with folded hands.
>
> Eight million four hundred thousand species of living beings, classified under four broad divisions, inhabit land, water and the air. Realizing the whole world to be pervaded by Sītā and Rāmā, I make obeisance with folded hands.[36]

The central ethical implication of divine immanence, that is, non-violence (*ahiṁsā*), is also echoed by Tulasīdāsa. In the *Uttarakāṇḍa,* Rāmā speaks about it to his brother Bharata.
"Brother, there is no religious duty like benevolence and no sin like oppressing others. I have declared to you, dear brother, the verdict of all the Vedas and the Purāṇas, and the learned also know it."[37]

If the teaching about *brahman*'s equal presence is to be saved from being an abstract and insignificant ideal, then the meaning of its central ethic, which is *ahiṁsā*, must be enlarged and used to challenge gender inequities. Contemporary Hindu ethics must become more cognizant of the ways in which social structures affect peoples' lives and not limit the application of ethics to the sphere of individual relationships. The systemic nature of gender inequality has to be understood and addressed with earnestness.

We must know *ahiṁsā* to be violated when women are forced, because of social values, to abort fetuses merely because the fetuses are female. *Ahiṁsā* is also violated when the cruel custom of dowry strains the precious economic resources of the families into which they were born and makes them feel guilty for being women. Women are degraded and demeaned by the practice of dowry, which signifies that the value of a woman is so low that she becomes acceptable to another only when her family is able to satisfy his greed for the latest gadgets of materialistic fancy. Her suffering continues in the home of her in-laws when she is resented because of dissatisfaction with the dowry and when she is subject to verbal and physical abuse in order to extort more from her poor family. Her life is often in danger, and she sometimes chooses to save her family by ending it herself. Women are not honored, and *ahiṁsā* is certainly not the paramount value in a society that inflicts suffering on her in so many ways. Such violent practices deny the truth of her identity with *brahman* and her identity with all of us.

Ahiṁsā and Justice for Women

In his understanding and interpretation of the meaning of *ahiṁsā*, Gandhi explained that in its negative form, it means abstention from injury to living beings physically or mentally. In its positive form, *ahiṁsā* also means love and compassion for all. For Gandhi, *ahiṁsā* also means justice toward everyone and abstention from exploitation in any form. "No man," claimed Gandhi, "could be actively non-violent and not rise against social injustice no matter where it occurred."[38] From this perspective, we have an obligation to accord women not only the value, dignity, and respect that stems from their embodiment of *brahman*, but also justice. Justice for women, in this context, requires that we ensure they have the same educational opportunities and liberties as men so that they can realize the fullness of their human potential.

There are numerous studies showing that the status of women increases with access to education and that the latter also leads to lower population growth and higher standards of living.[39] The Indian state of Kerala has achieved 92 percent literacy among girls and a fertility rate of 1.7.[40] This compares to general female literacy rate in India of 65.46 percent. Female literacy is improving, but a disproportionate percentage of the illiterate in India are still women.

There are many ancient traditions that can be creatively appropriated to support the education of women. The *Bṛhadāraṇyaka Upaniṣad* (4.4.18) recommends a ritual to householders to ensure the birth of a scholarly daughter.[41] There are also Vedic hymns that are attributed to women. Early "forest universities" in India were coeducational, and girls were entitled to commence the study of the Vedas after the *upanayana* or sacred thread ceremony. One class of female students was the *brahmavādinīs*, who committed themselves to lifelong study of liturgical and ritual texts and engaged in religious debates.[42]

Hindu classical texts, as we noted earlier, offer a one-sided emphasis on the obligations of women to men and are glaringly silent on the obligations of men to women. This imbalance needs to be redressed and mutual obligations emphasized. There are many ancient traditions that could be drawn upon to support gender equality and mutuality. The Ṛg Veda stipulates that the wife must be present at all domestic religious rituals. Young argues that this presence was not just a silent one because, in the absence of the men, the deities could not be left unattended, and the wife would have had to assume primary responsibility for making offerings.[43]

Justice as the Fulfillment of Mutual Obligations

While there has been an imbalance in the emphasis on female obligations and duties, the language of obligations and the significance that these have received in Hinduism are laudable and instructive. Justice, in the Hindu context, is more closely connected with the fulfillment of mutual obligation than with the assertion of rights. The contemporary emphasis on human rights often leads to an exaggerated individualism and needs to be balanced by a stress on human responsibilities and obligations. Freedom without a deep sense of responsibility does little to foster and nurture human communities. The value for the language of obligations in Hinduism arises out of its understanding of the unity and interrelatedness of all existence.

From a Hindu viewpoint, our lives are inextricably intertwined with, and dependent on, the universe as a whole, which includes the divine, the elements, and human and other life forms. As discussed earlier, the wheel of the universe revolves only if we recognize and fulfill our duties to the whole in response for its continuous sustenance of our individual lives. The Hindu understanding of the necessity of fulfilling mutual obligations is a rich resource for promoting gender equality. A doctrine of human rights and justice in Hinduism will be correctly inseparable from one of responsibility and obligations. Injustice is both selfish and blind to life's unity and interdependence.

In asking that the Hindu tradition emphasize mutual obligations between men and women, I wish to clarify that this is not an argument for exclusive and complementary roles. This argument is often used to relegate women to the domestic sphere and to deny them the freedom, to participate in all spheres of the human community. Our obligations to women include freedom and we must be aware of the many insidious arguments that are proffered to define their place. The following is one of many examples.

> Question: In these days women demand equal rights like men. Is it proper?
>
> Answer: No. It is not proper. In fact a woman has not the right of equality with man but she has a privilege. The reason is that she comes to her husband's house having renounced her parents, etc. She is called the mistress and the queen of the house. It is her husband who has a privilege outside the house. As a chariot moves with two wheels which are kept apart, so do the household

> affairs run smoothly with their separate rights. If the two wheels of the chariot are joined together, it can't be driven smoothly. If both of them have equal rights, how will a man like a woman conceive? Therefore right of equality in fact means separate rights of the two, and this is real freedom for both of them.[44]

Even Gandhi, who advanced the cause of women's freedom by drawing them into the struggle for national independence, argued conservatively for separate and complementary roles. Although he argued for spiritual equality, he also claimed that the vocations of the two are different and that the woman's place is in the home. "The duty of motherhood," wrote Gandhi, "which the vast majority of women will always undertake, requires qualities which men need not possess. She is passive, he is active. She is essentially the mistress of the house. He is the bread-winner. She is the keeper and distributor of the bread."[45] Such essentializing of the nature and role of women is one argument often advanced to limit their freedom.

What is necessary today is the creation of opportunities and a climate of attitudes in which women enjoy the freedom and right to self-development and are not constrained into roles that are demarcated for them by a patriarchal and androcentric culture. Our obligation to women is to become partners with them in the liberation of both genders from the constraints of patriarchy and to ensure that they enjoy freedom and autonomy. Swami Vivekananda articulated this succinctly in his view that women "must be put in a position to solve their own problems in their own way. No one can and ought to do this for them.[46]

The teaching about the identity of the self with *brahman* and the worth of the human person that follows from it must become the foundation of a Hindu challenge and critique of all attitudes, values, and actions that demean and trivialize women and reduce them to sexual objects and the property of males. Hinduism must resist and respond to the challenges of a materialistic and consumer-oriented culture in which people determine their own value and the value of others by the worth of the commodities they own. In a materialistic culture, human value varies with the worth of possessions and rises and falls with the upward or downward movements of the market. A tradition that affirms unequivocally that the significance of the human being is to be found in the fact that human nature embodies the divine infinite cannot condone the commercialization of human existence. It must champion the dignity of all human beings and attitudes of respect and reverence for all human life.

Feminine Images of God and the Empowerment of Women

One of the great contributions of feminist theology has been to demonstrate the relationship between patriarchy and male images of God. These images of God are predominant in male-dominated societies and reinforce, in turn, male authority roles and figures.[47] The images of God in any religious tradition are significant because they affect social structure and human consciousness. The Hindu experience, however, cautions us about positing any necessary relationship between the presence of feminine images and forms of God in a religion and the status of women. Even though the Mother Goddesses dominated some regions in India, this fact did not always translate into better status for women.

It must be of some significance, however, that the Hindu tradition has not hesitated to use a variety of feminine symbols and appellations for the sacred, and there are no theological problems in Hinduism with imaging the divine as feminine. Although many of the goddesses in Hinduism are subordinate to the god-figures and mirror the subordination of women to men, there are figures like Kālī and Durgā, who embody all the traditional features of God. A popular image represents the divine as *ardhanārīśvara* and shows God as the perfect integration of male and female characteristics. One-half of the image is male, and the other half is female. What is especially noteworthy about this icon is that the integration of the male and female is complete and equal.

The fact that the tradition uses both male and female metaphors for God underlines the truth that *brahman* is neither exclusively male nor female. *Brahman* is free from gender specificity, although embodied both in males and females. The challenge before us here, once more, is to see the implications of religious insight for social reality and to question the contradictions that result from their compartmentalization. The feminine images of God in Hinduism are a rich source to be retrieved and interpreted by advocates of gender justice and equality.

The Hindu tradition, as already noted, accords value and respect to women primarily in their roles as wives and mothers (of sons). In her role as mother, the woman is even more venerated than the father or the teacher. Her role as an educator and spiritual teacher of her children is clearly recognized.[48] In so many other ways, however, she is devalued and debased. The challenge for Hinduism is not to strip the mother of the sanctity and dignity it has traditionally reserved for her, but to help create the conditions under which women can freely choose their paths to self-development and to ensure that they are treated justly and with honor in non-traditional and traditional roles.

Scriptural Resources for Overcoming Patriarchy

Hinduism has traditionally distinguished between *śruti* and *smṛti* texts. *Śruti* literally means "that which is heard" and designates those scriptures that are considered to be revealed and that enjoy supreme authority. The term is regularly employed as a synonym for the Vedas. *Smṛti,* on the other hand, means "that which is remembered" and refers to sacred texts that have a human origin. The Dharmaśāstras or law books of Hinduism, such as the work of Manu, are classified as *smṛti.* These texts are secondary in authority to the *śruti* and, more importantly, deal with those aspects of the tradition that are contextual and limited to specific time periods and social conditions. Julius Lipner lucidly discusses the relationship between *śruti* and *smṛti.*

> Insofar as *smṛti* is humanly authored, it is generally fallible and liable to change. It is also liable to criticism. As such, it is a selective term. Sometimes, what is *smṛti* for you may not be recognized as such by me; or rather, though it may be necessary for both of us to recognize the authority of a particular slice of *smṛti,* we may weigh this authority differently according to the particular

> traditions out of which we come or the exigencies of the situation. *Smṛti* is the medium through which we hear the voice of *śruti;* it is interpretative, selective, collaborative, flexible.[49]

While the *śruti* texts are acknowledged to be revelation, the sphere of their authority is carefully defined and limited. The purpose of the *śruti,* as discussed in Chapter 2, is to reveal only those things that cannot be known through any of our ordinary means of knowledge, and its revelations should not contradict what we learn about the world through other sources of knowledge. For the Advaita tradition, the primary purpose of revelation is to inform us of the nature of absolute reality (*brahman*) and the relationship between specific ritual actions and their results.

The distinction between *śruti* and *smṛti* and the limits placed on the authority of the former are valuable and creative resources that must be utilized by Hindu interpreters for meaningfully addressing contemporary issues, including those of patriarchy. The problem here, however, is that androcentric views, although predominant, are not limited to those works that are regarded as *smṛti.* Katherine Young notes this.

> That Hindu reformers from the nineteenth century on have looked to the Vedas as the "Golden Age" for Hindu women may be based, consequently, not only on an appreciation of the values of this early society, but also on an early apologetic already structured into the texts. What the reformers often overlooked, however, was how the Vedic Age, especially the periods for the Brāhmaṇās and the Upaniṣads—also gave rise to many of the features of classical and medieval Hinduism that would eventually be criticized.[50]

Androcentric views in the *smṛti* texts must be dealt with by showing how they reflect social structures, beliefs, and patterns of authority in particular historical periods. Such texts must be replaced with new *smṛti*s that express the aspirations of women for justice. The explicit recognition that the *smṛti*s are contextual works grants the liberty to undertake this task. The challenge is greater, but not insurmountable, where androcentric views are expressed in the *śruti.* In dealing with such views, our approach may be twofold. We must affirm that the specific purpose of revelation is to inform us only of those things that cannot be known through other available sources. The purpose of revelation is to tell us of the nature of the absolute (*brahman*). The implications of this revelation for gender relationships must be inferred and applied by us. The Advaita tradition, as already discussed, posits that *brahman* exists equally and identically in all beings, and this must translate into a social order characterized by relationships of justice, mutual respect, and freedom from violence. This view of the purpose of revelation also gives us the freedom to see that there may be *smṛti* (contextual) texts within the *śruti,* and these do not have to be granted the same degree of authority. "A hundred *śrutis,*" says Śaṅkara, "may declare that fire is cold or that it is dark; still they possess no authority in the matter."[51]

Ignorance and Patriarchy

The Advaita tradition describes the fundamental human problem, as we noted in Chapter 1, to be one of *avidyā* or "ignorance." Human suffering is rooted in a fundamental misunderstanding of the true nature of reality. Human nature is not considered to be intrinsically flawed or defective. Ignorance can be overcome, and when it is and when we are awakened to the true nature of reality, there will be a corresponding transformation in the quality of our relationships and greater social harmony. In the Bhagavadgītā (18:20), knowledge of the highest kind is described as "that knowledge by which one knows one changeless existence in all things (and beings) and the undivided among the divided." Inferior to this way of knowing is "that knowledge by which one knows distinctly the manifold natures of different kinds of beings" (18:21). *Brahman,* existing in all beings, is identified in the Bhagavadgītā with the *ātmā* or the deepest level of the human self. It is here that true human fullness and freedom from wanting are discovered, and one learns to see oneself in all others.

Every human being, as discussed in Chapter 1, yearns for a fullness and freedom from want. This fullness is inherent in one's nature at the level of one's true self, where one is identical with the imperishable absolute. Ignorant of this, and driven by a sense of incompleteness, we seek to become full beings through the multiplication of our possessions and through power. Men seek self-gratification by treating women as objects of possession and by exercising power and control over them. Because the value of wealth or power comes from the fact that these are exclusive and unequally distributed, the one who seeks his happiness through these means lives in continuous anxiety and insecurity. He feels diminished by the power and wealth of others. "The spiritual problem with greed," David Loy observes, "—both the greed for profit and the greed to consume—is due not only to the consequent maldistribution of worldly goods (although a more equitable distribution is, of course, essential), or to its effects on the biosphere, but even more fundamentally because greed is based on a delusion: the delusion that happiness is to be found this way."[52] Loy will probably agree that his observation is also true of the greed to possess, dominate, and control women.

Although the historical roots of patriarchy are complex, we also must see that it is an expression of *avidyā*, a fundamental misunderstanding of the equality and unity of human beings and a false search for fullness through subjugating, dominating, and controlling women. Such an understanding helps us to see clearly that the liberation of women to become full beings is a necessary condition and expression of our own true liberation as men.

6

Liberation from Homophobia

"This is the bane of human nature, the curse upon mankind, the root of all misery—this inequality. This is source of all bondage, physical, mental and spiritual."

—CW 4, 329

The Reality of Homophobia

In 1998, *Fire*, a film by Canada-based producer Deepa Mehta, was released in India. *Fire* tells the story of two middle class sisters-in-law, Sita and Radha. Sita, after an arranged marriage, joins her husband and his family only to discover that his affections are centered on his Chinese girlfriend. Radha's husband, on the other hand, is on a spiritual quest and has chosen a life of celibacy. Spurned by their husbands, Sita and Radha turn to each other for support, and a love affair ensues. Although *Fire* is centrally concerned with the themes of patriarchy, repression, and rejection, the portrayal of a lesbian relationship ignited a hostile and violent reaction. Theaters screening the movie were burnt to the ground, the life of the producer was threatened, and, for a time, the Indian government banned the film.[1]

Hindu nationalist groups like the Shiva Sena and Rashtriya Seva Sangh led the agitation against *Fire.* The controversy reached the Indian parliament, where a heated debate ensued between opponents of the movie and those who defended the rights of the filmmaker. Protesters contended that homosexuality was a Western import and alien to the culture and traditions of India and denounced the movie as degrading and un-Indian. Shiva Sena leader Bal Thackeray (1926–2012) offered to end the agitation if the names of the women in the film were changed and they were given Muslim names! Mehta and others responded with the argument that homosexual relationships are part of the ancient heritage of India and condemned protesters for their homophobic behavior. Gay activist Ashok Row Kavi claimed that the criminalization of homosexuality was a legacy of British colonial rule and that the Hindu tradition does not condemn those who have different sexual preferences.

The violent response to *Fire* underlines a trend to disavow the reality of homosexuality in ancient India, represent it as a Western phenomenon, and deny its accommodation within Hinduism.[2] It highlights the sharp divisions that exist currently among Hindus over the status of homosexuals within the tradition. These differing positions are well illustrated in the experiences of Jim Gilman, a gay man and former member of the Chinmaya Mission, a popular Hindu Vedānta movement founded by the charismatic teacher Swami Chinmayananda (1916–1993).[3] As a disciple of Swami Chinmayananda, Gilman found complete acceptance at the feet of his teacher. His gayness was a nonissue. When questioned about his attitude toward homosexuality, Chinmayananda's response was sharp and brief. "There are many branches on the tree of life. Full stop. Next question."[4] After the death of Swami Chinmayananda in 1993, according to Gilman, he was asked by his successor, Swami Tejomayananda, to relinquish his position as a teacher (*acāryā*) and to leave the Chinmaya Mission. There were no criticisms of his work or behavior. Protestations about his observance of celibacy (*brahmacarya*) were to no avail. The issue was his gay identity and his past. Members of the Mission, as Gilman discovered, were concerned about his sexual orientation, "based in typical erroneous stereotypes of gay people as perverts and child molesters. I must say that it was one of the most painful experiences of my whole life."[5] A recent Hindu account represents homosexuality as "harmful to all parties," "against nature and the natural order of things," and as "known to cause the spread of diseases like AIDS."[6]

The Hindu openness to religious diversity can be a precious resource informing our reflection on matters of human sexuality. Historically, discussions among Hindu sub-traditions were dialogical, and there was a notable absence of systematic efforts to stamp out other alternative ways of religious thinking. The language of engagement was not militaristic, and differences, though important, were not seen as problematic. It would be a tragedy if, like the opponents of Deepa Mehta's *Fire*, Hindus were to privilege a single interpretation of the tradition and hatefully denounce alternative understandings. If Hindus respect and remain faithful to their pluralistic legacy, homosexuals, like heterosexuals, can be valued and accepted within the expansive embrace of the tradition.

Recognizing Third Sex Persons

Literary evidence contradicts the claim that homosexuality is a modern import into Hinduism. There are ancient references to the existence of three sexes in the Hindu tradition. These are male (*puṁs prakṛiti*), female (*strī prakṛiti*), and members of the third sex (*tṛitīya prakṛiti*).[7] The term *tṛitīya prakṛriti* seems widely employed by the fourth century.[8] In the Kāmasūtra, persons belonging to the third sex are described to be of two types "according to whether their appearance is masculine or feminine."[9] While some may argue that these references to a third sex in ancient Hindu literature ought not to be equated with the acceptance of homosexuals, it is important to take note of the fact that these references are free from homophobic hatred and anger, and, as will become clearer later, there are no denunciations of the third sex based on theological or religious argument.

Our understanding of the significance of a third sex in ancient Hindu literature is deepened by the specific terms used to designate this group of persons. While *tṛitīya* (third) *prakṛiti* is usually translated as "third sex," the Sanskrit term *prakṛiti* does not literally mean sex. It describes "the original or natural form of anything" and is used often as a synonym for "nature, character, constitution."[10] The use of this term highlights the understanding of the ancient thinkers that important aspects of one's sexuality, homosexual or heterosexual, are inherited at birth.[11] Manusmṛti

(3.49), for example, offers a biological explanation for sexual differentiation at birth: "A male child is produced by a greater quantity of male seed, a female child by the prevalence of the female; if both are equal, a third-sex child (*napuṁsaka*) or boy and girl twins are produced; if either are weak or deficient in quantity, a failure of conception results."[12]

Ancient Indian medical practitioners took a similar approach and sought their explanations for sexual identity in conception and fetal development.[13] Sexual identity is determined by the nature of and the respective proportions in which the father's semen and mother's blood combine at conception.

> Thus, a defect in the mother's seed may result in the birth of a baby that is female in appearance but not a true female (that is, an individual of the third gender), while a defect in the father's seed may result in a similarly defective male birth. A variation is the belief that a third-gender individual is conceived when amounts of the male and female seed are equal, as opposed to a preponderance of one or the other, which results in a child of the respective gender.[14]

Although the medicalization of homosexuality and treating it is as "embryological abnormality" are fraught with danger, including the assumption of heterosexual normativity, it is important to note that ancient Hindu thinkers appreciated the inherent dimension of sexual identity and did not view homosexuality as either deviant or unnatural. This may explain why no attempts were ever made to treat or confine homosexuals.[15] The appreciation that third sex orientation is congenital influences significantly our response to such persons. The Hindu tradition, as noted above, has cultivated a remarkable ability to accommodate diversity, and we can surely see third sex persons as part of this wonderful and enriching diversity of creation. Even as heterosexual persons are not called upon to justify their sexuality, third sex persons should not be burdened with the obligation to explain or defend their identities and with being mistakenly perceived as a disordered expression of other sexes.

The Case of Arjuna in Mahābhārata

One of the finest examples of such acceptance and fair treatment of third sex persons in ancient Hindu society concerns Arjuna, the Pāṇḍava leader, friend, and disciple of Krishna in the Bhagavadgītā and the hero of the Mahābhārata.[16] The Mahābhārata narrates the story of the conflict between two sets of cousins, the Kauravas and the Pāṇḍavas. The Pāṇḍavas were cheated out of their rightful share of the family kingdom, treated unjustly, and forced into exile. After losing a loaded game of dice against the Kauravas, the Pāṇḍavas were required, under the terms of the wager, to live for twelve years in the wilderness and spend the thirteenth year incognito. If their true identities were discovered during this year, they had to spend another twelve years in exile.

Arjuna, the warrior, chose to spend the thirteenth year in the court of a local ruler, King Virāṭa. He assumed the dress and personality of a member of the third sex, wearing the clothing and ornaments of a woman. Arjuna introduced himself to the king as Bṛihannaḍa, a teacher of dance and music.

> I sing and I dance and make fine music,
> I am good at the dance and master of song.
> Pray give me to Uttarā, sire, to serve her,
> I shall be the dance master of your queen.
> The reason I have this form—what profit
> Is there in recounting it but great pain?
> Bṛhannaḍa, sire is my name, deserted
> By father and mother as son and daughter.[17]

The king was initially skeptical of Arjuna's identity because he could not reconcile Arjuna's muscular build with his femininity. The King tested Arjuna in dancing and music and consulted with his ministers and the women of his court. Arjuna was allowed to live among the palace women and be an instructor.

> So in his disguise Dhanañjaya dwelled there
> In control of himself and doing them favors;

> And none of the people there found him out,
> Neither those in the house nor those outside.[18]

As a bona fide person of the third sex, Arjuna found acceptance, employment, and safety within the palace walls and among the women in the court. We must assume that Arjuna chose this particular guise knowing well that as a person of the third sex, he would not be rejected, humiliated, or demeaned. His choice had to be grounded in a wider social acceptance and role of third sex persons in Hindu society.[19]

Third Sex Persons in the Law Codes

Although there is good evidence that Hindu society acknowledged the existence of a third sex and had some appreciation for the biological basis of sexual identity, ancient codes of law specify sanctions against certain kinds of homosexual behavior and exclude homosexuals from ritual privileges and family inheritance.[20] One of the often-quoted texts is from Manu (11.175).

> "A twice-born man who commits an unnatural offence with a male, or has intercourse with a female in a cart drawn by oxen, in water, or in the day-time, shall bathe, dressed in his clothes."

This is a problematic verse highlighting many important exegetical issues. First, is the accuracy of the translation. The translator, G. Buhler, prejudicially renders *maithunaṁ puṁsī* (lit. sex with a male) as "unnatural offence with a male."[21] Second, the text appears to be more concerned with specifying a certain time and places where sexual relations are undesirable because it makes mention of both heterosexuality as well as homosexuality. It seems that the verse intends to curb public displays of sexuality. Third, the verse identifies the punishment as applying to the twice-born man.[22] The question of whether this verse should be read as applying to persons of the third sex remains doubtful.[23] Fourth, the punishment, a ritual bath, fully dressed, must be considered a relatively minor punishment.

Manu (11.68) also prescribes loss of caste for sexual relations between males. "Causing an injury to a priest, smelling wine or things that are not to be smelled, crookedness and sexual union with a man are traditionally said to cause loss of caste."[24]

Here we also see that sexual relations between males are not treated by themselves, but included with a variety of actions that seem to be of varying moral significance. In addition, as Sharma rightly notes, the loss of caste was not permanent and could be recovered by the performance of prescribed rites of expatiation.[25] The important point here, as Zwilling and Sweet rightly note, is that the "rabid homophobia of the Judeo-Christian West is absent—there are no exhortations to burn or to stone to death people who have queer sex, or who are otherwise different in their gender or sexual role. The Hindu law books do contain penalties for same-sex behavior, but these are for the most part minor fines and penances, comparable to similar heterosexual offences and other violations of ritual purity or social norms."[26] Most significantly, there is no evidence of any hateful persecution of third sex persons.

In the Laws of Manu, people of the third sex also are excluded from certain privileges accorded to others. These include making offerings to departed ancestors and deities (3:150, 165), from family inheritance (9:201, 203), and from making sacrificial offerings into the sacred fire (4:205–206):

> A priest should never eat at a sacrifice offered by a priest who does not know the Veda by heart, by someone who conducts sacrifice for every sort of person, or by a woman or an impotent man.
>
> Where an oblation is offered by such people there is bad luck for virtuous men; it goes against the grain of the gods, and therefore one should avoid it.

While the gender bias of Manu is revealed in his exclusion of women, some interpreters understand these exclusions to be connected with the fact that third sex individuals did not fulfill traditional Hindu obligations through marriage and bearing children.[27] The exclusion from inheritance may be a direct consequence of not having children to whom one may bequeath family property. Religious celibates, however, also give up rights to family property and do not participate in traditional rituals that are prescribed for householders. The exclusions that are mentioned in Manu therefore do not have to be construed as pertaining to homosexuals merely because of their sexual identity. These have to be seen in the light of the significance of procreation. The Hindu tradition places a very high value on having children, and raising a family discharges what is understood to be a debt to one's ancestors. A son is required for funeral rituals and to perform annual postmortem offerings on behalf of departed parents. Ritual worship in the Vedas presumes a heterosexual family with children. This is an issue to which we return later.

Divine Immanence and the Value of the Person

It is important to acknowledge that although the tradition recognizes the reality of a third sex and has argued for its biological basis, heterosexuality is still treated as normative, and third sex persons, especially in the law codes, are judged deficiently in relation to married, child-producing heterosexuals.[28] The challenge remains to move from acknowledgment of a third sex to an affirmation of the equal worth of and justice for all sexes.

There are important justifications in the Advaita tradition for such a movement and pivotal resources on which it must be grounded. The ultimate worth of the human person in Advaita is not located in his or her sexual identity. It proceeds from the claim that the human self (*ātmā*) is identical with the real and infinite (*brahman*). We are invited to see *brahman* in all and all in *brahman*. The profound significance that the Hindu tradition accords to this truth may be appreciated from the fact that its discernment is equated with liberation (*mokṣa*), the highest goal of human existence. *Mokṣa* is awakening to one's own identity and the identity of all beings with *brahman*. This vision does not call upon us to ignore or deny the uniqueness of individuals and communities, but to perceive the unity that underlies all and to realize the value of each one. One cannot profess value for the infinite and despise the multiplicity of beings that have emerged from the infinite and in which the infinite exists as self. This truth requires us also to regard all beings equally. As the Bhagavadgītā (5:19) states it: "Even here on earth, those whose minds are impartial overcome rebirth. *Brahman* is perfect and the same in all. Therefore, they always abide in *brahman*."[29]

Justice, understood as impartiality and equality of opportunity and treatment, is a consequence of the equal presence of the divine and is a condition for liberation and oneness with *brahman*. There is no good reason why this should not be applied to persons of the third sex.

The Advaita teachings about the unity of existence through *brahman* and the worth of all life are the sources of cardinal values such as *ahiṁsā* (non-injury), compassion (*dayā*), and generosity (*dāna*). Belief in divine immanence requires reverence and consideration for all and for relationships that are characterized by justice and freedom from violence. *Brahman* is identified as the ground of human selfhood and spoken of as non-different from the human self (*ātmā*) at its most fundamental nature. With this ultimate identity in mind, scriptural texts speak interchangeably of seeing the self (*ātmā*) in all beings and/or seeing the divine (*brahman*) in all beings.[30] For example, Īśa Upaniṣad (6) reminds us that the wise person who sees all beings in the self and sees the self in all beings is liberated from hate. The Bhagavadgītā (12:13) puts this same point positively and describes such a person not only as free from hate, but as friendly and compassionate to all. Freedom from fear is also a mark of wisdom and liberation.[31] Homophobia, characterized as it is by fear, hate, and denigration of third sex persons, finds no justification in Hinduism and betrays its most fundamental vision and values.

The Hindu ideal of seeing all beings in one's own self and one's self in all beings must not be interpreted passively. At heart, it is a call to enter compassionately into the lives of others, seeing through their eyes, sharing their emotions, understanding their thoughts, and responding to their needs. It is, as the Bhagavadgītā (6:32) explains, identifying with others in joy and in sorrow and learning to own their joys and pains as one's own. The requirement, in the case of third sex persons, is that through identity with them we know the pain that comes from being demonized, ostracized, excluded, persecuted, and denied the opportunities available to heterosexual persons. Knowing the pain of the other through an enlarged identity helps us to overcome an important source of homophobia, rooted as it is in the human tendency to devalue those who are defined as different and perceived, consequently, as a threat. As Ervin Staub points out in his seminal study *The Roots of Evil*, devaluation and the relegation of people to outgroups "serve as a basis for scapegoating and a precondition for harming."[32] Devaluation leads to the perception of people as objects and not as fellow beings who feel and suffer as we do. It provides the conditions for guilt-free violence and mistreatment. Humans are less likely to oppress those in whom they see themselves, and the Advaita ideal of "seeing oneself in all beings and all beings in oneself" is an important antidote to the poison of homophobia and all other prejudices.

Sex and Liberation (Mokṣa)

It is very important to take note of the fact that in relation to the attainment of *mokṣa* (liberation), the ultimate and highest goal of human existence in Hinduism, there is no difference between heterosexuality and homosexuality. Sexual identity does not debar a person from life's most desirable end.[33] Advaita, as discussed in Chapter 4, proposes that ignorance (*avidyā*) of the true nature of the human self (*ātmā*), the infinite (*brahman*), and the world (*jagat*) is the fundamental cause of suffering. Freedom or liberation cannot be attained without right knowledge of reality and the transformation of vision and action that this implies.

Advaita teaches that the self, in its essential nature, is timeless and full. Ignorant of this truth, one wrongly identifies entirely with the characteristics of body and mind, including sex. One assumes the limitations of these and considers oneself incomplete and wanting. *Mokṣa* is consequent on the right understanding of the nature of the self. It implies the recognition of the self to be more than the psychophysical composite.

This Hindu understanding of liberation, however, should not be interpreted to mean that the tradition is life denying or that it despises the body and human sexuality. Pleasure (*kāma*) is one of the legitimate goals of Hindu life so long as it is sought in accordance with the requirements of *dharma* (moral values) and its primary virtue, non-injury (*ahiṁsā*).[34] One of the recommended ways for contemplating God in the Taittirīya Upaniṣad (3.10.3–4) is as joy in sex, and sex is treated in the Upaniṣads as sacramental in nature.[35] It is ignorance (*avidyā*) and the immoderate and unethical life that stand as obstacles to liberation and not sexuality, heterosexual or homosexual. I am not aware of any authoritative (*śruti*) text that excludes a person from Hinduism's highest goal on the basis of sexual identity. As Kaṭha Upaniṣad (2:24) states it:

> "One who has not abstained from evil conduct, whose senses are not controlled and whose mind is not concentrated and calm cannot gain the Self through knowledge."[36]

One of the most remarkable examples of sexual inclusivity in the sacred texts of Hinduism, and perhaps in the religious literature of the world, occurs in the Rāmāyaṇa.[37] The context here is a story told by Rāma in which he likens God to a parent having numerous children. Although each child possesses a different gift, the parent loves all in the same way. The entire universe, Rāma explains, is his creation, and he is equally compassionate to all. "One who worships me in thought, word and action, relinquishing deceit, whether man, third sex person, or woman, is supremely dear to me."[38]

It is clear that, in the view of the author of the Rāmāyaṇa, human sexual identity, as well as other kinds of distinctions, do not matter to God. Love and purity of character are all important. While the above verse is the only one in the text referring specifically to third sex persons, the message about the centrality of love and the inclusiveness of God's love is unmistakable. Earlier in the text, there is a remarkable exchange with an outcaste woman who was apprehensive of approaching Rāma because of her sex and caste status. Rāma assured her that the relationship of love is the only one that binds God to human beings. "I recognize no relationship save that of love: neither lineage, family, religion, rank, wealth, power, connections, virtue or ability. A person without love is of no more account than a cloud without water."[39]

Similar passages can be found in other authoritative Hindu texts underlining the impartiality of God and the priority of a loving relationship. One well-known text is Bhagavadgītā (9:29): "I am the same to all beings; I do not favor or despise anyone; those who worship me with love are in me and I am in them."

Other sections of the text (2:55–72; 12:13–20;14:23–26) describing the character of the wise person and the servant of God make no reference to sex and speak only of virtues of the mind and heart such as delight in God, self-control, absence of hate and greed, friendliness, and compassion.

Procreation, Marriage, and the Third Sex

Although homosexuality is not regarded in Hinduism as a religious sin (*pāpa*), one of the principal reasons for stigmatization has to do with non-procreation through inability or disinterest. As Devadutt Pattanaik points out, "All hell breaks loose in a Hindu household not so much when a son or daughter displays homosexual tendencies, but when those tendencies come in the way of heterosexual marriage . . . non-heterosexuality is ignored or tolerated so long as it does not upset the heterosexual world order.[40] While the value of children should not by itself be thought of as problematic, it becomes so when those who for various reasons do not procreate are perceived as defective and of lesser worth.

As already noted above, the value and worth of persons in Advaita do not come from sexual identity or, we must now add, procreative ability or choice. The famous lines of the Kaivalya Upaniṣad (3) remind us that immortality is attained through renunciation and not by work, progeny, or wealth. Worth comes from the human embodiment of *brahman*, and liberation (*mokṣa*) is not contingent on procreation or its absence. The traditional value of procreation must be seen in the context of labor needs in an agricultural economy and a high rate of infant mortality. Today, these conditions have changed, and the need for offspring is no longer as urgent.

In addition to economic need and high infant mortality rates, male progeny, as discussed in Chapter 5, also is required for the performance of annual postmortem rituals (*śrāddha*) for the departed parent. This ritual, it is believed, saves the parent from suffering in the afterlife. I commented already on the fact that with the growth of nuclear families, both sons and daughters are leaving the family home, and a married daughter may be more interested and available to perform postmortem rituals. It is necessary today to reconsider the exclusion of Hindu women from such important family rituals. I noted also the need to emphasize the teaching of the tradition on *karma*, which makes each person responsible for his or her own destiny after death. As I have argued elsewhere, these rituals persist "in spite of the fact that they contradict the widely accepted worldview of *karma, saṁsāra* and *mokṣa*. They are based, not on the assumption of rebirth, but on the hope of the departed eventually joining the company of ancestors in an ancestral world. The emphasis is not on the moral law of *karma* determining the individual's future prospects, but on the ritual offerings of the descendant."[41] Returning to the theological roots of the tradition will avert the need for this emphasis in the Hindu tradition.

For various reasons, including the ones mentioned above, progeny and parenthood (*prajāpati*) became the central purpose of Hindu marriage. The tradition, however, has identified five purposes of marriage: pleasure (*rati*), parenthood (*prajāpati*), companionship (*sakhya*), worship (*yajña*), and spiritual bliss (*ānanda*). There are good reasons today for giving renewed emphasis to the goals of friendship and spiritual growth.[42] Hindu couples wishing to be married are not required to give proof of their procreative ability or intent, and older persons beyond the age of procreation are allowed to get married. Clearly the Hindu tradition recognizes that the purpose of marriage is not limited to procreation. Marriage also enhances religious growth and personal development through love, sharing, and control of sensual impulses.

There are ancient traditions in the Hindu world that may be cited and appropriated to point the way forward for our attitude toward marriage and procreation. One ancient text, the Nāradasmṛiti (1.12.15), advises against the marriage of homosexual men to women.[43] In addition, Kāmasūtra (2.9.36) records the practice of homosexual marriage in ancient India. "There are also citizens, sometimes greatly attached to each other and with complete faith in one another, who get married (*parigraha*) together."

The purpose of such marriages would not be procreation, but other goals such as friendship, mutual care, and spiritual development.

Recovering Indigenous Theological Resources

Many commentators note that the homophobia that exists today in India and among Hindus is a direct consequence of Western—in particular, British colonial—influence.[44] The criminalization of homosexuality came with British legislation in 1860 and remained in the law books until it was repealed on 2009. Section 377 of the Indian Penal Code, for example, reads: "Whoever voluntarily has carnal intercourse against the order of nature with any man, woman or animal, shall be punished with imprisonment for life, or with imprisonment of either description for a term which may extend to ten years, and shall be liable to fine."[45] Cross-dressing was outlawed and homophobia reinforced through prejudicial translation of ancient texts. Indigenous attitudes that recognized and accepted the reality of third sex persons and accorded them a place and role in society were displaced and replaced by guilt and condemnation. Gandhi, educated in England, sent groups to destroy erotic images on temples and had to be stopped by India's Nobel laureate poet, Rabindranath Tagore. Jawaharlal Nehru, India's first prime minister, also British educated, was upset by the publication of photographs by Alain Daniélou of sculptures dating from the eleventh century depicting homosexual relations. Nehru's contention was that such vices were the product of Western influence.[46] Today, the task of identifying authentic Hindu attitudes toward homosexuality also involves stripping away colonial accretions and puritanical attitudes to human sexuality that originate elsewhere.

Although ancient Hindu society stigmatized homosexuals and sought to debar them from certain privileges enjoyed by heterosexuals, there are important resources in the tradition for overcoming injustice and transforming our thinking about human sexuality. The highly decentralized Hindu tradition allows for great diversity of thought and religious choice. It is one of the earliest cultures to propose the category of a third sex (*tṛitīya prakṛiti*), with characteristics different from heterosexual males and females. It is true that "in the earliest speculations about a third gender there was a wavering between viewing it a true third category 'neither male nor female,' or assimilated to a defective (that is, female) pole of the male gender, erasing its uniquely androgynous characteristics."[47] The defect is primarily associated with the inability or unwillingness to procreate. The category of *tṛitīya prakṛiti*, however, provides us with a valuable resource that challenges and enlarges our thinking about sex categories that are generally thought to be binary in nature. It helps us to recognize the reality of a third sex, different from traditional male and female identities, and to accept such sexual diversity as a natural part of the diversity of the tree of life. The use of the term *prakṛiti* to describe the third sex is a suggestion that this category, contrary to the argument of one Hindu writer, is not "against nature and the natural order of things."[48]

The homophobia that is now discernible in sections of the Hindu community is absent in the ancient texts. While there are certain legal penalties for homosexual conduct mentioned in the law codes, these are fairly mild in nature, and there is no evidence in medical treatises of attempts to convert or cure homosexuals. One text explicitly forbids the compulsory marriage of homosexual men to women. While the stigmatization of homosexuals in Hindu society seems particularly connected with the value of male progeny, this desire is explicable in the context of labor needs in an agricultural economy and high infant mortality rates. The need for a male child to perform postmortem rituals that avert the suffering of the parent belies the core Hindu teaching about the doctrine of *karma*. Today, we need to put more emphasis on personal responsibility.

As far as the recognition of a third sex is concerned, it is also important to note that, as with heterosexuality, this does not imply a disregard for the necessity of attentiveness to ethical values in human relationships. There are certain common values (*sādhāraṇa dharma*) to which all are expected to subscribe. Among these are truth, forgiveness, sense control, and freedom from anger. Hindus are guilty, like people of other religions, of stereotyping persons of the third sex and wrongly equating homosexuality with promiscuity. Such stereotyping includes emphasis on sexual behavior. We need to remember also that the term "homosexuality," like "heterosexuality," should not be narrowly equated with sex. The issue, as with heterosexuality, is about preferences in relationships and the values of love, justice, loyalty, trust, caring, and friendship that are at the heart of all good relationships. We need to emphasize the importance of these values in all relationships.

Ultimately, in Advaita, persons are not valued for their procreative abilities or sex. Human worth is the outcome of the immanence of *brahman*, and the discerning of this truth is equated with liberation (*mokṣa*). The equal and identical presence of *brahman* in all is the ground for human dignity and equal justice. The tradition emphasizes the inclusivity of divine love and the accessibility of liberation. The significance of sexual identity, homosexual or heterosexual, has to be seen in relation to the teaching that the self (*ātmā*) is not bound or limited by sexual specifications. In affirming the sex-transcendent nature of the self, the Śvestāśvatara Upaniṣad (5:11), quite significantly, lists all three sexes: "It is not woman, man or third sex person. It identifies with whatever body it assumes."[49]

This inclusion of third sex persons in the Upaniṣad, as in the Rāmāyana, is a significant recognition in an authoritative text that human sexuality is not limited to heterosexual identities. It is also a challenge for us to reevaluate our contemporary attitudes and assumptions about homosexuality and to realize, appreciate, and enjoy the fact that, in the words of Swami Chinmayananda, "there are many branches on the tree of life."

7

Liberation from Anthropocentrism

> *"The Vedanta does not in reality denounce the world . . . it really means deification of the world—giving up the world as we think of it, as we know it, as it appears to us—and knowing what it really is. Deify it; it is God alone."*
>
> —CW 2, 146

Brahman as Ontological Ground of Nature

In this chapter, I consider the relationship between human beings and the rest of nature from the perspective of the Advaita tradition. Advaita, as discussed earlier, characterizes the relationship between the infinite (*brahman*), the world (*jagat*), and the human being (*jīva*) as not-two while affirming an ultimate ontological non-difference among all three. *Brahman* is the ultimate self of the world and the human being. Without any depletion, *brahman* brings forth the universe as an act of self-multiplication. The relationship between *brahman* as cause and world as effect is asymmetrical. The world, as an effect, shares in the nature of its cause (*brahman*), but *brahman* is not limited by the world. At the heart of the human problem is ignorance (*avidyā*) about the nature of *brahman* and the consequent assumption that the world's existence and reality are independent of *brahman.* This non-recognition of *brahman* as constituting the single ontological ground and being of the universe is the root of human suffering and lack of fullness. Liberation (*mokṣa*), attainable here and now, is synonymous with the overcoming of ignorance (*avidyā*) and the birth of a radically new understanding of self and world that ensues. In a liberative understanding, the world does not cease to exist, but its ontological unity and inseparable existence from *brahman* are recognized and celebrated.

Dualistic and Non-dualistic Views of Nature

Scholars and activists who have critically considered the relationship between human beings and nature in Western religious traditions identify a dualistic worldview as contributing significantly to our alienation from and devaluation and reckless exploitation of nature.[1] Dualistic traditions in general propose a radical distinction between self and world/nature, spirit and matter. The distinctions are hierarchical because self is identified with spirit/consciousness and considered superior to inert matter/nature. Nature is the realm of mortality and change, while spirit is accorded a higher value because it is regarded as immortal and unchanging. Commentators have argued that Christianity contributed to the desacralization of the world by describing a transcendental creator who is not present in the world in a way that makes the world sacred. Such a view make the exploitation of nature easier.[2] Nature is viewed also from a radical anthropomorphic standpoint that emphasizes the right of human control and domination. In searching for alternative philosophical viewpoints that overcome such dualisms, affirm the intrinsic worth of nature, and offer grounds for a positive relationship between human beings and nature, many have commended the Advaita tradition of Hinduism.[3]

The Advaita teaching about the fundamental ontological unity of *brahman*, world, and human beings is understood as promoting a reverence and value for nature that is conducive to sound environmental ethics. In the words of Crawford,

> The cosmic vision of Hinduism sees humans as an intrinsic part of nature. The fabric of life has many special strands, and human beings are special in their own rights by virtue of their moral character; but this does not place them outside nature or above nature. *Distinction*, not *separation* is the hallmark of the Hindu view of the position of humans in nature. The unitive

> thinking of Hinduism aligns it with a "deep ecology" which places people *in nature,* as opposed to a "shallow ecology" which is anthropocentric and which ascribes to *Homo Sapiens* a position of dominance and superiority over nature.[4]

This unitive view is understood as engendering respect for nature and prohibiting its heedless exploitation because the desacralization of nature and its destruction are related to seeing ourselves as separate and distinct from nature.

The Devaluation of Nature in Advaita

Although I concur with interpreters like Crawford and Deutsch that the non-dual Advaita tradition offers valuable resources for a more constructive relationship between human beings and nature and has the potential to overcome many of the problems that are traditionally associated with dualistic worldviews, such resources have not been a prominent part of the traditional understanding and articulation of Advaita. The tradition has been interpreted predominantly in ways that devalue nature and promote indifference to the world. The tradition seems to be more concerned historically with the negation of the world and not its sacralization or intrinsic worth. We must recognize also that classical Advaita interpreters were not concerned with articulating a theology of the natural world. Their focus was on describing the primary human problem of ignorance and specifying the way to its resolution. The lingering impression is that Advaita does not care about the world. Many share David Haberman's view. "The multiple world of appearance for Shankara's Advaita Vedanta, for example, is not ultimately real. It is an ever-changing cover which distorts and conceals the stable reality hidden beneath it. From this position the world of nature has no value in and of itself."[5]

In affirming the truth of a non-dual reality (*brahman*), many Advaita interpreters suggest that the knowledge of this reality requires and results in the eradication of the world. The world, it is argued, must be discarded before we can know *brahman*. "The complex world of our ordinary experience," writes Eliot Deutsch, "disappears in the pure white light of spiritual simplicity. All distinctions, contradictions and multiplicities are transcended and obliterated."[6] The world is likened to a sense-illusion, which we conjure and experience because of our ignorance. The most famous of these analogies equates the world with a snake that is mistakenly perceived in place of a rope. I cited earlier the words of T. M. P. Mahadevan that the world "is but an illusory appearance in *Brahman*, even as the snake is in the rope."[7] The implication here is that when the rope is properly known, the illusory snake will no longer exist. In addition, the disappearance of the snake is a condition for truly knowing the rope. Similarly, when *brahman* is known, the world ceases to be, and *brahman* cannot be known as long as the world of diversity is experienced. After the reality of the world is denied, it is easy to deny meaning and value for it. The words of Swami Nirvedananda, a monk of the Ramakrishna Order, which adheres to Advaita, are very powerful in this regard. He describes the world as having no value or meaning in its relation to *brahman.*

> Just as things and events seen in a dream vanish altogether and become meaningless when one wakes up, so does the universe with all its contents disappear when one finds the Real Self. One then becomes perfectly awakened to what really exists, the Absolute. Compared with that, the universe is no more than a dream. So long as one sees in a dream, the dream objects are intensely real. So also is the universe with all its contents to one under the spell of *avidyā* (ignorance). On awakening to Absolute Reality, however, all these have no value, no meaning, no existence.[8]

In his well-known work on Indian philosophy, Surendranath Dasgupta advances a similar interpretation of the view of Śaṅkara on the status of the world, although he is wrong in asserting that the many disappears when the truth of *brahman* is known.[9] "The Upaniṣads," in the words of Dasgupta, "held that reality or truth was one, and there was 'no many' anywhere, and Śaṅkara explained it by adding that the 'many' was merely an illusion, and hence did not exist in reality and was bound to disappear when the truth was known."[10] The denial of reality and value to the world extends to relationships within it, as the following story, told by the Hindu teacher Ramakrishna illustrates. Here the world is placed on the same level of reality as a dream.

> There was a farmer who lived in the countryside. He was a real *jñāni* (wise person). He was married and after many years a son was born to him, whom he named Haru. The parents loved the boy dearly. This was natural since he was the one precious gem of the family. On account of his religious nature, the farmer was loved by the villagers. One day he was working in the field when a neighbor came and told him that Haru had an attack of cholera. The farmer at once returned home and arranged for the treatment of the boy. But Haru died. The other members of the family were grief-stricken, but the farmer acted as if nothing had happened. He consoled his family and told them that grieving was futile. Then he went back to his field. On returning home, he found his wife weeping even more bitterly. She said to him: "How heartless you are! You haven't shed one tear for the child." The farmer replied quietly: "Shall I tell you why I haven't wept? I dreamt I had become a king. I was the father of eight sons and very happy with them. Then I woke up. Now I am greatly perplexed. Should I weep for these eight sons or for this one Haru?"[11]

When the reality of the world is denied in this manner, one may draw the inference that it is not consistent for one to be affected by events within it. To respond to the world is to grant reality to the world; it is to treat as real that which does not exist. Interpretations like these easily provide justification for world-renunciation rather than world-affirmation and have been most strongly and clearly articulated in the monastic and ascetic strands of Hinduism. Such strands show little or no interest in offering interpretations of the meaning of Advaita that grant value and significance to the world.

Taken to their extremes, these positions make it difficult to take the world of nature seriously. It is represented as beset with problems, and one is advised to cultivate an attitude of disgust toward it and to pray to be free from its clutches. Śaṅkara, the foremost exponent of Advaita, sometimes describes the world negatively. It is a place of suffering to be shunned, and the appropriate attitude toward it is one of disgust and repulsion. Such descriptions of the world may have the purpose of cultivating detachment and encouraging a turning toward *brahman*. The fact remains, however, that these do not encourage positive attitudes.

> Since the process of the Births and Rebirths is so beset with troubles, therefore, one should cultivate a feeling of disgust. That is because it is found that wretched creatures are every moment of their life taken up by the pangs of births and deaths and are thrust into illimitable terrible darkness—like the unnavigable ocean, and having no hope of going out—therefore one should cultivate feelings of disgust towards this process of Birth and Rebirth—avoid it, shun it, praying that "may I never fall into this terrible metempsyclic ocean."[12]

The world is further stripped of value when Advaita interpreters attempt to disconnect it from *brahman* and present it as a product of *māyā*. *Brahman* is presented merely as the support (*adhiṣṭhāna*) of *māyā*, which is represented as the direct material cause of the world. *Brahman* associated with *māyā* is spoken of *saguṇa brahman* or *iśvara* and regarded as lower than *nirguṇa brahman*, or *brahman* as disconnected and unrelated to the world of nature. *Māyā*, with its historical overtones of illusion, deception, untruth, and falsehood, is posited as the true cause of the world, and the world, as the product of *māyā*, is consequently devalued. Such interpretations make it difficult to justify an intrinsic value for nature and an attitude of reverence.

The predominant Advaita concern has been to explain the world away and to inculcate attitudes of world renunciation and detachment. If Advaita has the potential and resources to enrich our understanding of the human-world relationship, these resources will have to be highlighted and made more explicit through a new exegesis of the Upaniṣads and other authoritative texts. Such a task has not concerned the leading Advaita interpreters.

Affirming the Value of Nature in Advaita

Is it possible to formulate an understanding of the world within Advaita that can affirm its value, or must we be content with its devaluation and with interpretations that justify indifference to nature? This is one of the significant challenges for the non-dual tradition at this time, and I believe that alternative interpretations are necessary and possible. To present such alternatives, I return to some of the texts and constructive theological movements introduced in earlier chapters of this work, in particular Chapters 3 and 4. I read these, however, with the aim of discerning what we may learn about the value of the world.

Unlike Advaita interpreters who seem anxious to disconnect the world from *brahman* and to trace its origin to *māyā*, the Upaniṣads account for the world's origin in *brahman* alone. There is, in fact, a special concern to emphasize this origin for the world. In the Chāndogya Upaniṣad (6.2.1–2), for example, Āruṇi explains the origin of the world from *brahman* and not from non-being.

> In the beginning, son, this world was simply what is existent—one only, without a second. Now on this point some do say: "In the beginning this world was simply what is non-existent—one only, without a second. And from what is non-existent was born what is existent."
>
> But, son, how can that possibly be? How can what is existent be born from what is non-existent? On the contrary, son, in the beginning this world was simply what is existent—one only, without a second.

Similar texts are to be found in the Taittirīya Upaniṣad (2.6.1):

> He wished (*sokāmayata*), "Let me be many, let me be born." He undertook a deliberation. Having deliberated, he created all this that exists. That (*brahman*) having created (that), entered into that very thing. And having entered, it became the formed and the formless, the defined and the undefined, the sustaining and the

> non-sustaining, the sentient and the insentient, the true and the untrue. Truth became all this that there is. They call that (*brahman*) Truth.

Śaṅkara, following the Upaniṣads, is uncompromising in his view that the universe has its origin in *brahman* and in no other source. He does this most clearly when he is refuting the Sāṅkhya argument that the creation has its origin in insentient matter (*prakṛti*). In his commentary on the Brahmasūtra 1.1.2, for example, Śankara writes that "the universe cannot possibly be thought of as having its origin etc., from any other factor, e.g. *pradhāna* (primordial nature) which is insentient, or from atoms, or non-existence, or some soul under worldly conditions (viz. *hiraṅyagarbha*). Nor can it originate spontaneously; for in this universe people (desirous of products) have to depend on specific, space, time and causation." This argument, from Śaṅkara, is also an affirmation of *brahman as* a sentient being. Unlike *prakṛiti*, *brahman* is not inanimate; its nature is consciousness, and *brahman* can will the universe into existence.

The Upaniṣads also emphasize that *brahman* is not lost or depleted after creation. *Brahman* remains limitless and non-dual after the emergence of the world. Without any diminution or loss, therefore, *brahman* brings forth the world out of itself as an act of self-multiplication. The Upaniṣads are concerned with denying ontological dualism before and after creation. We read in Kaṭha Upaniṣad 2.1.10–11: "What indeed is here, is there; what is there, is here likewise. He who sees as though there is difference here, goes from death to death. This is to be attained through the mind indeed. There is no diversity here whatsoever. He who sees as though there is difference, goes from death to death."[13]

Affirming an ontological non-dual relationship between *brahman* and the world, however, is not the same as fully equating the world with *brahman*. The fact that *brahman* is described as cause (*kāraṇa*) and the world as effect (*kārya*) implies some difference. If there were no differences, the distinction would be meaningless. The relationship, as described in Chapter 3, may be understood as an asymmetrical one. The world partakes of the nature of *brahman*, but the limits of the world are not intrinsic to *brahman*.[14] At the same time, the world does not have an independent ontological identity distinct from *brahman*, and so the truth of non-duality is not compromised. The world does not have an existence of its own, whereas *brahman*'s existence is its own. Unlike many post-Śaṅkara commentators, Śaṅkara himself does not describe the world as illusory or unreal, and it is not often remembered that he argued strongly against the subjective idealists who reduce the world to a mere idea of the perceiving individual and who deny the world any existence outside the mind.[15]

To argue that the world, as an effect, is ontologically non-different from and dependent on *brahman* does not deny its meaning and value. The world does not have to exist independently of *brahman* to have value. Such an argument implies that only theologies of dualism can confer value to the world. On the contrary, because *brahman* has ultimate value, the non-dual relationship enriches the value of the world. Too much energy has been expended in Advaita in establishing the so-called unreality of the world and too little on seeing the world as *brahman*'s marvelous self-multiplication and as a celebrative expression of *brahman*'s fullness. Its value is derived from the fact that it shares the ontological nature of *brahman* even though, as a finite process, it can never full express *brahman*. Even as a clay pot does not exhaust the nature and potential of clay, the world does not exhaust the infinite.

Instead of focusing of interpretative strategies that seek to disconnect *brahman* from the world and thus devalue and ignore it, the tradition should return to the meaning of those texts that emphasize *brahman*'s deliberation (*īkṣaṇa*) and intentionality before and during the process of creating. It would be contradictory for the Upaniṣads to proclaim *brahman* as the source of the world and then trivialize the value of the world. A world that is presented as meaningless and without value for its intelligent creative source cannot have value for the created. If the world can be seen positively as the outcome of the intentional creativity of *brahman*, expressing and sharing the fullness of *brahman*, the world does not have to be renounced or negated. We may then speak of the meaning of life as participating in the celebration of existence by knowing *brahman* who brought all things into being and whose fullness is at the heart of everything. Such an understanding offers us also a different way of thinking about the meaning of liberation (*mokṣa*) in relation to the world.

Liberation and the Significance of Nature

Advaita commentators, as we have noted, suggest widely that liberation (*mokṣa*), synonymous with the knowledge of *brahman*, results in the negation of the world or the eradication of the experience of plurality. Such interpretations of the meaning of liberation follow from regarding the world as illusory or unreal.

How does one care for that which has no value, no meaning, no existence? In direct contrast to such interpretations of the meaning of liberation, a different reading of the Advaita tradition allows us to understand liberation as a way of seeing both *brahman* and the world, the one and the many, rather than the one alone. In the analogy of the clay and clay pot, the vision of the clay does not require the obliteration of the clay pot. There is no good ground for equating liberation in Advaita with the cessation of the experience of the world because there is no suggestion that the world becomes nonexistent in the vision of the liberated. Typical of such texts are the following from the Bhagavadgītā (13:27; 18:20).

> One who sees the great Lord existing equally in all beings,
> the imperishable in the perishable, truly sees.
>
> That knowledge by which one sees one imperishable being in all beings, indivisible in the divisible is the highest.[16]

Texts such as these invite a way of seeing reality that does not require negation of the world, but a celebration of its manyness and its ontological non-duality with *brahman*. Each being and object may be appreciated as a unique expression of *brahman*. Meaning and value are added, not taken from the world, when this ontological unity and inseparable existence from *brahman* are affirmed.

According to Śaṅkara (BRUBh 3.5.1:333), the world exists both for the one who knows *brahman* and the one who does not know *brahman*. The difference is that the knower of *brahman* understands the world, despite its appearance of independent existence, to be ontologically non-different from and dependent on *brahman*. In liberation, the world is not unseen but seen with new eyes; the many is seen as expressions of the One. Nature has an intrinsic value that derives from the fact of its connectedness to *brahman*. This is emphasized in several texts of the Bhagavadgītā that invite us to see and rejoice in nature as divine expression. These verses celebrate the beauty of nature as divine expression. There is no suggestion here that we should be disgusted or repelled by the world.

> I am the taste in water, the brilliance in the moon and sun, the sacred syllable (Om) in all the Vedas, the sound in air and virility in men.
>
> I am the pure fragrance in the earth, the radiance in fire, life in all beings and austerity in ascetics. (7:8–9)
>
> All is strung on me like jewels on a string. (7:7)[17]

In Bhagavadgītā (5:18), Krishna makes specifically mention of seeing the same (*sama*) *brahman* in humans as well as animals. No being is excluded.

> Wise persons see *brahman* in a learned person rich in knowledge and humility, in a cow, in an elephant, in a dog and even in a dog-eater.

Śvetāśvatara Upaniṣad (4:3) identifies *brahman* with the world of nature.

> You are the dark blue bird, the green one with red eyes, the rain-cloud, the seasons, and the oceans. You live as one without a beginning because of your pervasiveness, you, from whom all being are born.

Verses like these certainly invite us to a reverential attitude to nature and to caring practices. The world in this verse is not merely a pointer to *brahman* but is identified as *brahman*. Liberation, understood in this way, enriches rather than diminishes the meaning of the world, and all its positive implications for our relationship with nature need to be explored and celebrated.

Prominent among these is a deeper identity and affinity with the world of nature. It also allows the overcoming of alienation from and objectification of the natural world. This is the outcome of understanding *brahman* to be the single source, ground, and being of all that exists. Īśa Upaniṣad (6–7), cited earlier in the work, relates this knowledge of the unitive identity of God in all to freedom from hate, sorrow, and delusion.

> One who sees all beings in the self alone and the self in all beings, feels no hate by virtue of that understanding.
>
> For the seer of oneness, who knows all beings to be the self, where is delusion and sorrow?[18]

Liberation does not alienate, isolate, or separate one from nature and the community of beings, but awakens to life's unity. It fosters world-embrace and not world-rejection. The freedom from hate spoken of in this Īśa Upaniṣad verse certainly excludes revulsion and fear of nature. Although the Advaita tradition has not always pursued the implications of this understanding for life in the world and has interpreted the meaning of liberation in generally passive and world-negating ways, there are alternative interpretations that need to be affirmed.

In the Bhagavadgītā, the discussion on the identity of *brahman* in all is followed by a text (6:32) praising the liberated as one who owns the joy and suffering of others as her own. This verse, like many other texts, is notably free from anthropomorphism. On two occasions (5:25; 12:4), the text employs the expression "delighting in the well-being of all" (*sarvabhūtahite ratāḥ*) to describe the attitude of the liberated in relationships. Here again, there is no privileging of human beings. Liberation is equated with an empathetic way of being. It frees one from regarding oneself as engaged in competitive rivalry with other beings for dominance and control. Seeing the suffering of another as one's own, however, becomes impotently meaningless if this insight does not motivate compassionate action. Such compassionate action does not have to be limited to human beings. The Bhagavadgītā (3:20) commends action that is prompted by *lokasaṅgraha*, or concern for the well-being of the world. *Loka* is inclusive and embraces the entire creation.

Nature and the Yajña Mode of Being

The outcome of a unitive understanding of reality is a deep sense of interdependence and generosity. We cited in Chapter 4 the Bhagavadgītā's (3:13) commendation of relationships that are characterized by reciprocity and a sense of mutual obligations and spoke of this as a *yajña* way of being. The Hindu tradition gives emphasis to five of these relationships and speaks of the "Five Great Obligations" (*Pañca Mahāyajña*). These are obligations to God (*brahmayajña*), teachers (*ṛṣiyajña*), ancestors (*pitṛyajña*), humans (*manuṣyayajña*), and nature (*bhūtayajña*). It is significant that the world of nature is specified as a sphere of obligations for us. Because our lives are blessed by the dedicated giving of so many, we express our obligation and gratitude by our own self-giving. If we selfishly receive from and exploit the world without generous self-giving, the resources of the world, both human and natural, will be depleted. Such thoughtless exploitation results in suffering for the entire creation. As a way of relating to nature, both giving and receiving characterize *yajña*. Where people act in the spirit of *yajña*, the community thrives and prospers. When the *yajña* mode of being is violated and nature recklessly exploited, the community will not flourish.

The Bhagavadgītā (6:16–17) recommends a lifestyle of moderation in all matters and makes specific mention of consumption. We may certainly read "eating too much" to refer to the inconsiderate appropriation of our natural resources with disregard for consequences. It is appropriate to read a verse like this one as addressing a community's way of being.

> Yoga is not for one who eats too much or for one who does not eat at all; nor indeed, Arjuna, (it is) for the one who sleeps too much or who is always awake.
>
> For one who is moderate in eating and other activities, who is mindful in all activities, (and) to one's sleeping and waking hours, (for such a person) Yoga becomes the destroyer of sorrow.[19]

The significance of moderation in the Hindu tradition may be seen also in the four goals that are specified for a fulfilling human life (wealth, pleasure, virtue, and liberation). Wealth is necessary but must be guided by ethical considerations. Wealth that is accumulated through oppressive and exploitative means results in suffering to others and to oneself. Such exploitation also must include our use of nature's resources. Greed is overcome only by attentiveness to life's highest goal, liberation (*mokṣa*), which reminds us of the limits of wealth.

In a similar way, the Hindu conception of life as structured in and moving through four stages (student, householder, semi-retired, and renunciant) reminds us that certain goals are more appropriate at particular moments. In the student stage, the focus is on learning and the acquisition of life skills. In the householder stage, the pursuit of wealth through ethical means is a prominent goal. As we approach the evening of life, material concerns give way to a focus on religious growth through study and practice. There is a concern for balance and moderation in all stages, avoiding excess and immoderate consumption.

Nature and the Moral Order of the Universe

The Advaita tradition is rich in resources for the development of a relationship between human beings and nature in which nature is intrinsically valued, identified with, and wisely utilized. Traditional interpretations have not always highlighted these resources. On the contrary, nature is devalued by being disconnected from *brahman* and associated with the realm of the illusory from which one must seek freedom and release. The relationship between human beings and nature can be infused with new meaning by affirming the ontological non-duality at the heart of all reality and the sacred worth of creation as an expression of *brahman*. As we have seen, Upaniṣad accounts of creation trace its origin to the self-multiplication of *brahman* and present *brahman* as the intelligent cause and material ground of the universe. Muṇḍaka Upaniṣad (1.1.6) likens the emergence of the world from *brahman* to a spider projecting and withdrawing its web, sparks emerging from a fire, and plants sprouting from the earth. Even as sparks are of the same essence as the fire, and trees and plants share the essence of the earth, creation shares the essence of *brahman*. To see the world as originating from anything other than *brahman,* as existing independent from *brahman,* and as having a nature other than *brahman* is, in Advaita, to see under the veil of ignorance. The universe is the self-multiplication of *brahman* and gains its value and sanctity from this fact. To devalue the world is to devalue *brahman* and to overlook the meaning of non-duality.

Although the Hindu tradition has affirmed the uniqueness and privilege of human birth as offering the special opportunity for liberation (*mokṣa*), this is not articulated in a manner that confers upon us the right to dominate, possess, and make all other living forms subservient to our needs and wants. The uniqueness of the human being lies in our ability to discern life's unity in *brahman,* to practice self-control, and to cultivate value and reverence for creation.

The value and sanctity for life in the Hindu tradition is expressed in the centrality of the ethic of non-injury (*ahiṁsā*). *Ahiṁsā* reflects the Hindu emphasis on the interdependent unity of all existence and requires that we strive to minimize violence in our daily lives. The important point here is that the all life forms should be included within the ambit of human moral concern. We noted that among the five daily obligations is the service and care of non-human life forms (*bhūtayajña).* Non-violence must not be limited to our treatment of human beings but extended to all life forms. To hurt another is, in a fundamental way, to hurt oneself. One of the finest examples of an Advaitin living out the values of the tradition in relationships with nature is Ramana Maharshi (1879–1950). His consciousness of life's unity was not anthropocentric and extended to all beings. Biographical accounts record numerous incidents of his extraordinary identity with animals and the world of nature and his careful stewardship of resources.[20]

Karma and *saṁsāra,* two doctrines that are central to the Indian religious traditions, are also significant for our consideration of the human-nature relationship. *Karma* is the moral law of cause and effect, emphasizing that human actions at all levels produce results that are consequential for the performer or performers of those actions. The doctrine of *karma* affirms the ultimately just nature of the universe, because the consequences of human actions may not always be apparent in the short term. In the vision of *karma,* the consequences of our actions are not limited to the sphere of our relationship with other human beings. Because of the interconnectedness of reality, the moral law is all-inclusive and governs our relationships with all life forms. The character of our interactions with these is also consequential for us, because we are an inextricable part of the fabric of existence. Although the Hindu tradition shares with Buddhism a belief in the moral law of cause and effect, Buddhism has given special significance to the doctrine of interdependence. Living beings are not isolated or independent entities but are interconnected in a dynamic and all-pervasive circle of interdependence. Nothing happens outside the universal law of cause and effect, and our actions have consequences throughout a vast network of existence. A contemporary Buddhist author draws out some of the implications of this doctrine.

> Similarly, utilization of resources anywhere has repercussions throughout the entire planetary system. Often consumption of luxuries in one part of the world is directly related to poverty and suffering in other parts of the world. Thus the vision of universal and all-pervasive interdependence, which is so basic to Buddhism, requires moderation in all activities, especially reproduction and consumption, because of their impact on the rest of the universe.[21]

Closely related to the doctrine of *karma* is the belief in *saṁsāra,* that is, the cycle of birth, death, and rebirth. Birth is not a new beginning, just as death is not the end of existence. Birth is the entry onto the stage of the world, while death marks the point of exit. Living beings, however, have countless entrances and exits. Although there are differences in interpreting the doctrine of *saṁsāra,* the possibility of rebirth in a non-human form is widely believed. The Hindu tradition affirms a general evolution of life-forms from simple into more complex forms. We are related to other life-forms by the fact that *brahman* constitutes the ontological truth of all life, but also by the fact that we may have existed in these forms and may do so again in conformity with our desires and the operation of the law of *karma*. This is a further reason why other species ought not to be treated with cruelty and exploited recklessly to satisfy human greed. The doctrine of *saṁsāra*, along with *karma*, underlines the ties and bonds that connect all species. The belief in *saṁsāra* breaks down any sharp boundaries that differentiate one species from another and underlines the unity of all life forms.

Liberation from Greed and Stewardship of Nature

The Advaita tradition, as noted earlier, identifies greed as a fundamental cause of human suffering. Bhagavadgītā (3:37) identifies greed as a primary cause of evil. One important outcome of liberation is freedom from greed. Greed is a symptom of ignorance of the nature of self to be identical with the limitless *brahman*. The unreflective multiplication of desires is not conducive to human well-being and contentment. The Hindu tradition is not indifferent to the importance and significance of wealth. Hinduism does not celebrate involuntary poverty. *Artha* (wealth), as noted before, is the first of the four legitimate goals of human existence. Wealth, however, must always be pursued with attentiveness to *dharma*, which is, in its broadest sense, the regard for the well-being of the total community of living beings and the world of nature. Economic growth is desirable but cannot be measured only by profit. Its wider impact on human beings and on the environment must be taken into account. By the centrality given to *dharma*, the Hindu tradition obviously holds that wealth (*artha*) and *dharma* (virtue) can happily exist together. Fidelity to *dharma* requires the use of land, water, air, and other natural resources in ways that promote the well-being of all.

The tradition points out the limitations and dangers of uncontrolled consumerism and overconsumption and emphasizes that there are basic material needs that are necessary for human well-being. The ideal is moderation in consumption and the utilization of the world's resources in ways that preserve its integrity and promote the flourishing of all beings.

Meera Nanda has argued correctly that the wise use of nature does not necessarily flow from a "religious attitude of sacredness and reverence towards nature."[22] Nanda also points to the dangers of environmental activism when this is linked with religious nationalism ideology and symbols. She makes the case for environmental action based on secular motivations. I see no reason, however, why both approaches cannot be allies once the dangers of religious nationalism are identified and addressed.

8

Liberation from Childism

"Teach your children that they are divine, that religion is a positive something and not a negative nonsense; that it is not subjection to groans when under oppression, but expansion and manifestation."

—CW 1, 330

The Suffering of the Child

Two profoundly disturbing realities highlight the problem and challenges of the child in Hinduism and, more particularly, in India, where most Hindus live.[1] The results of a survey commissioned by the Ministry of Women and Child Development in association with UNICEF and Save the Children and released in 2007 revealed that more than 53 percent of children experience sexual abuse and that two of every three children are subjected to physical abuse. In more than 50 percent of child abuse cases, the suffering to the child was inflicted by persons known to the child and in positions of trust and responsibility. The survey, the first of its kind conducted in India, also revealed that approximately 65 percent of schoolchildren were physically punished in schools. Every second child was emotionally abused, with the parent usually being the perpetrator.[2]

The statistics of abuse are a sad component of a larger picture of suffering and neglect. The second tragic issue of concern is female feticide, which is estimated by the United Nations to be as high as two thousand each year. As noted in Chapter 5, many parents use medical diagnostic techniques, such as amniocentesis and ultrasound, to determine the gender of their unborn children and to abort female fetuses. We commented also on the implications of this for gender ratios.[3] Although some believe that the decline in the number of girls will lead to an improvement in their status through increasing demand, the reality seems different. Nita Bhalla cites a rise in polyandry in areas where women are fewer in number, as well as in the trafficking of women in states like Haryana and the Punjab, where men increasingly are looking outside native groups for brides.

Underlying these disturbing figures of female feticide and infanticide is an established preference for sons in Hindu families and the consequent devaluation of girls. This has to be seen in the context of a broadly patriarchal culture that has legitimized itself with religious appeals. In a report in the *International Herald and Tribune*, Amelia Gentleman noted the lamentation and disappointment that accompanied the birth of a girl child in Shravasti in North India.[4] The atmosphere is one of "reproachful silence" and not celebration. At the heart of the problem is the requirement that girls leave the homes of their parents at the time of marriage with a large dowry for their husbands and their families. The associated problems of early marriage, female illiteracy, and health neglect also are all present.

The Religious Value of the Child

In the light of these harsh childhood realities, what do the Advaita and the broader Hindu tradition tell us about the significance, status, and value of the child? Why must Hindus see the suffering and oppression of children as unacceptable and labor together for overcoming the causes? Are there resources within the tradition that enable us to develop a comprehensive vision of the well-being of the child? These are the questions and issues to which we now turn our attention.

To establish the religious value of the child in the Hindu tradition, we return once more to what is affirmed as having the highest value. In the perspective of Advaita, this value is attributed to *brahman*. As the unique and imperishable source of all that exists, *brahman* surpasses everything that is transient and impermanent. *Brahman* has the highest value because *brahman* is the highest reality, existing alone in all periods of time (past, present, and future) and ontologically independent. *Brahman* is self-existent, while the existence of everything else is contingent and dependent on *brahman*.

Along with affirming the existence of the one *brahman* before all else, the Advaita tradition understands *brahman* alone to be the source of all creation. As we have seen in earlier chapters of this work, the Upaniṣads describe the creation as originating in a wish on the part of *brahman* for self-multiplication. Taittirīya Upaniṣad (2.6.1) presents the divine urge in the following words: "He wished, 'Let me be many, let me be born.' He undertook a deliberation. Having deliberated, he created all that exists. That (*brahman*), having created (that), entered into that very thing."

Chāndogya Upaniṣad (6.2.3) also mentions the desire of *brahman* for self-multiplication and birth. "That Being willed, 'May I become many, may I grow forth.' "

The Taittirīya Upaniṣad text cited above, speaking of the entry of *brahman* into all that is created, is especially significant for understanding the value of the child. This is the insight of the text that we want to emphasize here. In creation, *brahman* enters into every created form, and as a result, each form gains value and significance.[5] The value of the child is derived from having her origin in *brahman* and from the fact of embodying *brahman*, the reality of ultimate value.

Birth Replicates Cosmic Creation

The birth of every child repeats the cosmic creative process described in the Upaniṣads where *brahman* creates and enters into everything created. The Yajur Veda speaks of the womb as the birthplace of the divine.

> He is the Deity who pervades all regions,
> born at first, he is also within the womb.
> Verily, he who is born and is to be born,
> Meets his offspring facing him on all sides.[6]

The child is valuable not only because *brahman* is the creator and source of life, but, most important, because *brahman* is present in every child as self. The Advaita understanding of *brahman* emphasizes *brahman*'s immanence as well as transcendence. Although emphasizing that *brahman* exists in everything and everything exists in *brahman*, Advaita does not equate *brahman* simplistically with the world or limit *brahman* to the world. As the Īśā Upaniṣad (5) states, "That (*brahman*) moves. That does not move; that is far off, that is near; that is inside all this, and that is also outside all this." The famous *Puruṣa Sūkta* hymn of the Ṛg Veda underlines the transcendence of *brahman* by stating that *brahman* pervades the world by a fourth of *brahman*'s being, while three-fourths remain beyond it.

Brahman Is Present Equally in All Beings

The Upaniṣad teaching about *brahman*'s immanence is always carefully specified by two significant disclosures, both of which are logical and consistent with the nature of *brahman*. Bhagavadgītā (13:27) expresses succinctly both insights. "The one who sees the Lord, as remaining the same in all beings, as the one who is not being destroyed, in the things that are perishing, he alone sees."

The first disclosure is that *brahman* is present in all beings. With regard to the presence of *brahman*, therefore, all beings must be equally regarded. No one is excluded, and there are no qualifications that can be justified. Age and intellectual maturity or rationality are not requirements for embodying *brahman*. The child is not excluded. The second disclosure about *brahman*'s presence is the emphasis on the equality or sameness of that presence. There are no fluctuations of degree or differences of any kind in the manner of *brahman*'s presence. *Brahman*'s immanence is not greater or lesser in beings. The Śvetāśvatara Upaniṣad (4:3–4), in emphasizing the inclusivity and equality of *brahman*'s presence, makes specific mention of the child, female and male. The intention of the text is clearly to rule out sex and age differences as far as *brahman* is concerned by specifying women and men, boys and girls, and the aged. Note also that this text, like the Ṛg Veda hymn cited above, speaks also of the birth of *brahman* in each child. "You are a woman; you are a man; you are a boy and also a girl. As an old man, you totter along with a walking stick. As you are born, you turn your face in all directions."

The significance of this teaching must be appreciated from the fact that seeing the divine existing equally in all beings is considered to be the sin qua non of wisdom and liberation. "Because of seeing the Lord as the same, as the one who obtains in the same form everywhere, he does not destroy himself by himself. Therefore, he reaches the ultimate end." (BG 13:28) The Bhagavadgītā (18:20) commends the knowledge that enables us to see "one changeless existence in all beings and the undivided among the divided." A false and inferior way of seeing is to regard things as disconnected, isolated, and independent of each other and to see only difference (18:21–22). Īśā Upaniṣad (1) opens with the famous exhortation to see the world clothed in *brahman*: "All this—whatever moves on this earth is covered by the Lord." It speaks of *brahman* as being within all things as well as outside of everything (5).

Value for Brahman Expressed in Compassion

For the discerning, *brahman* has ultimate value and is deserving of our deepest reverence. It is *brahman*'s existence in all beings that gives them value and significance. The dignity and worth of the human being is the consequence of this embodiment of the infinite. Because Advaita understands *brahman* to be intimately present at the heart of all that is created ("The Lord abides in the heart of all beings," Bhagavadgītā 18:61), we profess and express our value and commitment to *brahman* by our care for all in which *brahman* is present. Our awakening to *brahman* leads to a deeper identity and affinity with all. It awakens us to the truth of life's indivisibility and interrelatedness. It enables us to own the pain and suffering of others as our own and to take delight in the flourishing of others.

In his comment on Bhagavadgita (6:32), Śaṅkara writes that the liberated person "sees that whatever is pleasant to himself is pleasant to all creatures and whatever is painful to himself is painful to all beings. Thus seeing that what is pleasure or pain to himself is alike pleasure and pain to all beings, he causes pain to no being; he is harmless. Doing no harm and devoted to right knowledge, he is regarded as the highest among all *yogins*."[7] On two occasions (5:25; 12:4), the text employs the expression "delighting in the well-being of all" (*sarvabhūtahite ratāḥ*) to describe the outlook of the liberated in relation to others. Wisdom is equated with an empathetic way of being. What is especially important for us here is that the tradition unmistakably connects our understanding of *brahman*'s presence in the human being with a compassionate way of being (*dayā*). Our knowledge of *brahman* should find expression in a commitment to work for the overcoming of suffering in others. Delighting in the well-being of others has little meaning otherwise.

Ahiṁsā (Non-injury) and the Value of the Child

Śaṅkara's connection between the unity and identity of *brahman* in all and non-injury (*ahiṁsā*) is not arbitrary. *Ahiṁsā*, the cardinal principle of Hindu ethics, expresses positively the value and reverence for life that is at the heart of the Advaita ideal. Belief in divine immanence requires us to demonstrate reverence and consideration for life in all its forms and to avoid injury to others.

The value for life, as far as the child is concerned, is exemplified traditionally in several important ways. Feticide is regarded as killing, and abortion is treated as sinful.[8] The condemnation of feticide and abortion includes both male and female. Children are immensely desirable, and one of the purposes of marriage in the Hindu tradition is parenthood.[9] Raising children is categorized as one of the three obligations of human beings arising from the condition of indebtedness (*ṛṇa*) in which we all live. Our indebtedness to God is fulfilled through contemplation and worship, to teachers through study and teaching, and to ancestors by raising children and ensuring the continuity of generations. We express gratitude for the care received as a child by caring for a child. Epic texts such as the Rāmāyaṇa and Mahābhārata make reference to a complex ritual (*putrakāmesti yajña*) for the purpose of conceiving children, and the Upaniṣads speak about procedures for producing a famous male child or a learned daughter. The Rāmāyaṇa begins with the story of Daśaratha, king of Ayodhya, who is in deep sorrow because he does not have a child. After the performance of the *putrakāmesti yajña*, he is blessed with four sons, suggesting that his children were divine gifts.

The concern for the child's well-being is powerfully evident in the traditional Hindu life-cycle sacraments. The purpose of these sacraments (*saṁskāras*) is to bless, protect, and seek divine grace for the flourishing of the child. What is significant about the Hindu sacraments is that they, as Laurie Patton notes, commence before the physical birth of the child.[10] The first, *garbhādhāna* (gift to the womb), is performed by parents for conception.[11] The second, *puṁsavana* (begetting a male child), is performed during the third or fourth month and reflects the unfair gender preference to which we have already pointed. The third, *sīmantonnayana* (parting of the hair), is meant for the healthy mental and physical growth of the child and for the protection of the mother. These prenatal ceremonies, expressing concern for the conception, survival, and well-being of the child, are followed by postnatal ceremonies marking birth (*jātakarma*), naming (*nāmakaraṇa*), journeying outdoors (*niṣkramaṇa*), first solid food (*annaprāśna*), cutting of the hair (*cūḍākaraṇa*), and education (*upanayana*). These sacraments all underline a tremendous value of the child and his or her happiness, well-being, and education. Laurie Patton, cited above, reminds us that rituals such as the naming, feeding, and tonsure ceremonies included girls.

Honoring the Divinity in the Child

The value of the child, derived from *brahman*'s immanence and birth, as it were, in every child, is also emphasized in the special way in which Hindus celebrate the divine as child. The tradition allows for a variety of relationships with God. One may relate to God as servant, friend, or lover. One of the most popular and special relationships, however, is where God is adored and worshipped as child (*vātsalya bhāva*). This is most obvious in the celebration of the childhood of incarnate (*avatāra*) figures such as Krishna and Rama. Sacred texts such as the Śrīmad Bhāgavatam and the Rāmāyaṇa, describing their lives and teaching, spend considerable time on the minute details of their childhood, and childhood incidents are among the most popular narratives. Hindus delight in the childhood of Krishna, in his love of butter, his innocence and spontaneity, childish mischief, and freedom from the constraints of adult life. Poetic compositions focusing on Krishna's childhood are extremely popular among Hindus, and the festivals celebrating the birthdays of Krishna and Rama are widely observed. It is traditional, for example, to mark the birth of Krishna by gently rocking an icon (*mūrti*) of baby Krishna in a crib to the accompaniment of birth songs. Hindus take delight in identifying their children with such deities, and this is often signified by the choice of a name such as the child-Krishna (*Bālakrishna*) or the child-Rama (*Bālarāma*) or the naming of a girl after one of the feminine forms of God such as Lalitā, Mīnākṣi, Rādhā, Sītā, and Pārvatī. It is customary during the great Hindu festival of Durgā Pūja or Navarātri to offer worship to the Goddess of the universe in the form of a girl child. The Goddess is worshipped in the girl child with traditional rituals such as the offering of water, flowers, incense, and light. In the most orthodox form of this practice, nine girls representing various manifestations of the divine are honored by the washing of the feet and the offering of gifts of clothing.

All of these rituals and practices testify to a strong sense of divine immanence leading to reverence and value of the child. It is not problematic or blasphemous to associate the divine in this intimate way with the child. By becoming a child in the forms of Rama and Krishna, with all the characteristics of the human child, the life of the child is honored and celebrated.

The Girl Child in the Hindu Perspective: Ideal and Reality

In the light of our discussion on the religious value of the child in Hinduism, it is important to return to the issue that we highlighted earlier in this chapter. This is the fact of the preference for sons in Hindu families, the abortion of female fetuses, and disparities in accessibility to those necessities that are required for her well-being. Evidence indicates disparities in access to food, health care, and education for girls. A recent study verifies that women visit antenatal clinics and receive tetanus shots more often if they are pregnant with a male child. This leads to higher female neonatal mortality rates.[12]

It is clear that in terms of the fundamental value of the child, the Advaita tradition cannot distinguish between female and male. *Brahman* is present equally in all beings, and all deserve equal dignity and worth. In articulating this truth, sacred texts do not make gender exceptions or distinctions, and we must not, either. When the implications of this teaching are enunciated, these are done in terms of equality. This equality is meaningless unless expressed in equality of treatment.

At the same time, it is clear that, in practice, the girl child is the tragic victim of gender injustice. The roots of gender injustice toward the girl child are to be found in the assumptions of a patriarchic culture that does not value the female and male equally as embodying the divine. One of the characteristics of a patriarchal culture is that the female is not understood as having equal and intrinsic value, but a value that is derived from a subservient relationship to the male. We must emphasize in the strongest terms that there is no religious ground to justify this in the teachings of the Advaita tradition.

This culture of patriarchy and inequality finds expression in a number of practices that make girls less desirable than boys and contribute to the unequal opportunities and access to resources. At the forefront of such practices, noted already, is the continuing practice of giving and receiving dowries. It is an insidious custom that makes a girl less desirable than a boy in many families. From birth, "a girl is viewed as a burden and a liability and is likely to be given a meager share of the family's affection and resources. This is because the investment made on her brings no return. Instead, when she gets married, a sizeable dowry has to be given to her, draining valuable family resources."[13] As one villager confessed to Amelia Gentleman, cited above, "The minimum is 25,000 rupees for dowry, which includes the price of a bicycle that you have to give to the groom and various ornaments. And then there's the cost of the wedding itself, another 20,000. Even when you look at the baby for the first time you have these thoughts." The increasing demands of the dowry system make daughters unwanted economic liabilities. The Indian constitution specifies that the giving and receiving of dowries is illegal, but the law has not been vigorously or successfully enforced. Hindus, however, cannot look only to legal remedies for gender injustice, but must advocate vigorously for a change in values and attitudes on the basis of normative religious teachings. Dowry practices are wrong because these devalue women. We commented also, in Chapter 5, on the preference for the male child rooted in the belief that a son is necessary for performing funeral rituals and making annual ritual offerings on behalf of the departed parents. We also suggested reasons why this preference must be changed.

Hindus must understand and affirm unequivocally that the unequal value and treatment of the girl child, as manifested in dowry demands, female infanticide, and abortion, violates the central teachings of Hinduism about *brahman*'s equal presence and its primary ethical requirement, non-injury (*ahiṁsā*). Hindu teachings and ethics are violated and girls are oppressed when they are deprived of the opportunity for life and aborted because they are girls. The same happens when the cruel custom of dowry reduces the girl child to a commodity for bargaining. A girl is not honored as embodying *brahman* when she is demeaned in this way. Those who are indifferent to the suffering of the girl child cannot claim to be faithful to the Hindu teaching about divine embodiment in every human being.

Religious Value and the Provision of Needs

Having established the religious value of the child in the Hindu tradition, a value too often betrayed and contradicted in practice, we turn now to ways in which this value must be expressed in the provision of those needs that every child requires for her or his well-being. The profound value of the child in Hinduism matters very little unless it leads to practices that nurture and allow for the flourishing of the child. It is important for religious value to become the basis for awakening compassion and concern for the child, questioning injustice and oppression of the child and inspiring action for improving the life of the child. A religious value that is disconnected from reality soon becomes irrelevant. The Hindu teaching about the divine value and equality of the child must find expression in practices that enable the flourishing of the child in society.

When a utopian society was imagined in Hinduism, it was visualized as a community free from suffering and violence of all kinds. The saintly poet Tulasīdāsa provides one of the finest descriptions of such an ideal existence when he recounts the life of Rama. His vision of the kingdom of God (*rāmrājya*) is practical and speaks of both material and religious realities.

> "There was no premature death or suffering of any kind; everyone enjoyed beauty and health. No one was poor, sorrowful or in want; no one was ignorant or devoid of auspicious marks."[14]

It is a primary responsibility of parents, in the Hindu tradition, to secure the material and emotional well-being of their children by forming nurturing and loving relationships, ensuring education, and providing for the nutritional and health needs of the child. Communities must support parents in the fulfillment of these obligations.

Keeping in mind the specific problems of the child in India and the universal needs of all children, we may now specify the following as the most basic needs of the child as required in the Hindu tradition. Because the language of the Hindu sacred texts does not advocate rights but speaks of mutual duties and obligations, we speak of fulfilling these needs as our basic obligation and duty to all children.

The Obligation to Life

The employment of life-enhancing medical procedures, such as amniocentesis and ultrasound for sex selection and abortion, is contrary to the unequivocal Hindu understanding of feticide as sinful, the tradition's value for life as embodying the divine, and the ethical principle of non-injury (*ahiṁsā*), regarded in the Hindu tradition as the highest virtue (*parama dharma*). It is a blatant rejection and disregard of the divine presence in the girl child. The abortion of the female fetus after a sex determination test is a deprivation of a child's right to life and equality of treatment. For the same reasons, the Hindu tradition must be uncompromising and vocal in its opposition to female infanticide. A study conducted by the Community Service Guild of Madras found that female infanticide in the Salem District of Tamil Nadu is "rampant" and confined to Hindus. "Of the 1,250 families covered by the study, 740 had only one girl child, and 249 agreed directly that they had done away with the unwanted child. More than 213 of the families have more than one male child whereas half the respondents had only one daughter."[15]

The problem of female feticide was highlighted in a unique manner when two couples in the state of Haryana, a state with one of the lowest sex ratios in India, added a marriage vow promising not to kill their girl child.[16] This vow preceded all of the traditional seven vows. Villagers welcomed the couples' decision, and the priest who conducted the marriages pledged to have all couples take this vow. "For me," the priest is quoted as saying, "this is the most sacred vow and I will administer this oath to every couple whose weddings I oversee." The scarcity of brides in Haryana may be the pragmatic motive for this new marriage vow, but one hopes that the religious value of the child will be a sufficient and powerful reason for forbidding female feticide.

Patton, in a well-crafted discussion, uses traditional exegetical arguments to establish that there is no scriptural justification for female infanticide. Although acknowledging that there are current "rites" performed for female infanticide, it is clear that these lack traditional authority.

> These include the "feeding of milk" to the baby, which is actually drowning the baby in a pot or vat of milk. They also involve the feeding of a grain husk that could slit the throat of a small baby, or the mixing of food with "medicine" that is actually an overdose. All of these rites are given names that make it seem as if the work is innocuous and even dharmic. It is a very straightforward and helpful case to argue . . . that according to the principles of orthodox Vedic ritual thinking, these rites are not authoritative in any way, and against dharma.[17]

The Obligation for a Healthy Life

The Hindu value for life is complemented by the value for health and longevity. In the Atharva Veda, for example, the well-known prayer is for a life of one hundred years.

> For a hundred autumns, may we see
> For a hundred autumns, may we live,
> For a hundred autumns, may we know,
> For a hundred autumns, may we rise,
> For a hundred autumns, may we thrive,
> For a hundred autumns, may we be,
> For a hundred autumns, may we become,
> Aye, and even more than a hundred autumns.[18]

The Kena Upaniṣad begins with a prayer for health and strength in all of the organs of the body. One of the fundamental goals for all human beings is *artha* (wealth), which includes the basic necessities that every human being requires for a good and healthy life. It is important to emphasize today that *artha* must include access to health care. It is rather meaningless to prescribe *artha* as a basic requirement for the good life for all human beings and not be concerned about the fact that children, the most vulnerable and dependent among us, lack access to these necessities.

The recognition of *artha* as a fundamental human need underlines the important fact that the religiosity of Hinduism must not to be disconnected from recognizing and securing basic human needs. The focus on health as integral to human well-being is evident in the existence of the ancient medical science of Ayurveda. The Sanskrit term *ayur* specifies that the purpose of the system is the preservation and extension of life, and *veda* locates this medical practice centrally within the religious tradition. Āyurveda is traditionally associated with the Atharva Veda. Hindu religiosity is not anti-materialistic and cannot condone or be indifferent to poverty whereby large numbers of children are malnourished, ill, or do not have the opportunity to attain adulthood. Our inability to care for the health of our children is a failure to meet our religious obligation to them. We do not value life if we do not act to sustain and care for our children, the most dependent and vulnerable among us.

The Obligation to Education

The Hindu tradition sees learning as necessary for fulfilling one's human potential and for participating and contributing to the community. The Advaita tradition, in fact, sees knowledge as indispensable for liberation (*mokṣa*). The Hindu value for education is most evident in the fact that in its conceptualization of life as moving rhythmically through four stages (*āśramas*), it has designated the first as the stage of learning (*brahmacarya*). Although educational opportunities were limited by gender and caste constraints, there is no valid reason for such unjust exclusions, and a learning stage must be seen as necessary for the development of every child.

The value of the education of the girl child is evident in the Bṛhadāraṇyaka Upaniṣad (6.4.14) ritual for giving birth to a learned daughter (*paṇḍita*). On the basis of the principle of divine equality and value, that which was seen as necessary for a few must be understood as our obligation to all. Early marriage is an impediment to the opportunity for education. It deprives women of the right to make one of the most important decisions in their lives. In the Hindu scheme of life, marriage follows the stage of learning, and this must be true for both women and men. In the Rāmāyaṇa's vision of an ideal society (*rāmrajya*), everyone is learned.

The Obligation to Leisure and Happiness

Forcing children into a life of arduous work is contrary to Hindu teaching for multiple reasons. First, it is opposed to the Hindu ideal of a fourfold life scheme in which work belongs properly to the second or householder (*gṛhastha*) stage of life. The stage of work follows the stage of learning. A life of work without the opportunity for learning is contrary to the Hindu scheme of sequential life stages. Second, it deprives the child of the opportunity to go through the stage of learning and thus prepare intellectually, emotionally, and physically for work. Third, it takes away from the child the opportunity for appropriate childhood experience of one of the four goals of Hindu life, *kāma* (pleasure). In the case of the child, pleasure is associated with the opportunity for play with peers and siblings, delighting in the innocent joys of childhood without fear.

It is precisely this childhood period that is celebrated in the life of Krishna. Images of Krishna as a child are popular in Hindu homes and temples. One of his adorable names is *mākhan chor* (stealer of butter), describing his mischievous love for butter, and his mother's failure to keep her containers concealed from him. There are occasions when toys are part of the holy offerings made to Krishna. Our delight in Krishna's childhood and our celebration of his play must also awaken us to the suffering of millions of children who have no opportunity for the joys of childhood when they are thrown prematurely into the harsh world of work. Children must not be robbed of the delights of childhood by exploitation as prostitutes and slave laborers.

One of the leading religious figures in the struggle against child labor in India is Swami Agnivesh. He is the founder of Baal Mukti Aandolan (Movement Against Child Labor). It is estimated that India has 65 million bonded child laborers working in agriculture, manufacturing matches, locks, carpets, stone quarries, brick kilns, and tanneries. They are denied "their fundamental rights to childhood, to education, to play and to dream like a normal child."[19]

The Obligation to Non-Injury and Freedom from Exploitation

We started our study by citing a survey revealing the widespread emotional, sexual, and physical child abuse in India. In addition to abuse inflicted by persons in positions of authority and trust, the statistics reveal a heartless exploitation of children as sexual objects.

The abuse of children and our failure to protect them from exploitation are incompatible and at variance with the most basic Hindu teachings. The Hindu teaching about the unity of existence in *brahman* and the sacredness of life that is an expression of the divine is the foundation of its cardinal ethical principle, non-injury (*ahiṁsā*). *Ahimsa*, as already noted, is regarded as the highest virtue (*parama dharma*), and this is true not only of Hinduism, but also of other traditions originating in India, such as Buddhism and

Jainism. In the Bhagavadgītā, for example, it is listed as a virtue four times, and in three of these references, it tops the list.[20] The Rāmāyaṇa speaks of hurting another as the most fundamental violation of religious law (*dharma*). Mahatma Gandhi, arguably the greatest champion of *ahiṁsā* in our times, emphasized that it should be understood not only negatively as avoiding injury to others but positively as love that expresses itself in compassion and caring for others.

While the ethic of non-injury is all embracing, it is unfortunate that contemporary discussions seem to focus only on war. We need, however, to see the abuse of the most defenseless and vulnerable among us as a fundamental violation of *ahiṁsā*. The centrality of *ahiṁsā* must become the foundation on which we build a vigorous campaign against child abuse and exploitation of every kind. Eradication of child abuse and child exploitation must become the measure of our commitment to the core values of the Hindu tradition. Even the child Krishna has to be protected from the violence of his uncle, Kamsa, by being taken across the raging waters of the Yamuna River to the safety and security of his foster parents, Nanda and Yashoda. The well-being of the child was paramount, even when this required separation from the biological parents.

The value of the child is derived from having her or his source in *brahman* and from the fact that *brahman* exists equally in every child as self (*ātmā*). We express our value and commitment to *brahman* by our value and care for children. Knowledge of *brahman*'s immanence requires us to demonstrate reverence and consideration for children and to avoid injury and abuse.

The Hindu tradition especially honors the presence of *brahman* in the child. There is no religious justification in Hinduism for treating the female child unequally and for regarding her as having a lesser worth than the male child. The profound value of the child in Hinduism matters very little unless it leads to practices that nurture and allow for the flourishing of the child. It must inspire efforts to combat violence toward children found in sex selection, sexual abuse, child labor, dowry demands, and early marriage. The Hindu teaching about the divine value and equality of the child must find expression in the flourishing of the child in society through the provision of fundamental needs such as nutrition, health care, education, play, and leisure.

Female feticide, infanticide, and abortion are contradictory to the tradition's value for life as embodying the divine and the ethical principle of non-injury (*ahiṁsā*). Hindu spirituality is not anti-materialistic and does not glorify the life of poverty whereby children are malnourished, ill, or do not have the opportunity to attain adulthood. The Hindu tradition sees learning as necessary for fulfilling one's potential in life and for participating in and contributing to one's community.

Marriage in the Hindu scheme of life should follow the stage of learning. A life of work without the opportunity for learning is contrary to the Hindu scheme of sequential life stages. Early marriage, especially for girls, deprives them of the opportunity to go through the stages of learning and to prepare intellectually, emotionally, and physically for work and family. Children must not be robbed of the delights of childhood. This occurs when they are thrown prematurely into the world of work and family life. The centrality of non-injury must become the foundation on which Hindus build a vigorous campaign against child abuse of every kind. Eradication of child abuse and exploitation and commitment to the well-being of children must become the measure of our commitment to the Hindu tradition.

9

Liberation from Caste

"See that you do not lose your lives in this dire irreligion of 'Don't-touchism.' Must the teaching ātmavat sarvabhūtesu—(looking upon all beings as your self)—be confined to books alone?"

—CW 6, 319–320

A Personal Encounter

In February 2006, I was invited as a Hindu guest at the 9th Assembly of the World Council of Churches in Porto Alegre, Brazil. I had attended previous assemblies in Vancouver, Canada (1983); Canberra, Australia (1991); and Harare, Zimbabwe (1998). At the very first discussion that I attended in Brazil, a session focused on interreligious relations, the presence and participation of Hindus in the assembly were vigorously challenged and denounced by a Christian bishop from South India. He passionately chastised the World Council of Churches for giving legitimacy to Hindus and their tradition by inviting us to the assembly. He described us as his oppressors and characterized the Hindu tradition as intrinsically unjust and bereft of any redeemable features. He concluded his contribution by issuing an invitation to everyone to work for the eradication of Hinduism and not its validation. I learned later that the bishop came from the Dalit (oppressed) community, the name preferred by many who have been relegated historically to the lowest rungs of the hierarchical caste ladder and demeaned as untouchables.[1]

The bishop's angry denunciation of Hinduism for the oppression of the caste system was not, of course, the first time I had heard such a rebuke. The caste system is a feature of the tradition that is highlighted prominently in textbook accounts and in interreligious conversations. Yet his words struck me with a special force. I had never before heard anyone describe me as an oppressor, and I never struggled with the fact that I am perceived as an oppressor in the eyes of another.

I was born of Hindu parents and raised in Trinidad and Tobago. My great-grandparents migrated from Northern India in the late nineteenth century as indentured workers to escape hunger and poverty in India by taking the place of freed African slaves on sugar plantations. Paradoxically, their living conditions, especially life in plantation barracks, contributed to the erosion of caste differences and exclusion. In the shared and common living space of a barrack, the observation of caste strictures was rendered very difficult. Caste, therefore, although not entirely absent, was a minimal feature in our everyday lives. We were aware that most of the Hindu priests claimed status as *brahmins*, but other traditional features of caste, such as hereditary work specialization and regulations governing interdining, intermarriage, and social relations, were minimal or nonexistent. Our friendships in school and in village playgrounds were spontaneous and free and not constrained by caste considerations. Hindu temples were open to all. Labels such as "Dalit," "untouchable," or *harijan* were unknown to us.[2] We never thought that identifying with a caste was necessary or central to what it meant to be Hindu. Our experience of the Hindu tradition was, by and large, caste free.

Because the Hindu community and tradition in which I was raised had shed the most unjust and brutal features of the caste system, I found it disconcerting to be called an "oppressor." In my mind, the word conjured a person who intentionally inflicted suffering on others, curbed their freedom, and took perverse delight in the exercise of power and domination. I did not recognize myself as an oppressor.

I was challenged, however, by the bishop's denunciation of my tradition to recognize that he encountered it in ways that were radically different from my own experience. His context—historical, cultural, and social—was India, and he encountered Hinduism, in the practice of caste, as an oppressive tradition that negated the dignity and self-worth of his community. I had to see my tradition through his eyes and understand the source of his pain and anger. The same tradition that affirmed my self-value denied his own. His experiences had convinced him that caste injustice was intrinsic to Hinduism.

The Reality of Caste Oppression

The experience of being oppressed is a reality in the lives of Dalits like Ramlal Ram. On October 4, 2003, Ram, accompanied by his son, Khelaw, and three other family members, headed for the Shiva temple in the village of Bahera, located in the north Indian state of Uttar Pradesh. With flowers and sweets in hand, they wanted, like everyone else, to offer worship to the Goddess Durga on the occasion of her festival. Although some local leaders gave assurances that his visit to the temple would not be problematic, Ram's presence immediately unleashed a storm of verbal abuse and violent efforts to physically expel them. Ramlal Ram and his family stood their ground and edged closer to the Goddess. Blows rained, stones were thrown, and a rifle was discharged. Ram was hit in the chest and, bleeding profusely, died. "We only demanded," commented one villager, "that we be allowed to pray. It is the people of our caste who build the deity with mud, ink and color. But when it comes to offering *puja,* we are left out," said one villager.[3]

All the details of historical developments that explain the murderous hate and violent outrage against Ram may never be precisely documented. These belong to a past that is complex and inaccessible. We do know enough, however, to understand that this brutality is rooted in a worldview that represented Ram as the negativized other: inferior, impure, and threatening.

Caste Privileges and the Negativized Others

Although there is a developing and serious critique of the so-called Aryan Invasion hypothesis calling into question some of its fundamental assumptions, it is clear, from the evidence of the Ṛg Veda, that there was an early polarization between those who regarded themselves as of noble descent (*ārya*) and those, named the *dasyus*, who were regarded as lacking in virtue, inferior, and observing different customs. They were likened to a famine and excluded from sacred rituals.[4] Evidence suggests that by approximately 800 BCE, those regarding themselves as *ārya*s had consolidated themselves in relation to other groups and systematized their relationship in the form of a hierarchically structured system (*varṇa*). The *brāhmaṇa*s (priests) occupied the top, followed by the *rājanya/kṣatriya* (soldiers), *vaiśya*s (merchants and farmers), and *śūdra*s (laborers). The first three groups were regarded as the *dvija*s or twice-born and were entitled to perform and participate in Vedic ritual. Generally, male members of these *varṇa*s alone underwent the initiatory ritual (*upanayana*) that enabled them to study the Vedas. The incorporation of the *śūdras* into the *varṇa* system, and especially their subservient role in relation to the other groups, supports the hypothesis that they represent the "others" who were gradually included into the complex social order. It is also possible that a policy of appeasement was practiced that rewarded cooperative groups with elevation to membership in the upper *varṇas*.[5]

Not all groups, however, were assimilated and incorporated. It is likely that some groups resisted or were not offered the "privilege" of becoming part of the hierarchical order. Such groups, such as the *cāṇḍāla*s and *śvapacas*, were declared ritually impure (*aśuchi*) and segregated. The *cāṇḍāla*s, for example, were equated with animals and considered unfit even to eat the remnants of others' meals. By the time of Manu (ca. 150 BCE), it was believed that birth into a particular caste was the consequence of *karma* or the maturation of past moral actions in the present life. For bad deeds in this life, one could be reborn as a dog, a boar, or a *cāṇḍāla*, in that order. From its early use to refer to a specific group, *cāṇḍāla* became a general term for the untouchable other.

Numerous injunctions, such as the polarity of purity and impurity, hereditary occupations, and the idea of the *dvija* (twice-born), led to the institution of innumerable injunctions against those groups now branded as *aspṛśya* (lit. untouchable). By the period between 400 BCE and 400 CE, standard features of untouchability such as physical segregation, non-commensality and non-connubiality were firmly in place. The Vedas were not to be studied in a village where *cāṇḍāla*s resided. Food offered in ritual was defiled if seen by a *cāṇḍāla*, and sacrificial vessels were rendered impure by their touch. Food and ritual vessels also were polluted if seen and touched by dogs, crows, and donkeys; the implication is that untouchables are grouped with animals.

Omprakash Valmiki, in his powerful autobiographical account, *Joothan*, comments on the fact that "while it was considered all right to touch dogs and cats or cows and buffaloes, if [a higher-caste person] happened to touch a Chuhra, one got contaminated and polluted. . . . The Chuhras," as Valmiki notes, "were not seen as human. They were simply things for use. Their utility lasted until the work was done. Use them and throw them away."[6] An upper-caste person coming into contact with an untouchable was required to take a purificatory bath. Untouchables were to have separate wells and to enter villages at night or during the day only if they identified themselves by sound or appropriate marks. For food, they had to depend on others. A person stealing the animal of an untouchable was required to pay only half of the required fines. As Wilhelm Halbfass has rightly noted, the *cāṇḍāla*s are part of the *dharma* system through their exclusion from sacred ritual. "They participate in it insofar as they accept their exclusion; they subject (or ought to subject) themselves to the ritual norms of exclusion and prohibition, and they are recognized as negative constituents of the system."[7]

Today, approximately 15 percent of the population of India, consisting of approximately 160 to 180 million people, are labeled "untouchable" or members of the "Scheduled Castes" in the terminology of the Indian constitution. The same constitution also specifies that "the State shall not discriminate against any citizen on grounds of religion, race, caste, sex, place of birth." Special laws, such as the Protection of Civil Rights Act, 1976, have been enacted to give meaning to the constitutional provisions. In spite of such measures, however, the phenomenon of untouchability persists in contemporary India, and many Hindus continue to define the meaning of Hindu identity over and against those who are deemed impure and, for this reason, marginalized. The sharp distinctions between self and other, the boundaries of the pure and impure, are still drawn sharply in Indian villages, where the character of human and economic relationships are still governed by the hierarchies of caste and where reports of violence against persons of lower castes are common. Although the conditions of life in Indian cities are quite different from those in rural areas, cities are not free from the travails of caste and untouchability. In urban areas, discrimination expresses itself in more subtle forms and in limited job choices that push untouchables into menial tasks. In a city like Hardwar, on the banks of the Ganges, physical segregation is evident in the fact that the upper-caste dwellings are closer to the pure water of the river, while the lower castes are relegated, depending on relative degree of purity, to locations farther away from the river.[8] Similar conditions have been reported in Nepal. The entry of untouchables into upper caste homes is forbidden, and the latter still think it necessary to have a bath of purification if contact is made with an untouchable. Tea shops in western Nepal use separate utensils for untouchables and require them to wash their own glasses. They are regularly debarred from temples and denied access to water sources. The legal prohibition of untouchability has not done much to ameliorate the conditions under which the community lives.[9]

It is the indignity and violence of a life where one is not called by a personal name that Omprakash Valmiki narrates in *Joothan*. Schooling became possible for him only after his father repeatedly begged the principal to teach him "a letter or two." At school, he was never allowed to forget his caste status, and violence, for no specific reason, was a constant threat and reality.

> I had to sit away from the others in the class, and even that wasn't enough. I was not allowed to sit on a chair or a bench. I had to sit on the bare floor; I was not allowed even to sit on the mat. Sometimes I would have to sit away behind everybody, right near the door. From there, the letters on the board seem faded.[10]

The labor of the lower castes was regarded as a right of the upper castes, whether it was reaping the wheat harvest, cleaning the *baithak*s (outer room used by men for chatting), or removing dung from the cattle sheds.

The rewards of labor, in a barter system centered on crop production, were minimal and took the form of wheat and *joothan*, scraps of leftover food, the eating of which is taboo and assiduously avoided by upper castes. It is an ultimate indignity.

> During a wedding, when the guests and the *baratis*, those who had accompanied the bridegroom as members of his party, were eating their meals, the Chuhras would sit outside with huge baskets. After the bridegroom's had eaten, the dirty *pattlas*, or leaf plates were put in the Chuhras' baskets, which they took home, to save the *joothan* that was sticking to them. The little remnants of *pooris*, puffed bread; bits of sweetmeats; and a little bit of vegetable were enough to make them happy. They ate the *joothan* with a lot of relish. They denounced as gluttons the bridegroom guests who didn't leave enough scraps on their leaf plates. . . . During the marriage season, our elders narrated, in thrilled voices, stories of the bridegroom's party that had left several months of *joothan*.[11]

Valmiki's father, who invested precious family resources in his education, hoped that his son's caste status would be improved by education. Omprakash discovered, through one humiliating experience after another, that even when it is possible to get past poverty and want, it is not possible to get past caste. Unlike many educated Dalits who changed their surnames to avoid the stigmatization of caste, Omprakash refused to take what he regarded as an easy way out, although his worth as a person was continuously devalued because of his surname. Omprakash concluded his story with a question, perhaps rhetorical from his perspective, but one that all Hindus must ask themselves with urgent concern.

> Times have changed. But something somewhere continues to irk. I have asked many scholars to tell me why *savarnas* hate Dalits and Sudras, the lower castes, so much. The Hindus who worship trees and plants, beasts and birds, why are they so intolerant of Dalits? . . . As long as people don't know that you are a Dalit, things are fine. The moment they find out your caste, everything changes. The whispers slash your veins like knives. Poverty, illiteracy, broken lives, the pain of standing outside the door, how would the civilized *savarna* know it?[12]

Change, Conversion, and Leadership

We must acknowledge that changes, though occurring at a slow pace, are under way. The impact of legislation, urbanization, democracy, freedom, equality, and feminism are transforming age-old attitudes and customs. In addition, the modern era is also witness to increasing self-awareness among the untouchables and their readiness to organize themselves to agitate for justice. They are also prepared to embrace alternative religious options. The conversion of untouchables to traditions such as Buddhism, Christianity, and Islam has evoked concern among several Hindu groups, and some have responded with *shuddhi* (purifying) rituals to admit them back into the fold of Hinduism.

There is an urgent need, however, on the Hindu side to understand the meaning and attraction of other religions to the convert. It must be instructive that the largest numbers of converts from Hindu traditions come from the so-called untouchable castes. They experience the tradition as oppressive and as negating their dignity and self-worth. For such persons, the message of human equality, though not easy to realize in practice, even in the traditions they adopt, is received as liberating. In a social context where occupation may still be determined by caste and where the ability to change one's identity and work must await future birth, the opportunity for a new identity that may afford dignity, choice, and better economic opportunities is compelling. For such persons, the argument that the religion into which one is born is best only adds to the oppression and is seen as part of a deliberate effort to deny them freedom and control over their lives. Hindus must be challenged by conversion to understand the many ways in which the tradition is failing to meet the legitimate needs of those who are born into its fold. Hindus must continue to labor for a religious and social system that attests to their dignity and self-determination.

The difficulty of such self-critical reflection is, in part, the consequence of the fact that Hindu leadership is still dominated by men from the upper castes who have always experienced power and privilege within the tradition. Having never experienced religiously justified oppression and injustice, they assume wrongly that the tradition that has been good to them is good for all who are born within its fold. They resist the questioning of a system that guarantees them power and privilege. Conversion is an opportunity for Hindu leaders to consider the relationship between religious doctrine, especially the theological assumptions of caste, and systemic social and economic structures that condemn millions to lives of poverty, indignity, and marginalization. The tradition needs to stop treating converts like childlike people who always need to be always protected from the lures and deceptive practices of missionaries. This is a demeaning condescension that denies them agency and self-determination.

Dalits and Hindu Identity

The question of whether or not the Dalits are Hindus is central to determining Hindu responses to the injustices of untouchability. It was one of the questions that sharply divided the approaches of the Dalit leader B. R. Ambedkar (1891–1956) from that of Mahatma Gandhi. Gandhi believed that the untouchables belong to the Hindu fold and that untouchability is an aberration that must be expunged. He argued, however, for the retention of the four *varṇas* and the performance of hereditary occupations. Ambedkar, on the other hand, argued that untouchables are not Hindus because they are not included in the *varṇa* system. As Hindus continue to consider this issue, we must be especially attentive to Dalit voices who question and are deeply suspicious of what they see as another effort to define their identity.

> I was not born a Hindu for the simple reason that my parents did not know that they were Hindus. This does not mean that I was born a Muslim, a Christian, a Buddhist, a Sikh or a Parsee. My illiterate parents, who lived in a remote South Indian village, did not know that they belonged to any religion at all. People belong to a religion only when they know that they are a part of the people who worship that God, when they go to those temples and take part in the rituals and festivals of that religion. My parents had only one identity and that was their caste: they were Kurumaas.[13]

Dalits issue an important challenge to those who claim them as Hindus to tell them which morality is Hindu morality. Ilaiah's questions, though uncomfortable, cannot be ignored by Hindus. "Which values," he asks, "do they want to uphold as right values? The 'upper' caste Hindu unequal and inhuman cultural values or our cultural values? What is the ideal of society today? What shall we teach the children of today? Shall we teach them what has been taught by the Hindus or what the dalitbahujan masses of this country want to learn?"[14]

The primary challenge for Hindus is not just claiming Dalits as Hindus but the more demanding one of owning responsibility for the historical physical and psychological brutalization of the Dalits by representing them as the untouchable other in relation to whom Hindu identity is affirmed. It is the task of identifying and repudiating doctrines and customs that profess the unequal worth of others and legitimize their dehumanization and humiliation. It is the task of moving from defensive apologetic to self-criticism and articulating a vision of the tradition that affirms human dignity and worth. It is responding to Ilaiah's challenge by clearly defining the core values of the tradition, especially in relation to systems like caste. Defensive arguments that suggest a harmonious and noble original intention underlying caste do nothing to define those values or deal with the reality of oppression.

Self-Value and the Devaluation of Others

While the specific origins of untouchability are historically complex, we cannot dispute the fact that it is rooted in the more general human tendency to affirm self-value by devaluing the other who is branded as different and by exercising power and control over him. Devaluation leads to the perception of people as objects and not as fellow beings who feel and suffer as we do. It provides the conditions for guilt-free violence and mistreatment. Humans are less likely to oppress those with whom they self-identify and whom they value for this fact.

Hindus must acknowledge the inhumanity, injustice, and oppression of the caste system and the fact that the system has been widely legitimized by the tradition and its practitioners. Many Hindus still, unfortunately, consider the practice of caste to be a religious requirement. We need to see caste as one historical expression of a system of human oppression and domination, present in many societies, that sanctified itself in the garb of religious validation. Hindus are not exempt from this susceptibility to the corruption of power and the tendency to affirm self-value by devaluing others. Regardless of its origins in antiquity, our challenge today is the urgent one of responding to a hierarchical ordering of human beings that ascribes unequal value based on identities imposed at birth.

Affirming Equal Worth and Justice of All

Where I must differ, however, with the Dalit bishop with whose challenge I started this chapter, and with interlocutors like Ilaiah, is over the claim that untouchability is intrinsic to the Hindu tradition and that the tradition has no resources to redeem itself. As I have argued throughout this work, there is a theological vision at the heart of Advaita that invalidates the assumptions of inequality, impurity, and indignity that are the foundations of caste belief and practice. From the perspective of Advaita, it is clear that the highest value is attributed to *brahman*. In creation, *brahman* enters into every created form, and it is the presence of *brahman* that gives value and significance to the human being. The dignity and worth of the human being is the consequence of the fact that she embodies the infinite. *Brahman* includes everyone; caste excludes.

The teaching on divine immanence and the consequent equal worth of all human beings must inspire and impel Hindus to identify and overcome the exploitative and oppressive caste structures. We cannot be content with merely offering concessions to those who have been disadvantaged and who have not traditionally enjoyed the privileges accorded to members of the upper castes. While supporting such measures, the tradition must also get to the heart of the matter by questioning the very legitimacy of a hierarchical social system that assigns different privileges and value to human beings on the basis of exclusive notions of purity and impurity. The role of religious doctrine and ritual in providing legitimacy for the system of caste must be examined. A self-critical sincerity is needed to acknowledge the ways in which many, especially those from the so-called untouchable castes, experience the tradition as oppressive and as negating their dignity and self-worth. The fact that the religion into which one is born may not be experienced as liberative must be admitted. The acknowledgment of past and present injustices by those who have enjoyed the benefits of caste is a necessary step. There also must be the will for the reform and reconstruction of Hindu society on the basis of those central insights and values of Hinduism that promote justice, dignity, and the equal worth of human beings.

Discerning the unitive presence of *brahman* in all creation results in a deeper identity and affinity with all. It leads to the empathetic owning of the pain and suffering of the other as one's own. It challenges attitudes of indifference toward the suffering of others with whom we do not identify because of caste boundaries. It enables us to see all beings as constituting a single community and provides a theological basis for a compassionate and inclusive community where the worth and dignity of every human being is affirmed and where justice at all levels is sought. Caste inflicts suffering on millions of our fellow human beings, and the Advaita tradition insists that we see this suffering as our own. Hindus must respond to caste as an urgent problem, as fundamentally incompatible with Hinduism's most profound teachings and necessitating a unanimous and unequivocal repudiation. The meaning of being Hindu must not continue to require the demeaning of another human being. As with the issue of gender injustice, legal remedies are necessary, but there is an urgent need for an unambiguous Hindu theological repudiation of caste.

Although Gandhi's views on caste are not without controversy and are rejected by prominent Dalit leaders, his understanding of the theological implications of the divine equality is still important for the Hindu tradition. "No scripture," he contended, "which labels a human being as inferior or untouchable because of his or her birth can command our allegiance; it is a denial of God and Truth, which is God."[15] Gandhi's understanding of non-injury (*ahiṁsā*) as negatively implying abstention from injury and positively requiring the practice of compassion and justice is relevant to the overcoming of caste. The degradation of others is violence. "No man," said Gandhi, "could be actively nonviolent and not arise against social injustice no matter where it occurred."[16]

The Story of Śaṅkara and the Untouchable

The Advaita recognition of the fundamental contradiction between the teaching about the equal presence of *brahman* in every being and the practice of caste exclusion is powerfully articulated in a well-known story about Śaṅkara's encounter with an untouchable (*cāṇḍāla*) in the sacred city of Varanasi. After taking a bath in the Ganges, Śaṅkara was walking toward the temple of Shiva when he saw an untouchable man standing in the narrow lane. Fearing pollution from contact with the untouchable, Śaṅkara shouted for him to move away. To Śaṅkara's surprise, the untouchable held his ground and interrogated him. "O great among the twice-born, what is it that you want to move away by saying, 'Go, Go?' Do you want the body made up of food to move away from another body made up of food? Or do you want consciousness to move away from consciousness?"[17]

Most accounts of this meeting speak of the untouchable as an incarnation of Shiva. Because Śaṅkara himself is regarded by many in the Advaita tradition as an incarnation of Shiva, the encounter becomes an engagement between two forms of Shiva for the purpose of teaching the essentials of Advaita. In this way, its impact is muted. Our translator, for example, speaks of the story as not important and cautions about deriving any conclusions from it.[18] The untouchable's questions to Śaṅkara, however, are a profound indictment of the caste system and a sharp refutation of its assumptions. Śaṅkara's call to the untouchable to move out of his way sprang from fears of losing purity by contact with another regarded as impure. This concern is at the core of the practice of untouchability. The untouchable's questions are an incisive and targeted refutation from the fundamental teaching of Advaita of the assumptions of superiority based on claims to purity.

Following a discussion in Taittirīya Upaniṣad 2.5, the Advaita tradition distinguishes the *ātmā* from the five sheaths.[19] The outermost of these, the physical body, is referred to as the food sheath (*annamaya kośa*) because the body is composed of, sustained by, and returns to food (*anna*). The rhetorical question from the untouchable ("Do you want the body made up of food to move away from another body made up of food?") is a statement of fact about the identity of the physical matter that constitutes all bodies. His question is a subversive one that undermines all caste practices, including rules of commensality and other forms of physical exclusion predicated on differences.

Assuming, with sarcasm, that an Advaitin cannot make a rational argument for differences between one physical body and another, the untouchable asks whether the great teacher is requesting consciousness to move away from consciousness (*caitanyameva caitanyāt*). Consciousness (*caitanya*), in Advaita, is the very nature of the self (*ātmā*) and identical in all beings. It is not-two. But there is something even more significant here. Śaṅkara shouted for the untouchable to "Go, Go" (*gacca, gacca*). Movement in space, however, is possible only for a finite entity. Advaita teaches that the self pervades and fills everything that exists, including space. It cannot "go" anywhere. If the self is the object of the verb "go," then Śaṅkara would be contradicting fundamental Advaita teachings that the self is identical in all beings and not limited by space.

With his two questions, the untouchable interlocutor of Śaṅkara unmasks the contradictions between caste practices and Advaita teaching, challenging the tendency in some Advaitins to separate teaching and social reality. There is no ontological basis, physically or in the nature of ultimate reality, to justify human hierarchy and fear of the other. The implication of the untouchable's response is that caste is rooted in ignorance (*avidyā*). The response of Śaṅkara, reputedly expressed in the five verses of *Manīṣāpañcakam*, reiterates the core teachings of Advaita but also reveals the challenge to the tradition.

> If a person has attained the firm knowledge that he is not an object of perception, but is that pure consciousness which shines clearly in the states of waking, dream and deep sleep, and which, as the witness of the whole universe, dwells in all bodies from that of the Creator Brahma to that of an ant, then he is my Guru, *irrespec-*

tive of whether he is an outcaste or a Brahmana. This is my conviction.[20]

The fundamental Advaita teachings highlighted here are the nature of the *ātmā* as consciousness, the ultimate subject that is present in all states of experience as witness (*sākṣi*) and present identically in all beings. One who knows this truth, says the poet, is my teacher, "irrespective of whether he is an outcaste or a Brahmana." Śaṅkara's verse leaves open the possibility that the knower of the *brahman*, though a teacher, does not entirely overcome his or her outcaste status in the eyes of the other. The label of outcaste is not undermined. Caste identity, in other words, is not true at the level of the individual's ultimate identity, but it still persists in the social sphere. The highest truth (*pāramārthika sattā*) still does not transform social reality or structures (*vyāvahārika satta*).

The Exegesis of Bhagavadgītā 5:18

Bhagavadgītā 5:18 speaks also of the wisdom of seeing *brahman* in all beings, making mention of the outcaste. "Wise people are indeed those who see the same (Brahman) in a *brāhmaṇa* who is endowed with knowledge and humility, in a cow, in an elephant, in a dog, and (even) in a dog eater."

Most contemporary commentators on this Bhagavadgītā verse do not interrogate or problematize the category of outcaste. Generally, the verse is read as a description of the seeing of *brahman* in all by the wise person. Swami Chidbhavananda characterizes the different forms as "unreal," underplaying their social significance. "He cognizes the same Omniscience present in all these forms which are unreal. The *jñāni* sees truly while the worldly sees erroneously."[21] The problem here is that when social categories and physical forms are treated as unreal, there is little incentive to change or to transform these. Swami Chinmayananda reads this verse as emphasizing the vision of the wise who "can find in no way, any distinction in the outer world of names and forms."[22] Such a reading of the text, however, implies that the liberated will not see the distinctions that are in fact made and the suffering inflicted on the basis of such distinctions. One may argue that the liberated can (and should) see the underlying unity of all beings but also the tragedies that follow in the world when this unity is not discerned and its social implications not discussed. If liberated persons do not see injustice, they can never become agents for social change, and religious teaching becomes irrelevant to social reality.

Jayadayal Goyandaka, in his popular commentary on the Bhagavadgītā, admits that even the wise person will perceive distinctions and respond differently to these.

> A wise man does observe in his dealings all such distinctions as are necessary and proper in the eyes of the world. He will treat a Brāhmaṇa even as a Brāhmaṇa should be treated and will deal with the pariah as one ought to do; even so he will use a cow, an elephant and a dog as well in a befitting way. Nevertheless, he perceives God alike in everybody and bears the same love towards all.[23]

Goyandaka does not specify in his commentary what is appropriate treatment for a so-called outcaste person, but he makes a clear argument for different treatment. The closest he comes to any specification is in his claim that the scriptures "enjoin that a good Brāhmaṇa should be respected and adored, but prescribe no such thing in respect of a pariah." His argument in the rest of his commentary on this verse employs the analogy of treating and utilizing the various parts of one's own body in different ways while still regarding these as one's own. This analogy is not helpful because there is no similarity between the different functions served by the parts of the human body and the inequalities and indignities of caste. Goyandaka still speaks of the wise person as perceiving God in all beings and as bearing the same love toward all. Yet this does not appear to make any difference in the way that human beings are treated socially. Here also, a transformed vision does not challenge the status quo or behavior in the social sphere. Equality in the religious realm is disturbingly seen as compatible with inequality in the social realm. This is a critical issue that I have identified repeatedly in this discussion.

Swami Ramsukhdas raises the question of how the wise person can treat people differently while still seeing with eyes of equality. He also turns to the problematic analogy of the body, arguing that "we see all the parts of our body with an equal eye and think of their welfare, yet our dealings with these are different."[24] Similarly, claims Ramsukhdas, "the wise also have different dealings with different beings according to the difference in their food, qualities, conduct and caste, and it is proper." Religious vision here again accommodates itself to social hierarchies without even theoretically challenging such structures. It is quite likely that both Ramsukhdas and Goyandaka have in mind the Puruṣasūkta hymn of the Ṛg Veda (10.90), where the cosmos described as emerging from the body of the cosmic person. The four *varṇas* are connected, respectively, with the mouth (*brahmins*), arms (*kṣatriyas*), thighs (*vaiśayas*), and feet (*sūdras*) of this primeval being.

Caste and the Authority of Scripture

The Advaita understanding of the scripture as a *pramāṇa* and the distinction between *śruti* and *smṛti* also are valuable resources for interrogating the structure of caste. If one cites scripture to make the argument, using the example of the human body and its different parts, that human beings are qualified by birth for different occupations and must be treated differently, then the question about the basis of such differences arises. The authority of other *pramāṇas*, like perception and inference, challenges the claim that birth decisively determines one's occupational aptitude and competence. It is a well-known fact that there is no necessary correlation between birth in a particular family and one's qualification for a particular kind of work. The availability of opportunities, educational and economic, is critical in determining work choices. Any argument, therefore, based on scripture that birth qualifies a person for particular occupations is refuted by empirical evidence. The Advaita view, as we clarified in Chapter 2, is that if scripture contradicts a well-established fact of everyday experience, it cannot be considered authoritative because such a matter is outside its authoritative sphere. The purpose of scripture is only to inform us of matters that cannot be known through conventional ways of knowing. There are valid empirical methods for determining human occupational abilities. This is not a matter that is outside the sphere of perception and inference. If the prescription of occupational choices is outside the authoritative concern of the *śruti,* then all such efforts, wherever occurring, must be understood as humanly authored systems of thought and practice (*smṛti*) that are subject to interrogation and change. In a similar way, arguments about physical purity and impurity cannot be justified by appeal to *śruti* because such claims can be refuted empirically by establishing that there is no difference in the matter that makes up different bodies. This is the point of the untouchable question to Śaṅkara. Why are you asking one material form, constituted of food, to move away from another form similarly constituted? Scripture is not authoritative if it reveals anything that is contradicted by the evidence of other valid sources of knowledge, and it is clear that the fundamental premises of the hierarchical ordering of human beings, exemplified by caste, have no empirical justification.

From an Advaita perspective, it is not good enough to cite scriptural verses to justify social systems. For each verse cited, we are obliged, following the definition of the scripture as a source of valid knowledge (*pramāṇa*), to ask at least two sets of questions: First, does the passage reveal something that cannot be known otherwise? If so, what is it, and why cannot it be known otherwise? In relation to caste, we must ask: What specifically does the scripture reveal that is not otherwise knowable? Second, does the text contradict anything known through other valid sources? If it does, it is not an authoritative revelation. The fundamental assumptions of caste are refuted empirically and so cannot be justified by appeal to scripture.

Dharma, Caste, and Liberation

At various points in this book, I have referred to the four goals of Hindu life: wealth, pleasure, virtue, and liberation. The four goals have the potential for universal applicability, and their attainment should be a measure of the moral and just character of any community and its progress. In reality, however, these goals have been circumscribed by the boundaries of a hierarchical social system that privileged the worth of some human beings over others, limited their access to certain goals, and interpreted *dharma* as requiring order rather than justice. On the whole, *dharma* was primarily and narrowly identified with the rigid order of the caste system. In the interpretation of *dharma*, emphasis was placed on the faithful performance of duty as determined by one's birth-derived location in the caste. The maintenance of caste order and stability, not justice, became the unquestioned overriding concern. This limited identification of *dharma* with caste constricted and obscured its more radical and challenging implications for critiquing social structures and engendering compassionate concern and action for liberation from suffering.

At its heart, however, the goal of *dharma* is satisfied only through actions that are undertaken with attentiveness to the good of all beings and not to specific groups. *Dharma* derives from an understanding of the universe as an interdependent and interrelated whole. It emphasizes that existence and the realization of our human potential are possible only in the context of this whole and the benefits derived from the generous giving of all constituents of reality. The meaning of *dharma* as duty, broadly conceived, and not conflated with caste requirements, requires a lifestyle that is deeply informed by a sense of obligation and generous self-giving for all that one receives. Although *dharma* has been explicated almost singularly with reference to caste obligations (*varṇa dharma*), the tradition recognized the necessity for universal ethical norms (*sādhārana dharma*) binding on all human beings and governing their relationships. There are various lists offered in sacred texts, and these include non-violence, compassion, self-control, truthfulness, concern for the welfare of all beings, justice, forgiveness, and non-stealing. The Golden Rule, "not doing to others what one would not like done to one's self," is an effective summary of the meaning of *sādhāraṇa dharma*.[25] Today, the need is for an explication of the liberative meaning of these universal ethical norms and a rejection of *dharma* as implying the unequal rights and privileges of caste. *Dharma* must become synonymous with the common good, what the Bhagavadgītā (3:20) refers to as *lokasaṅgraham*, and applied rigorously in the quest for justice against all forms of injustice and oppression.

Conclusion

> *"The Vedanta. . . . as a religion must be intensely practical. We must be able to carry it out in every part of our lives. And not only this, the fictitious differentiation between religion and the life of the world must vanish, for the Vedānta teaches oneness—one life throughout."*
>
> —CW 2, 291

The first part of this work considered the human problem from the perspective of the Advaita tradition. We identified it as suffering (*duḥkha*), expressing itself most acutely in a persistent sense of self-inadequacy, anxiety over mortality, and the fleeting nature of pleasurable experiences. We seek to overcome suffering through the multiplication of desires, hoping by finite gains to enhance our self-worth. Such gains, however, consistently fail to solve the problem of self-lack and leave us wanting. The understanding of this predicament leads the human being, in the Advaita tradition, to a qualified teacher who names the fundamental human want as a desire for the limitless (*brahman*). Because we are not separated spatially or temporally from *brahman*, who is the very nature of the seeking self, the problem is characterized as one of ignorance (*avidyā*). Ignorance can be dispelled only by right knowledge, and the Advaita tradition identifies the source of valid knowledge for *brahman* with the teachings of the Upaniṣads, the final sections of the four Vedas. It is with these teachings that the teacher instructs the student who has approached him for a resolution to the human problem.

In Part One, we also considered the Advaita understanding and arguments for the Upaniṣads as a source of valid knowledge for *brahman* and the reasons why a teacher is seen as necessary for fruitful instruction. Advaita is a teaching tradition that relies on the willingness of a student to inquire earnestly under the teacher's guidance. With the aid of a variety of pedagogic strategies (knower-known distinction, effect-cause identity), the skillful Advaita teacher helps the student to see that she is identical in nature with *brahman,* the uncreated and eternal reality, free from the limits of space and time, present in all beings and lacking nothing. The student also understands that *brahman* is the truth of the universe, analogically similar to clay as the truth of all objects made of clay. Seeing clearly the truth of one's nature frees from the suffering and anxiety of erroneously taking oneself to be a limited and wanting being.

We considered also in Part One the implications for life in the world of a liberated understanding. The world should not be problematized in Advaita because at the heart of the human predicament is a mistaken understanding of one's nature and a consequent misunderstanding of the world. Liberation is a new understanding of self and world. The consequence of knowing oneself to be a full being is freedom from greed. One shares the most profound identity with all beings when one knows oneself to be the self of all. Wisdom blossoms in compassion, that is, the seeing of oneself in the sorrows and joys of others, in generosity, and in self-control.

In Part Two of this work, we applied the core teaching and values of the Advaita tradition to several issues of contemporary significance: patriarchy, homophobia, anthropocentrism, childism, and caste. In each case, our aim was to establish that the Advaita tradition offers teachings that are in conflict with and challenge the assumptions of these beliefs and practices. Advaita also offers a wisdom about human beings and the world that requires and enables us to affirm the equal worth and dignity of every human being and inspires work for justice and the overcoming of suffering.

We are now in a position, as we conclude, to offer a summary of the insights of this study.

1. The world has its origin in *brahman,* the uncreated, single, indivisible, and infinite reality. It does not

emerge from non-being, pre-existent matter, or a personal being or beings limited by time and space.

2. The emergence of the world from *brahman* is the consequence of an intentional act of self-multiplication. It does not occur spontaneously. Because *brahman* exists alone before creation and because *brahman* is the sole cause of the universe, Advaita understands *brahman* to be both intelligent cause and material ground for everything that exists. *Brahman*, however, is not transformed pantheistically into the world and is not depleted or lost in the process of bringing forth the many. Advaita argues for a distinctive cause and effect relationship in which the infinite, without being subject to time, loss of nature, or limitation of any kind, brings forth the world out of itself as an act of self-multiplication.

3. The relationship between *brahman* and the world is best described as not-two (*advaita*) because the existence of the many cannot be denied, yet these have no substantial reality apart from *brahman*. In analogical terms, the relationship is like that of clay pots and clay or waves and water.

4. As the single ontological source and ground for the universe, *brahman* is identical to and exists as the human self (*ātmā*), the ultimate subject, and non-objectifiable awareness that is the ground of all cognitive processes. *Brahman* is also the ontological truth of every object in the universe, the self of everything.

5. Advaita traces the root of the human problem to ignorance (*avidyā*). Not knowing that *brahman* is identical to the self and the substantial truth of the universe, we see everything as existing separately and take ourselves to be limited, isolated, and incomplete. We search in futility for the attainment of fullness. Paradoxically, the human problem is

that we search to become that which we are. The full and limitless *brahman* constitutes the nature of the seeking self from which we are separated only by ignorance.

6. Ignorance gives rise to greed, which, in turn, leads to greedful actions. Ignorance has personal, social, and institutional outcomes. Our search for self-value by asserting our superior worth over others finds social expression in group identities, formed on the basis of nation, ethnicity, religion, tribal, class, or caste, which profess exclusive value over other groups. Greed also motivates corporations and institutions whose single motive is the maximization of profits and that are willing to employ measures that are reckless and detrimental to the public good.

7. Liberation (*mokṣa*) is the clear comprehension of one's identity with *brahman*, the self of all and the constituent truth of everything. Ignorance is thinking that we are isolated and limited entities, distinct and different from every other self. Liberation is knowing that the self is not limited by space or time and that it is free and the self of all. Liberation is to be sought and gained here in this world. The world, as world, must not problematized in Advaita; the problem is an erroneous understanding of world and self.

8. Liberation frees from greed, a condition of insatiable self-lack. This freedom is the consequence of knowing the self to be full. This, in turn, frees from greedful actions. Freedom from ignorance, greed, and greedful actions transforms motivation and liberates us to work for the well-being of others.

9. Liberation, like ignorance, has social implications. Liberation is the seeing of one's own self as the self of all beings, a vision that frees from hate. It is the deepest identity that one can have with another, expressing itself as love. Love is identification

with others in suffering and in joy. The vision of life's unity also finds expression in compassion, generosity, and self-control.

10. *Brahman* has the greatest value because it is the highest reality. The human being derives value from the fact that *brahman* is present equally and identically in everyone. The worth of every woman is an intrinsic one and is not derived indirectly through relationships with males. Patriarchy is an expression of *avidyā,* a fundamental misunderstanding of the equality and unity of human beings. It is also a false search for fullness through subjugating, dominating, and controlling women. The oppression of women is an expression of ignorance that blinds to the presence of *brahman.*

11. The cardinal ethical value that expresses the Advaita teaching about the identity of self in all beings is non-injury (*ahiṁsā*). *Ahiṁsā* is reverence and consideration for life in all forms. *Ahiṁsā* is violated and women devalued when they are forced to abort female fetuses and when dowries are demanded as the price of marriage.

12. *Ahiṁsā* must not be construed only negatively as abstention from injury. Positively, it requires the practice of compassion and justice. Justice for women, in this context, requires that we ensure them the same opportunities and liberties as men in order that they realize the fullness of their human potential. They must not be constrained into roles demarcated for them by a patriarchal and androcentric culture.

13. Homosexuality is not a modern import into the Hindu tradition. There are ancient references specifying that sexual identity is more complex and diverse than the categories of female and male. These discussions also suggest that fundamental aspects of sexual identity are inherited with birth.

Homosexuality was not regarded as unnatural or deviant behavior.

14. The ultimate worth of the human person in Advaita is not located in his or her sexual identity or procreative ability or choice. It proceeds from the teaching that the human self (*ātmā*) is identical with the real and infinite (*brahman*). One cannot profess value for *brahman* and despise the multiplicity of beings into which the divine has entered willingly. Homophobia, characterized as it is by fear, hate, and denigration of third-sex persons, finds no justification in Hinduism and betrays its most fundamental vision and values.

15. In relation to the attainment of *mokṣa* (liberation), the ultimate and highest goal of human existence in Hinduism, there is no difference between heterosexuality and homosexuality. Sexual identity does not debar a person from life's most desirable end.

16. The Advaita truth of seeing oneself in the other requires that we know the pain that comes from being demonized and persecuted because of one's sexual identity. Knowing the pain of the other through an enlarged identity helps us to overcome an important source of homophobia, rooted as it is in the human tendency to devalue those who are defined as different.

17. The stigmatization of homosexuals in Hindu society seems particularly connected with the value of male progeny. This desire, however, is explicable in the context of labor needs in an agricultural economy and high infant mortality rates. Some Hindu traditions assert the need for a male child to perform postmortem rituals that avert the suffering of the departed parent. Hindu traditions need to give more emphasis to the core Hindu teaching

about the doctrine of *karma,* which emphasizes personal responsibility.

18. The Advaita understanding of the world as ontologically non-different from and dependent on *brahman* enriches the value of the world. It enables us to see the world not as an illusion or a product of ignorance (*avidyā*), but as a marvelous self-multiplication and as a celebrative expression of *brahman*'s fullness. In liberation, the world does not become nonexistent, but is understood as existing in a non-dual relationship with *brahman.* The world is seen with new eyes; the many is seen reverentially as expressions of the one and individual expression valued.

19. The Advaita identity with all beings includes the world of nature. It enables us to overcome alienation from and objectification of the natural world. It fosters world-embrace and not world-rejection.

20. Although Advaita affirms the uniqueness of human life as offering the special opportunity for liberation (*mokṣa*), this is not articulated in a manner that confers upon us the right to dominate, possess, and make all other living forms subservient to our needs and wants. The uniqueness of the human being lies in our ability to discern life's unity in *brahman* and to cultivate value and reverence for creation and all forms of life.

21. The freedom from greed that follows the understanding of the self's fullness results in moderation in consumption and the avoidance of excess. The reckless exploitation of nature's resource is a consequence of ignorance and a cause of suffering to self and others. Wealth must always be pursued with attentiveness to *dharma,* that is, in its broadest sense, the regard for the well-being of the total community of living beings and the world of nature.

22. *Ahiṁsā* (non-injury), the cardinal ethical expression of life's unity, requires that all life forms be included in the ambit of one's moral concern. The commitment to avoid suffering is not limited by species. In a similar way, the moral law of *karma* is all-inclusive. The character of our interactions with nature is also consequential for us because we are an inextricable part of the fabric of existence. To violate nature is to violate ourselves.

23. The value of the child is derived from having her origin in *brahman* and from the fact of embodying *brahman* as the universal reality of ultimate value. The birth of every child repeats the cosmic creative process described in the Upaniṣads, where *brahman* creates and enters into the created.

24. In terms of the fundamental value of the child, the Advaita tradition does not distinguish between female and male. *Brahman* is present equally in all beings, and all deserve equal dignity and worth. In articulating this truth, sacred texts do not make gender exceptions or distinctions. There is no religious ground in Advaita for preferring a male child or for gender injustice toward the girl child.

25. Hindus must understand and affirm unequivocally that the unequal value and treatment of the girl child, as manifested in dowry demands, female infanticide, and abortion, violate the central teachings of Hinduism about *brahman's* equal presence and its primary ethical requirement, non-injury (*ahimsa*). *Ahiṁsā*, construed both as avoiding injury and positively as love and compassion, must become the measure of our commitment to the child.

26. The profound value for the child in Hinduism matters very little unless it leads to practices that nurture and allow for the flourishing of the child. The Hindu teaching about the divine value and

equality of the child must find expression in the flourishing of the child in society.

27. Our obligations to children are expressed in the protection of life, in the provision of health care and education, in ensuring opportunities for leisure, and in ensuring that they are not abused and exploited.

28. Marriage should follow the stages of learning. Early marriage of children deprives them of the opportunity for learning and the delights of childhood. It leaves them mentally, emotionally, and physically unprepared for a life of work and family.

29. Hindus must acknowledge the inhumanity, injustice, and oppression of the caste system and the fact that the system has been legitimized by many in the tradition. Hindus must own responsibility for the physical and psychological suffering of the Dalits caused by representing them as the untouchable other in relation to whom Hindu identity is affirmed.

30. The teaching on divine immanence and the consequent equal worth of all human beings must inspire and impel Hindus to identify and overcome the exploitative and oppressive caste structures. Hindus cannot be content only with offering concessions to those who have been disadvantaged and who have not traditionally enjoyed the privileges accorded to members of the upper castes. We must question the very legitimacy of a hierarchical social system that assigns different privileges and value to human beings on the basis of exclusive notions of purity and impurity. Caste is rooted in ignorance (*avidyā*), and there is no ontological basis physically or in the nature of ultimate reality to justify this human hierarchy.

31. Caste inflicts suffering on millions of our fellow human beings, and Advaita requires that we see this suffering as our own. Hindus must respond

to caste as an urgent problem, as fundamentally incompatible with its most profound teachings and necessitating a unanimous and unequivocal repudiation. The meaning of being Hindu must not continue to require the oppression and demeaning of another human being.

32. Scripture is not authoritative if it reveals anything that is contradicted by the evidence of other valid sources of knowledge. The fundamental premises of the hierarchical ordering of human beings, exemplified by caste, are refuted empirically and so cannot be justified by appeal to scripture.

There is a theological vision at the heart of Advaita that affirms the identity and unity of *brahman* in all beings as the self (*ātmā*). *Brahman* is the indivisible ground of all that exists. This vision invalidates the assumptions of inequality, impurity, and indignity that are the foundations of patriarchy, caste, and homophobia. It also provides the insights and values for advocating for justice, dignity, and the equal worth of human beings.

Notes

Introduction

1. Advaita subscribes to the widely shared Hindu teaching about divine embodiment and views Krishna, the teacher of the Bhagavadgītā, as an embodiment of the creator. Śaṅkara's understanding of the purpose of Krishna's birth is explained in his introduction to his commentary on the Bhagavadgītā.

2. Sarvepalli Radhakrishan, *Indian Philosophy*, 2 vols. (Bombay: Blackie and Son Publishers, 1977), vol. 2, 445.

3. Ibid., 446. Italics added.

4. Swami Prabhavananda, *The Spiritual Heritage of India* (Hollywood: Vedanta Press, 1979), 293.

5. M. A. Buch, *The Philosophy of Śaṁkara* (Baroda: A. G. Widgery, 1921), 274.

6. S. K. Belvalkar, *Vedānta Philosophy* (Poona: Bilrakunja Publishing House, 1929), 15–16.

7. Y. K. Menon and R. F. Allen, *The Pure Principle: An Introduction to the Philosophy of Śaṅkara* (East Lansing: Michigan State University Press, 1960), 17–18.

8. Ibid., 18

9. Radhakrishnan, *Indian Philosophy*, vol. 2, 518.

10. This is the principal focus of my first study, *Accomplishing the Accomplished: The Vedas as a Source of Valid Knowledge in Śaṅkara* (Honolulu: University of Hawaii Press, 1991).

11. I do not claim this as a novel argument. It was advanced earlier by R. V. de Smet. See R. V. de Smet, "The Theological Method of Śaṅkara," PhD thesis, Gregorian University, 1953. Francis Clooney has also made similar arguments. See Francis X. Clooney, *Comparative Theology* (Malden, MA: Wiley-Blackwell, 2010), 77–86.

12. See Deane William Ferm, "Third World Liberation Theology: Challenge to World Religions," in Dan Cohn-Sherbok, ed., *World Religions and Human Liberation* (Maryknoll, NY: Orbis Books, 1992), 1.

13. Marcus J. Borg, *The Heart of Christianity* (New York: HarperCollins, 2003), 201.

14. Some of the concerns of liberation theology have found expression in Buddhism though the movements of engaged Buddhists. The focus here is also to apply the wisdom and practices of the Buddhist tradition to overcome suffering caused by injustice and oppression in the sociopolitical and economic spheres. See Thich Nhat Hanh, *Interbeing: Fourteen Guidelines for Engaged Buddhism* (Berkeley: Parallax Press, 1987).

15. There are, of course, prominent contemporary Hindus involved in the struggle for justice. Swami Agnivesh is a good example. See Swami Agnivesh, *Religion, Spirituality and Social Action* (Delhi: Hope India Publications, 2003). I will also add Swami Vivekananda and Mahatma Gandhi as examples of Hindus in the recent past who championed the concerns of liberation theology.

16. T. M. P. Mahadevan, *Outlines of Hinduism* (Bombay: Chetana Limited, 1977), 28.

17. See Anantanand Rambachan, *The Advaita Worldview: God, World and Humanity* (Albany: State University of New York Press, 2006). See especially chapter 5.

Chapter 1: The Quest for the Fullness

1. My translation.
2. Translation by Swami Dayananda Saraswati.
3. See Bhagavadītā 5:13, 5:21, and 5:23.
4. See *Bhagavadgītā* 6:28.
5. For my exegesis on the meaning of *ānandam* in relation to *brahman*, see Anantanand Rambachan, *The Advaita Worldview*, 40–43.
6. Dalai Lama, *Ethics for the New Millennium* (New York: Riverhead Books, 1999), 4–5.
7. Swami Dayananda Saraswati, *Talks and Essays of Swami Dayananda* (Rishikesh: Sri Gangadhareswar Trust, 2004), 20.
8. Ernest Becker, *Escape from Evil* (New York: The Free Press, 1975), 3.
9. Ernest Becker, *The Denial of Death* (New York: Free Press, 1973), 66.
10. Becker, *The Denial of Death*, 87.
11. Translation by Swami Gambhirananda.
12. Translation by Swami Madhavananda.
13. Translation by Swami Dayananda Saraswati.

14. Translation by Swami Dayananda Saraswati.

15. Translation by Swami Dayananda Saraswati.

16. Becker, *The Denial of Death*, 4.

17. Becker, *The Denial of Death*, 4

18. See, for example, the narrative of Maitreyī in Bṛhadāraṇyaka Upaniṣad (chapter 4) and the encounter between Naciketa and Yama at the beginning of Kaṭha Upaniṣad.

19. Translation by Patrick Olivelle.

20. Becker, *Escape from Evil*, 3.

21. Translation by Swami Dayananda Saraswati.

22. Becker, *Escape from Evil*, 12–13.

23. Huston Smith, *The Religions of Man* (New York: Harper and Row Publishers, 1965), 20. Italics mine.

24. Becker, *Escape from Evil*, 12

25. Swami Dayananda Saraswati, *Introduction to Vedānta* (Delhi: Vision Books, 1995), 21.

26. Greed, of course, must be distinguished from legitimate human needs that can be fulfilled.

27. Translation by Swami Dayananda Saraswati.

28. Translation by Swami Dayananda (modified).

29. Becker, *The Denial of Death*, 58.

30. Translation by Swami Gambhirananda (modified).

31. Becker, *The Denial of Death*, 58.

32. Becker, *The Denial of Death*, 185.

33. *Vedāntasāra of Sadānanda*, trans. M. Hiriyanna (Poona: Oriental Book Agency, 1962), 47.

34. Translation by Swami Swahananda.

35. Swami Dayananda Saraswati, *Introduction to Vedanta*, 38–39.

36. Walpola Rahula, *What the Buddha Taught* (New York: Grove Press, 1974), 40.

37. Quoted in Antony Fernando and Leonard Swidler, *Buddhism Made Plain* (New York: Orbis Books, 1985), 53.

Chapter 2: The Validity of Non-Duality

1. The justification for each one of these to be considered a valid source of knowledge is a matter of detailed discussion in Advaita. I have treated each one separately in my earlier work. See Anantanand Rambachan, *Accomplishing the Accomplished: The Vedas as a Source of Valid Knowledge in Śaṅkara*. See chapter 1. Also see D. M. Datta, *Six Ways of Knowing* (London: Allen and Unwin, 1932).

2. The word "upaniṣad" is derived from the root "*sad*" meaning "to reach" or "to destroy." The prefixes "*upa*" and "*ni*" mean "near" and "well-ascertained." The name therefore points to a well-ascertained knowledge of oneself that destroys suffering and is gained from inquiry with a teacher. As with the word "Veda," "Upaniṣad" signifies knowledge first, and its meaning as a book is secondary.

3. Translation by Swami Dayananda (modified).

4. These statements are taken, respectively, from the Sāma, Atharva, and Yajur Vedas.

5. I have discussed some the distinctive Advaita methods of using words in *Accomplishing the Accomplished*, chapter 3.

6. Cited in D. Venugopal, *Pujya Swami Dayananda* (Anaikatti: Arsha Vidya Gurukulam, 2008), 53–54.

7. Translation by Swami Dayananda Saraswati.

8. See Rambachan, *Accomplishing the Accomplished*, 64–65.

Chapter 3: The Full Self

1. My translation.

2. *Dakśiṇamūrti Stotra of Śaṅkaracārya*, 3rd ed., trans. Alladi Mahadeva Sastry (Madras: Samata Books, 1978).

3. Walpola Rahula, *What the Buddha Taught* (New York: Grove Press, 1974), 23

4. Translation by Swami Dayananda.

5. Translation by Swami Dayananda.

6. Translation by Swami Dayananda (modified). In the thirteenth chapter, the Bhagavadgītā uses the terminology of field (*kṣetra*) and knower of the field (*kṣetrajña*) to speak of the world of objects and *ātmā* as the awareness that illumines everything known.

7. See also Īśā Upaniṣad 6–7.

8. Swami Dayananda Saraswati, *Talks on Who Am I?* (Rishikesh: Sri Gangadhareswar Trust, 1984), 35. In reading an argument of this kind, one must keep in mind that its purpose is explanatory, and the intention is not to offer an independent, conclusive argument for the all-pervasive nature of awareness. This would contradict the claim that the Upaniṣads are the valid source of knowledge.

9. Translation by Ganganatha Jha.

10. Translation by Ganganatha Jha (modified).

11. Existent here means existing independently.

12. Although the Upaniṣad texts offer various accounts of the emergence of the universe from the infinite *brahman*, it is important to note

that the Advaita tradition does not regard this as one of the functions of the Upaniṣads as a valid source of knowledge. Details about the order of the creation are the subject matter of other *pramāṇas*, such as perception and inference.

13. See also Aitareya Upaniṣad 1.1.1

14. See Taittirīya Upaniṣad 2.6.1 and Chāndogya 6.2.1–6.2.4.

15. Translation by Swami Swahananda.

16. My translation. The sequence continues with references to the eyes, ears, and breath.

17. "That Thou Art" (Chāndogya Upaniṣad 6.8.7; Sāma Veda); "This *ātman* is *brahman*" (Māṇḍukya Upaniṣad 2; Atharva Veda); "Awareness is *brahman*" (Aitareya Upaniṣad 5.3; Ṛg Veda); and "I am *brahman*" (Bṛhadāraṇyaka Upaniṣad 1.4.10; Yajur Veda).

18. See Rambachan, *The Advaita Worldview*, 72–76

19. For my difficulties with the translation of *ānanda*, see Rambachan, *The Advaita Worldview*, 40–43.

20. I read *līlā* in Brahmasutra 2.1.33 as suggesting such a celebrative self-expression.

Chapter 4: The Liberated Life

1. There is a history of discussion in Advaita that, unfortunately, treats *avidyā* as existing independently and as beginningless and uncaused. It is sometimes equated also with *māyā* and regarded as the material cause of the universe.

2. My translation.

3. It should be emphasized that the gain of knowledge, in Advaita, is a demanding process that also requires the cultivation and nurturing of virtue. As Kaṭha Upaniṣad 2.24 puts it, "One who has not abstained from evil conduct, whose senses are not controlled and whose mind is not concentrated and calm cannot gain the Self through knowledge." I have discussed this requirement in detail in chapter 2 of *The Advaita Worldview.*

4. See also Kaṭha Upaniṣad 2.3.14, which speaks of the falling away of the heart's desires. Translation by Swami Gambirananda.

5. Translation by Swami Dayananda (modified).

6. It is interesting to note that the Buddhist tradition, in detailing the chain of dependent origination, begins with ignorance.

7. My translation.

8. My translation.

9. I have treated this matter in detail in chapter 2 of *The Advaita Worldview.*

10. Sin (*pāpa*) refers here to an action generating a unpleasant result for the performer; it is an action causing suffering.

11. Translation by Ganganatha Jha (modified).

12. A comprehensive list of these virtues is offered in Bhagavadgītā 13:7–11.

Chapter 5: Liberation from Patriarchy

1. All references are taken from Swami Vivekananda, *The Complete Works of Swami Vivekananda* (abbreviated CW), 8 vols., Mayavati Memorial Edition (Calcutta: Advaita Ashrama,1964–1971). Volume and page numbers are indicated after the letters CW.

2. In recent years, the Hindu Dharma Acharya Sabha, founded in 2002, has been making an effort to speak with a common voice on matters of concern to the Hindu community.

3. Some of the material in this discussion appeared first in a chapter on Hinduism that I contributed to John C. Raines and Daniel C. Maguire, eds., *What Men Owe to Women: Men's Voices from World Religions* (Albany: State University of New York Press, 2001), 17–40.

4. The caste (*varṇa*) system is a hierarchical ordering of society into four occupational groups. At the apex of the social order are the *brahmins* (priests and scholars), followed by the *kṣatriyas* (rulers and warriors), *vaiśyas* (merchants and traders), and *śūdras* (laborers and servants of the first three groups). Those who do not belong to one of these four groups constitute the outcastes or untouchables. They are considered ritually impure and do not enjoy the rights and privileges of the higher castes. In practice, the four main groups are divided into many subgroups that are referred to as *jātīs*.

5. Katherine K. Young, "Women In Hinduism," in Arvind Sharma, ed., *Today's Woman in World Religions* (Albany: State University of New York Press, 1994), 115.

6. Swami Ramsukhdas, *How to Lead a Household Life* (Gorakhhpur: Gita Press, 1994), 56.

7. G. Buhler, trans., *The Laws of Manu* (Oxford: Oxford University Press, 1886), 5:147–149; 154–156.

8. Buhler, *The Laws of Manu*, 3:55–57.

9. See Vasudha Narayanan, "Hindu Perceptions of Auspiciousness and Sexuality," in *Women, Religion and Sexuality* (Philadelphia: Trinity Press International, 1991), 64–92.

10. Klaus K. Klostermaier, *A Survey of Hinduism* (Albany: State University of New York Press, 1994), 89.

11. *Śrī Rāmacaritamānasa*. trans. R. C. Prasad (Delhi: Motilal Banarsidass, 1991), 270.

12. Ibid., 506.

13. Ibid., 354.

14. Swami Ramsukhdas, *How to Lead a Household Life,* 50.

15. Rāmacaritamānasa, *Ayodhyākāṇḍa*, 468

16. The story of Sāvitrī is told in the *Mahābhārata*. Sāvitrī decided to marry Satyavān, although he was destined to live only one more year. On the day appointed for his death, she followed him to his place of work and stayed at his side. When the deity of death, Yama, came to claim Saytavān, Sāvitrī refused to let her husband go alone and followed him to the realm of the departed. To dissuade Sāvitrī, Yama offered to fulfill any of her wishes except the return of her husband to the world of the living. He quickly consented to her first two wishes. Her third wish was for many sons. Yama readily granted it, but Sāvitrī kept following him. When he told her to return, she reminded him that a widow could not remarry. Yama had no choice but to return Satyavān. For a retelling of this story, see Sister Nivedita, *Cradle Tales of Hinduism* (Calcutta: Advaita Ashrama, 1975).

17. Sakuntala Narasimhan, "India: From Sati to Sex Determination Tests," in Miranda Davies, ed., *Women and Violence* (London: Zed Books Ltd., 1994), 45–50.

18. Narayanan, "Hindu Perceptions of Auspiciousness and Sexuality," 85.

19. A. S. Altekar, *The Position of Women in Hindu Civilization* (Delhi: Motilal Banarsidass, 1938), 71.

20. S. Cromwell Crawford, *Dilemmas of Life and Death* (Albany: State University of New York Press, 1995), 35.

21. *Hinduism Today*, November 1994.

22. "Indian Dowry Deaths on the Rise," *The Telegraph*, February 27, 2012, accessed September 17, 2012, http://www.telegraph.co.uk/news/worldnews/asia/india/9108642/Indian-dowry-deaths-on-the-rise.html.

23. See Elisabeth Bumiller, *May You Be the Mother of a Hundred Sons* (Delhi: Penguin Books, 1990), 48–49.

24. Narasimhan, "India: From Sati to Sex Determination Tests," 51.

25. "India Abortions of Girls on the Rise: Study," *Huffington Post*, May 24, 2011, accessed September 17, 2012, http://www.huffingtonpost.com/2011/05/24/india-abortions-of-girls-_n_866067.html. See also Anita Raj, "Sex-Selected Abortion in India," *The Lancet* 378, no. 9798 (2011): 1217–1218.

26. Vasudha Narayanan, "One Tree Is Equal to Ten Sons: Hindu Responses to the Problems of Ecology, Population, and Consumption," *Journal of the American Academy of Religion* 65, no. 2 (1997): 314.

27. See Buhler, *The Laws of Manu*, 9:138.

28. Narayanan, *Hindu Perceptions of Auspiciousness and Sexuality*, 85–88.

29. See Buhler, *Laws of Manu*, 9:18.

30. See David R. Kinsley, *Hinduism, A Cultural Perspective* (Upper Saddle River, NJ: Prentice Hall, 1993), 164.

31. From V. L. Manjul, "Women Priestesses," *Hinduism Today*, January 1997, https://www.hinduismtoday.com/modules/smartsection/item.php?itemid=4774.

32. Translation by Swami Dayananda Saraswati. The Hindu view of God is not a simple polytheism that affirms a multiplicity of independent deities. Hinduism affirms the oneness of God while maintaining a multiplicity of God-forms and figures, both male and female. Hindus enjoy the freedom to choose a particular God-form as the focus of their religious life. Ultimately, the divine transcends any form and name attributed by human beings.

33. Translation by Swami Dayananda Saraswati. See also Īśa Upaniṣad 6–7.

34. Translation by Patrick Olivelle.

35. Arthur Osborne, *Ramana Maharshi and the Path of Self Knowledge* (York Beach, ME: Samuel Weiser, 1970), 79.

36. Rāmacaritamānasa, *Bālakāṇḍa*, 8–9.

37. Ibid., 719.

38. Mahatma Gandhi, *All Men Are Brothers* (New York: Columbia University Press, 1958), 89.

39. For some statistics in the Indian context, see Narayanan, "One Tree Is Equal to Ten Sons," 312–316.

40. See "Map of Literacy Rate in India," Maps of India, accessed September 17, 2012, http://www.mapsofindia.com/census2011/literacy-rate.html. Accessed September 17, 2012.

41. See Altekar, *The Position of Women in Hindu Civilization*, 3.

42. See Ellison Banks Findly, "Gārgī at the King's Court: Women and Philosophic Innovation in Ancient India," in *Women, Religion and Social* Change, ed. Yvonne Yazbeck Haddad, and Ellison Banks Findly (Albany: State University of New York Press, 1985), 37–58.

43. Katherine K. Young, "Hinduism," in *Women in World Religions*, ed. Arvind Sharma (Albany: State University of New York Press, 1987), 62.

44. Swami Ramsukhdas, *How to Lead a Household Life*, 55.

45. Gandhi, *All Men Are Brothers*, 161.

46. CW 7, 214. Women, argued Vivekananda, needed the freedom to determine their own destinities.

47. See Mary Daly, *Beyond God the Father* (Boston: Beacon Press, 1973).

48. See Buhler, *The Laws of Manu*, 2:145.

49. Julius Lipner, *Hindus: Their Religious Beliefs and Practices* (London: Routledge, 1994), 75.

50. Katherine Young, "Hinduism," 71–72.

51. BGBh 18:66.

52. David Loy, "The Religion of the Market," *Journal of the American Academy of Religion* 65, no. 2 (1997): 286.

Chapter 6: Liberation from Homophobia

1. For a summary of the controversy generated by *Fire*, see newspaper articles at www.sawnet.org/news/fire.html, Accessed September 24, 2012.

2. See Amara Das Wilhelm, *Tṛitīya-Prakṛti: People of the Third Sex* (Philadelphia: Xlibris, 2003), 33. Some of this material appeared first in a chapter on Hinduism in Marvin M. Ellison and Judith Plaskow, eds., *Heterosexism in Contemporary World Religion* (Cleveland: Pilgrim Press, 2007), 201–224.

3. For a life of Swami Chinmayananda, see Nancy Patchen, *The Journey of a Master: Swami Chinmayananda, the Man, the Path, the Teaching* (Bombay: Central Chinmaya Mission Trust, 1989).

4. Arvind Kumar, "Many Branches on One Tree: Reflections on Vedanta, Homosexuality and Swami Chinmayananda," *Trikone Magazine* (July 1996), 6.

5. Ibid., 7.

6. Nawal K. Prinja, ed., *Explaining Hindu Dharma: A Guide for Teachers*, 2nd ed. (Surrey: Vishwa Hindu Parishad, 2001), 169.

7. Examples of this classification offered by Wilhelm include Buhler, *The Laws of Manu* (3.49); and the *Śrīmad Bhāgavatam* (4.17.26, 4.28.61, 8.3.24). The *Śrīmad Bhāgavatam* (ca. 800–900) is attributed to the poet-compiler Vyāsa and focuses on the life of Krishna, revered by many Hindus as an incarnation (*avatāra*) of God. See Wilhelm, *Tṛitīya Prakrti*, n. 4, 178.

8. See Leonard Zwilling and Michael J. Sweet, "'Like a City Ablaze': The Third Sex and the Creation of Sexuality in Jain Religious Literature," *Journal of the History of Sexuality* 6, no. 3 (1996): 359–384. These authors suggest that the three-sex model originated in the speculation of Sanskrit grammarians who sought to find a connection between

grammatical genders (male, female, and neuter) and human gender. See also Leonard Zwilling and Michael J. Sweet, "In Search of Napuṁsaka," *Trikone Magazine* (July 1996), 14.

9. The Kāmasūtra (ca. 400 CE) is attributed to Vātsyayana. While not an authoritative scripture, it gives us an important glimpse into sexuality in ancient India. The word *kāma* means "pleasure" and includes both sensual and aesthetic enjoyment. It is one of the four legitimate goals of Hindu life. The other three are *artha* (wealth), *dharma* (virtue), and *mokṣa* (liberation). Vātsyayana focuses primarily on sexual relationships and defines *kāma* as "the mental inclination toward the pleasures of touch, sight, taste, and smell, to the extent that the practitioner derives satisfaction from it." See *The Complete Kama Sutra*, trans. Alan Danielou (Rochester: Park: Street Press, 1994), 2.9.1, 183, and 1.2.11, 28–29. Hinduism emphasizes that the pursuit of wealth and pleasure is subject to the norms of virtue (*dharma*).

10. See Monier Monier-Williams, *A Sanskrit-English Dictionary* (Oxford: Oxford University Press, 1974), 654.

11. This interpretation of the meaning of *prakṛti* is not meant to suggest that all aspects of sexuality are biologically determined. Today, we understand much more clearly the significance of socialization in the shaping of sexual identity and roles. Wilhelm sees a further significance in the use of the term, *prakṛti*. "Generally," he writes, "the word "sex" refers to biological sex and "gender" to psychological behavior and identity. The term *prakṛti* or nature, however, implies both aspects together as one intricately woven and cohesive unit. . . ." See Wilhelm, *Tṛtīya Prakṛti*, 4.

12. The Sanskrit term, *napuṁsaka* (lit. not male), widely used for a homosexual, reflects the patriarchal bias of Hindu society and its emphasis on procreation. Male identity was synonymous with the ability to procreate. Other terms include *ṣaṇḍa* (half-male, half-female) and *klība* (non-reproductive). These terms are commonly translated as "eunuch," but it must be noted that castration was rare in ancient India and never recommended for persons of the third sex. See Arvind Sharma, "Homosexuality and Hinduism," in *Homosexuality and World Religions*, ed. Arlene Swidler (Valley Forge: Trinity Press International, 1993), 48. In *Tṛtīya-Prakṛti*, Wilhelm argues that the practice of castration became popular with the advent of Islam into India in the eleventh century (49–51). As noted by Sweet and Zwilling, "[c]astration, either of men or of animals, was regarded with disapproval and at times legally forbidden in Indian tradition prior to Muslim rule. Therefore the use of "eunuch" as an equivalent translation for terms found in classical texts denoting individuals who are not normative in their sexual or gender-role behavior is rarely appropriate." See Michael Sweet and Leonard Zwilling, "The First Medi-

calization: The Taxonomy and Etiology of Queerness in Classical Indian Medicine, *Journal of the History of Sexuality* 3, no. 4 (April 1993): 590–607.

13. The most important of these are the manuals of Cāraka (Cārakasaṁhitā) and Suśruta (Suśrutasaṁhitā). Both are dated around the second century CE. See Priyavrat Sharma, ed. and trans., *Cārakasaṁhitā*, 3 vols. (Varanasi: Chaukambha Orientalia, 1981); and P. Ray, H. Gupta, and M. Roy, eds., *Suśrutasaṁhitā: A Scientific Synopsis* (New Delhi: Indian National Science Academy, 1980).

14. Sweet and Zwilling, "The First Medicalization: The Taxonomy and Etiology of Queerness in Classical Indian Medicine," 604.

15. Ibid., 606. Sweet and Zwilling compare the Indian approach with that of Europe and the United States, where efforts were made, with medical support, to treat and confine homosexuals.

16. The Mahābhārata (ca. 400 BCE–400 CE) consists of 100,000 verses and is popularly referred to as the fifth Veda. Within it occurs the Bhagavadgītā (Song of the Lord), a dialogue between Krishna (*avatāra*) and Arjuna. The Bhagavadgītā is one of the most popular scriptures of Hinduism and is regarded as a philosophical pillar of the Hindu tradition.

17. J. A. B. van Buitenen, trans. and ed., *The Mahābhārata* (Chicago: University of Chicago Press, 1978), 4:40–41.

18. Ibid., 41.

19. For other summaries of this story, see Devadutt Pattanaik, *The Man Who Was a Woman* (New York: Harrington Park Press, 2002), 95–96; and Wilhelm, *Tṛitīya-Prakriti*, 22–23.

20. It is very important to note that the law codes in the Hindu tradition fall under the classification of *smṛti* texts. These are distinguished from revealed texts, referred to as *śruti*. *Smṛti* texts are secondary in authority to *śruti* texts and are explicitly understood to reflect the views of a particular human author and the times when the author lived. The four Vedas are the paramount examples of *śruti* texts in Hinduism, while the law code of Manu is an example of a *smṛti* text.

21. See Buhler, *The Laws of Manu*, 466. Recent translators have shed such prejudices and are more faithful to the original text. See, for example, Wendy Doniger and Brian K. Smith, trans., *The Laws of Manu* (London: Penguin Books, 1991), 268. Sharma, "Homosexuality and Hinduism," offers a comment on this issue of translation. Alain Daniélou, *The Complete Kāma Sūtra*, points out that the Sanskrit term for lesbians, *svairīi* (lit. independent women), becomes "corrupt women" (6).

22. Twice-born refers to the male members of the first three castes—*brahmins*, *kṣatriyas*, and *vaiśyas*. A twice-born person alone is entitled to the study of the Vedas through the sacrament of being invested with the sacred thread.

23. Wilhelm claims that there are no verses in the law books that forbid sexual relations between people of the third sex. See *Tṛitīya Prakṛti,* 17–18.

24. The translation is by Doniger and Smith. Buhler again uses the expression "unnatural offence with a male."

25. Sharma, "Hinduism and Homosexuality," 54. Moreover, it also is not clear if this verse is referring to third sex persons or heterosexual men who engage in homosexual behavior.

26. Leonard Zwilling and Michael J. Sweet, "In Search of the Napuṁsaka," *Trikone Magazine* (July 1996): 15. For the severity of punishments for certain kinds of heterosexual offenses, see Manu (8:359–368). Manu (8:369–370) also stipulates harsher punishment for lesbian sexual relations. We may account for this by reference to the influence of patriarchy and greater concern in traditional Hindu society for feminine virginity.

27. See Wilhelm, *Tṛitīya Prakṛiti,* 18–19.

28. As already noted, it is not clear if the verses apply to heterosexual persons who engage in homosexual behavior or if these are applicable to third sex persons.

29. My translation.

30. See, for example, Bhagavadgītā 6:29–32.

31. See Bhagavadgītā 17:1 and Taittirīya Upaniṣad 2.7 and 2.9.

32. Ervin Staub, *The Roots of Evil: The Origins of Genocide and Other Group Violence* (Cambridge: Cambridge University Press, 1989), 48.

33. This is not to deny that there are patriarchal Hindu traditions that suggest that being a woman is disadvantageous for the attainment of liberation. My contention is that when one looks at the Hindu understanding of the fundamental human problem and the nature of liberation, sexual identity cannot be an impediment.

34. In the Bhagavadgītā (7:11), for example, Krishna identifies himself with pleasure that is not in opposition to virtue.

35. See, for example, Bṛhadāraṇyaka Upaniṣad, 6.2.9–16; 6.4.2–3; Chāndogya Upaniṣad 2.13.1–2.

36. My translation.

37. See F. S. Growse, trans., *The Rāmāyaṇa of Tulsi Das* (Delhi: Interprint, 1983), *Doha* 87, 541.

38. My translation. I translate *napuṁsaka* as "third sex person." Some translators render it as "eunuch," which, for reasons already mentioned, is inappropriate. One translator speaks of "one lacking the characteristics of both (man and woman)."

39. *The Rāmāyaṇa of Tulsi Das,* 90. Growse translation (amended).

40. Pattanaik, *The Man Who Was a Woman,* 8.

41. See Anantanand Rambachan, "The Hindu Way of Death," in *Handbook of Death and Dying*, 2 vols., ed. Clifton D. Bryant (Thousand Oaks: Sage Publications, 2003), 2:647.

42. See S. Cromwell Crawford, *Dilemmas of Life and Death* (Albany: State University of New York Press, 1995), 196.

43. Cited in Wilhelm, *Tṛitīya Prakṛti*, 20. It is possible that this text may be responding to the social practice of forced marriages, but it is difficult to make sound historical judgments based on this textual evidence.

44. See Pattanaik, *The Man Who Was a Woman*, 10; Daniélou, *The Complete Kāma Sūtra*, 10–11; and Wilhelm, *Tṛitīya Prakṛti*, 47–48.

45. This section of the Indian penal code was overturned on July 2, 2009, by the Delhi High Court. Hindu, Muslim and Christian leaders protested the decision. See "Delhi HC Okays Consensual Sex between Gays," *IBN Live*, accessed September 24, 2012, http://ibnlive.in.com/news/delhi-high-court-legalises-consensual-gay-sex/96148-3.html. On December 3, 2013, India's Supreme Court overturned this decision, making sex between consenting homosexual adults illegal and punishable by imprisonment.

46. See Daniélou, *The Complete Kāma Sūtra*, 10.

47. Sweet and Zwilling, "The First Medicalization," 601.

48. Nawal K. Prinja, *Hindu Dharma*, 169.

49. My translation.

Chapter 7: Liberation from Anthropocentrism

1. See, for example, Rosemary Reuther Radford, *New Woman, New Earth: Sexist Ideologies and Human Liberation* (New York: Seabury, 1975).

2. See David Kinsley, *Ecology and Religion* (Upper Saddle River, NJ: Prentice Hall, 1995).

3. See, for example, S. Cromwell Crawford, *Dilemmas of Life and Death: Hindu Ethics in a North American Context* (Albany: State University of New York Press, 1995); Eliot Deutsch, "Vedanta and Ecology," *Indian Philosophical Annual* 7 (1970): 79–88.

4. Crawford, *Dilemmas of Life and Death*, 177.

5. David Haberman, *Journey through the Twelve Forests: An Encounter with Krishna* (New York: Oxford University Press, 1994), 126.

6. Eliot Deutsch, *Advaita Vedanta: A Philosophical Reconstruction* (Honolulu: University of Hawaii Press, 1985), 28.

7. T. M. P. Mahadevan, *Outlines of Hinduism* (Bombay: Chetana Limited, 1977), 28.

8. Swami Nirvedananda, *Hinduism at a Glance* (Calcutta: Ramakrishna Mission, 1979), 172.

9. I have addressed this issue in *The Advaita Worldview.*

10. See S. Dasgupta, *A History of Indian Philosophy* (Delhi: Motilal Banarsidass, 1975), I:442. This is the most widely advocated interpretation of Śaṅkara. For similar views, see P. Deussen, *System of the Vedanta* (Delhi: Oriental Reprint, 1979), 459; M. Hiriyanna, *Essentials of Indian Philosophy* (London: Unwin Paperbacks, 1978), 158; and Swami Prabhavananda, *The Spiritual Heritage of India* (Hollywood: Vedanta Press, 1979), 284. Prabhavananda contends that with knowledge of *brahman,* the world is not experienced and ceases to exist.

11. *The Tales and Parables of Sri Ramakrishna* (Madras: Sri Ramakrishna Math, 1980), 52–54.

12. See CUBh 5.10.8, 272.

13. Translation by Swami Gambhirananda

14. See BSBh 3.2.21, 620.

15. See BSBh 2.2.28, 420.

16. My translation.

17. Translation by William Sargeant (modified).

18. My translation.

19. Translation by Swami Dayananda Saraswati (modified).

20. See Arthur Osborne, *Ramana Maharshi and the Path of Self Knowledge,* chapter 11.

21. Rita Gross, "Buddhist Resources for Issues of Population, Consumption and the Environment," in *Population, Consumption and the Environment,* ed. Harold Coward (Albany: State University of New York Press 1995), 159.

22. See Meera Nanda, *The Wrongs of the Religious Right: Reflections on Science, Secularism and Hindutva* (New Delhi: Three Essays Collective, 2005), 88.

Chapter 8: Liberation from Childism

1. Hindus constitute more than 80 percent of India's population of 1 billion.

2. "Over 53% Children Face Sexual Abuse: Survey." *The Times of India,* April 10, 2007, accessed September 19, 2012, http://timesofindia.indiatimes.com/NEWS/India/Over_53_children_face_sexual_abuse_Survey/articleshow/1881344.cms.

3. The Indian journalist Nita Bhalla recently highlighted this issue. See "Rise in India's Female Feticide May Spark Crisis," Reuters, August 31, 2007, accessed September 19, 2012, www.reuters.com/article/healthNews/idUSDEL22936620070831?feedType=RSS&feedName=healthNews.

4. See Amelia Gentleman, "In India, a Terrible Place to Be Born a Girl," *International Herald and Tribune*, Asia-Pacific, November 30, 2007.

5. Because *brahman* is unlimited by space, *brahman* does not literally enter into anything. The language of entry is meant to signify that everything exists and is created in *brahman*. It is another way of emphasizing that *brahman* is all pervasive.

6. A. C. Bose, *Hymns from the Vedas* (Bombay: Asia Publishing House, 1966), 301.

7. BGBh 6:32, 199–200.

8. See S. Cromwell Crawford, *Dilemmas of Life and Death* (Albany: State University of New York Press, 1995), 11–36.

9. I am not limiting the meaning of parenthood to biological children. This goal also may be satisfied through adoption.

10. See Laurie Patton, "Hindu Rituals on Behalf of Women: Notes on First Principles," in *Women and Goddess in Hinduism: Reinterpretations and Re-envisionings*, ed. Tracy Pintchman and Rita D. Sherma (New York: Palgrave Macmillan, 2011), 163.

11. See Raj Bali Pandey, *Hindu Saṁskāras* (Delhi: Motilal Banarsidass, 1969).

12. See Prashant Bharadwaj and Leah K. Lakdawala, "Discrimination Begins in the Womb: Evidence of Sex Selective Prenatal Investments, "*Journal of Human Resources* 48, no. 1 (2013): 71–113.

13. Adarsh Sharma and Shanta Gopalakrishnan, in *Girl Child in Indian Society*, ed. Mita Bhadra (Jaipur: Rawat Publications, 1999), 24.

14. See *Rāmacaritamānasa*, 705. Rama is identified by Tulasīdāsa with God and presented as a divine incarnation (*avatāra*).

15. Malavika Karlekar, "The Girl Child in India: Does She Have Any Rights," *Canadian Women's Studies* (March 1995): 55–57. Also, see B. D. Miller, *The Endangered Sex: Neglect of Female Children in Rural North India* (New Delhi: Oxford University Press, 1997). For a discussion in South India, see Sabu George, Rajaratnam Abel, and B. D. Miller, "Female Infanticide in Rural South India," in *Economic and Political Weekly* 27, no. 22 (May 1992), 1153–1156.

16. *The Times of India*, January 2008. Patton also points to ancient rituals for couples desirous of girl children. See "Hindu Rituals on Behalf of Women," op. cit., 163.

17. Patton, "Hindu Rituals on Behalf of Women," op. cit., 165.

18. Atharva Veda 19.67.1–8.

19. See "Swami Agnivesh—To Bring Spiritual Values in Politics and Social Responsibility in Religions," Accessed September 19, 2012, www.swami agnivesh.com/bonded.htm.

20. See Bhagavadgītā 10:5, 13:7, 16:2, and 17:14.

Chapter 9: Liberation from Caste

1. I narrated this account in Jennifer Howe Peace, Or N. Rose, and Gregory Mobley, eds., *My Neighbor's Faith* (Maryknoll, NY: Orbis Books, 2012), 154–158.

2. Gandhi referred to the so-called untouchables as *harijans* (children of God). This reminds us that "Dalit" is one of many names used for members of the lower castes.

3. "Dalit Dares Puja Ban, Shot Dead in Temple," *The Telegraph*, October 8, 2008, accessed November 27, 2012, http://ambedkar.blogspot.com/2003/10/dalit-dares-puja-ban-shot-dead-in.html.

4. See Prabhati Mukherjee, *Beyond the Four Varṇas: The Untouchables in India* (Shimla: Indian Institute of Advanced Study, 1988), 19–20. For a critique of the Aryan Invasion theory, see Klaus K. Klostermaier, *Hinduism: A Short History* (Oxford: Oneworld Publications, 2000), chapter 3.

5. Ibid., Chapter 2.

6. Omprakash Valmiki, *Joothan*, trans. Arun Prabha Mukherjee (New York: Columbia University Press, 2003), 2.

7. Wilhelm Halbfass, *India and Europe: An Essay in Understanding* (Albany: State University of New York Press), 126–127.

8. See Julius Lipner, *Hindus: Their Religious Beliefs and Practices*, 116–117.

9. Keshab Poudel, "One World South Asia," November 12, 2003.

10. Omprakash Valmiki, *Joothan*, 3.

11. Ibid., 10.

12. Ibid., 154

13. Kancha Ilaiah, *Why I Am Not a Hindu* (Delhi: Samya, 1996), 1.

14. Ibid., 1.

15. Louis Fischer, *The Essential Gandhi* (New York: Vintage Books, 1962), 252.

16. Mahatma Gandhi, *All Men Are Brothers*, 89.

17. *Manīṣāpañcakam*, translated by S. N. Sastri, accessed November 4, 2012, http://www.celextel.org/adisankara/manishapanchakam.html. This poem of five verses is traditionally attributed to Śaṅkara; its composition is believed to be occasioned by Śaṅkara's encounter with the untouchable.

18. Ibid., Introduction.

19. See Anantanand Rambachan, *The Advaita Worldview*, 58.

20. Verse 1. Italics mine.

21. *The Bhagavadgītā*, translation and commentary by Swami Chidbhavananda (Tamil Nadu: Sri Ramakrishna Tapovanam, 1982).

22. *The Holy Geeta*, commentary by Swami Chinmayananda (Bombay: Central Chinmaya Mission Trust, n.d.).

23. *Śrīmadbhagavadgītā*, commentary by Jayadayal Goyandaka (Gorakhpur: Gita Press, 2002).

24. *Śrīmad Bhagavadgītā*, commentary by Swami Ramsukhdas, 2 vols. (Gorakhpur: Gita Press, 2001).

25. See Troy Wilson Organ, *The Hindu Quest for the Perfection of Man* (Athens: Ohio University Press, 1970), 215–221.

Bibliography

Primary Sources in English Translation

Bhagavadgītā with the Commentary of Śaṅkarācārya. Translated by Alladi Mahadeva Sastry. Madras: Samata Books, 1977.

Bhagavadgītā. Translated by Winthrop Sargeant. Albany: State University of New York Press, 1984.

Bhagavadgītā. Translated by Swami Dayananda Saraswati. Chennai: Arsha Vidya Centre, 2007.

Brahmasūtra Bhaṣya of Śaṅkarācārya. Translated by Swami Gambhirananda. Calcutta: Advaita Ashrama, 1977.

Bṛhadāraṇyaka Upaniṣad with the Commentary of Śaṅkarācārya. Translated by Swami Madhavananda. Calcutta: Advaita Ashrama, 1975.

Chāndogya Upaniṣad with the Commentary of Śaṅkara. Translated by Ganganatha Jha. Poona: Oriental Book Agency, 1942.

Chāndogya Upaniṣad. Translated by Swami Swahananda. Madras: Sri Ramakrishna Math, 1975.

Dakśiṇamūrti Stotra of Śaṅkaracārya. 3rd ed. Translated by Alladi Mahadeva Sastry. Madras: Samata Books, 1978.

Eight Upaniṣads with the Commentary of Śaṅkarācārya. Translated by Swami Gambhirananda. 2 vols. *Īśa, Kena, Kaṭha,* and *Taittirīya* in vol. I; *Aitareya, Muṇḍaka, Māṇḍūkya* and *Kārika* and *Praśna* in vol. II. Calcutta: Advaita Ashrama, 1965–1966.

Laws of Manu. Translated by G. Buhler. Oxford: Oxford University Press, 1886.

Śrī Rāmacaritamānasa. Translated by R. C. Prasad. Delhi: Motilal Banarsidass, 1984.

Śvetāśvatara Upaniṣad. Translated by Swami Gambhirananda. Calcutta: Advaita Ashrama, 1986.

The Complete Kāma Sūtra. Translated by Alan Danielou. Rochester: Park Street Press, 1994.

Upadeśasāhasrī of Śaṅkarācarya. Translated by Swami Jagadananda. Madras: Sri Ramakrishna Math, 1984.

Upanishads. Translated by Patrick Olivelle. Oxford: Oxford University Press, 1996.
A Thousand Teachings: The Upadeśasāhasrī of Śaṅkara. Translated by Sengaku Mayeda. Albany: State University of New York Press, 1992.
Vedāntasāra of Sadānanda. Translated by M. Hiriyanna. Poona: Oriental Book Agency, 1962.
Vivekacūdāmaṇi. Translated by Swami Madhavananda. Calcutta: Advaita Ashrama, 1978.

Bibliography (Selected)

Agnivesh, Swami. *Religion, Spirituality and Social Action*. Delhi: Hope Publications, 2003.
Altekar, A. S. *The Position of Women in Hindu Civilization*. Delhi: Motilal Banarsidass, 1938.
Becker, Ernest. *Escape from Evil*. New York: The Free Press, 1975.
Becker, Ernest. *The Denial of Death*. New York: The Free Press, 1973.
Belvalkar, S. K. *Vedānta Philosophy*. Poona: Bilrakunja Publishing House, 1929.
Bhadra, Mita, ed. *Girl Child in Indian Society*. Delhi: Motilal Banarsidass, 1999.
Borg, Marcus. *The Heart of Christianity*. New York: HarperCollins, 2003.
Buch, M. A. *The Philosophy of Śaṁkara*. Baroda: A. G. Widgery, 1921.
Bumiller, Elisabeth. *May You Be the Mother of a Hundred Sons*. Delhi: Penguin Books, 1990.
Chapple, Christopher Key, and Mary Evelyn Tucker, eds. *Hinduism and Ecology*. Cambridge: Harvard University Press, 2000.
Clooney, Francis X. *Comparative Philosophy*. Malden, MA: Wiley-Blackwell, 2010.
Crawford, Cromwell, S. *Dilemmas of Life and Death*. Albany: State University of New York Press, 1995.
Dalai Lama. *Ethics for a New Millennium*. New York: Riverhead Books, 1999.
Daly, Mary. *Beyond God the Father*. Boston: Beacon Press, 1973.
Dasgupta, S. *A History of Indian Philosophy*. 5 vols. Delhi: Motilal Banarsidass, 1975.
Datta. D. M. *Six Ways of Knowing*. London: Allen and Unwin, 1932.
De Smet, R. V. "The Theological Method of Śaṅkara. PhD diss., Gregorian University, 1953.
Deutsch, Eliot. "Vedanta and Ecology." *Indian Philosophical Annual* 7 (1970): 79–88.
Duessen, P. *The System of Vedānta*. Delhi: Oriental Reprint, 1979.

Ferm, D. W. "Third World Liberation Theology: Challenge to World Religions." In *World Religions and Human Liberation*, edited by Dan Cohn-Sherbok. Maryknoll, NY: Orbis Books, 1992.

Fernando, Anthony, and Leonard Swidler. *Buddhism Made Plain*. New York: Orbis Books, 1985.

Findly, Ellison Banks. "Gārgi at the King's Court: Women and Philosophic Innovations in Ancient India." In *Women, Religion and Social Change*, edited by Yvonne Yazbeck and Ellison Banks Findly, 37–58. Albany: State University of New York Press, 1985.

Fischer, Louis. *The Essential Gandhi*. New York: Vintage Books, 1962.

Gandhi, Mahatma. *All Men Are Brothers*. New York: Columbia University Press, 1958.

Gross, Rita. "Buddhist Resources for Issues of Population, Consumption and the Environment." In *Population, Consumption and the Environment*, edited by Harold Coward. Albany: State University of New York Press, 1995.

Halbfass, Wilhelm. *India and Europe: An Essay in Understanding*. Albany: State University of New York Press, 1988.

Hanh, Thich Nhat. *Interbeing: Fourteen Guidelines for Engaged Buddhism*. Berkeley: Parallax Press, 1987.

Hiriyanna, M. *Essentials of Indian Philosophy*. London: Unwin Paperbacks, 1978.

Ilaiah, Kancha. *Why I Am Not a Hindu*. Delhi: Samya, 1996.

Jain, Pankaj. *Dharma and Ecology of Hindu Communities*. Surrey: Ashgate, 2011.

Karlekar, Malavika. "The Girl Child in India: Does She Have Any Rights?" *Canadian Women's Studies* (March 1995): 55–57.

King, Sallie B. *Being Benevolence: Social Ethics of Engaged Buddhism*. Honolulu: University of Hawaii Press, 2006.

Kinsley, David. R. *Hinduism: A Cultural Perspective*. Upper Saddle River, NJ: Prentice Hall, 1993.

Klostermaier, Klaus. K. *A Survey of Hinduism*. Albany: State University of New York Press, 1994.

Knitter, Paul F. *Without Buddha I Could Not Be a Christian*. Oxford: Oneworld Publications, 2009.

Lipner, Julius. *Hindus: Their Religious Beliefs*. London: Routledge, 1994.

Loy, David. "The Religion of the Market." *Journal of the American Academy of Religion* 65, no. 2 (1997): 275–290.

Mahadevan, T. M. P. *Outlines of Hinduism*. Bombay: Chetana Publications, 1977.

Menon, Y. K., and R. F. Allen. *The Pure Principle: An Introduction to the Philosophy of Śaṅkara*. East Lansing: Michigan State University Press, 1960.

Mukherjee, Prabhati. *Beyond the Four Varnas: The Untouchables in India*. Shimla: Indian Institute of Advanced Study, 1988.

Nanda, Meera. *The Wrongs of the Religious Right: Reflections on Science, Secularism and Hindutva*. New Delhi: Three Essays Collective, 2005.

Narasimhan, Sakuntala. "India: From Sati to Sex Determination Tests." In *Women and Violence*, edited by Miranda Davies, 45–50. London: Zed Books, 1994.

Narayanan, Vasudha. "One Tree Is Equal to Ten Sons: Hindu Responses to the Problems of Ecology, Population, and Consumption." *Journal of the American Academy of Religion* 39, no. 2 (1997): 291–332.

Narayanan, Vasudha. "Hindu Perceptions of Auspiciousness and Sexuality." In *Women, Religion and Sexuality*, edited by Jeanne Becher, 64–92. Philadelphia: Trinity Press International, 1991.

Nivedita, Sister. *Cradle Tales of Hinduism*. Calcutta: Advaita Ashrama, 1975.

Omprakash, Valmiki. *Joothan*. Translated by Arun Prabha Mukherjee. New York: Columbia University Press, 2003.

Osborne, Arthur. *Ramana Maharshi and the Path of Self Knowledge*. York Beach, ME: Samuel Weiser, 1970.

Pandey, Raj Bali. *Hindu Saṁskāras*. Delhi: Motilal Banarsidass, 1969.

Patchen, Nancy. *The Journey of a Master: Swami Chinmayananda, the Man, the Path, the Teaching*. Bombay: Central Chinmaya Mission Trust, 1989.

Pattanaik, Devadutt. *The Man Who Was a Woman*. New York: Harrington Park Press, 2002.

Patton, Laurie. "Hindu Rituals on Behalf of Women: Notes on First Principles." In *Women and Goddess in Hinduism: Reinterpretations and Re-Envisionings*, edited by Tracy Pintchman and Rita D. Sherma. New York: Palgrave Macmillan, 2011.

Prabhavananda, Swami. *The Spiritual Heritage of India*. Hollywood: Vedanta Press, 1979.

Prinja, Nawal K, ed. *Explaining Hindu Dharma: A Guide for Teachers*. 2nd ed. Surrey: Vishwa Hindu Parishad, 2001.

Radford, Rosemary Reuther. *New Woman, New Earth: Sexist Ideologies and Human Liberation*. New York: Seabury, 1975.

Radhakrishnan, Sarvepalli. *Indian Philosophy*. 2 vols. Bombay: Blackie and Son Publishers, 1977.

Rambachan, Anantanand. *The Advaita Worldview: God, World and Humanity*. Albany: State University of New York Press, 2006.

Rambachan, Anantanand. *Accomplishing the Accomplished: The Vedas as a Source of Valid Knowledge in Śaṅkara*. Honolulu: University of Hawaii Press, 1991.

Ramsukhdas, Swami. *How to Lead a Household Life*. Gorakhpur: Gita Press, 1994.

Saraswati Dayananda, Swami. *Talks on Who Am I?* Rishikesh: Sri Gangadhareswar Trust, 1984.

Saraswati Dayananda, Swami. *Introduction to Vedānta*. Delhi: Vision Books, 1995.

Saraswati Dayananda, Swami. *Talks and Essays of Swami Dayananda*. Rishikesh: Sri Gangadhareswar Trust, 2004.

Sharma, Arvind. "Homosexuality and Hinduism." In *Homosexuality and World Religions*, edited by Arlene Swidler. Valley Forge: Trinity Press International, 1993.

Smith, Huston. *The Religions of Man*. New York: Harper and Row Publishers, 1965.

Staub, Ervin. *The Roots of Evil: The Origins of Genocide and Other Group Violence*. Cambridge: Cambridge University Press, 1989.

Sweet, Michael J., and Leonard Zwilling. "The First Medicalization: The Taxonomy and Etiology of Queerness in Classical Indian Medicine." *Journal of the History of Sexuality* 3, no. 4 (1993): 590–607.

Venugopal, D. *Pujya Swami Dayananda*. Anaikatti: Arsha Vidya Gurukulam, 2008.

Vivekananda, Swami. *The Complete Works of Swami Vivekananda*. 8 vols. Mayavati Memorial Edition. Calcutta: Advaita Ashrama, 1964–1971.

Walpola, Rahula. *What the Buddha Taught*. New York: Grove Press, 1974.

Wilhelm, Amara Das. *Tṛitīya-Prakṛti: People of the Third Sex*. Philadelphia: Xlibris, 2003.

Young, Katherine K. "Hinduism." In *Women in World Religions*. Albany: State University of New York Press, 1987.

Young, Katherine K. "Women in Hinduism." In *Today's Woman in World Religions*, edited by Arvind Sharma. Albany: State University of New York Press, 1994.

Zwilling, Leonard, and Michael J. Sweet. "Like a City Ablaze: The Third Sex and the Creation of Sexuality in Jain Religious Literature." *Journal of the History of Sexuality* 6, no. 3 (1996): 359–384.

Index

Printed in Great Britain
by Amazon

38022981R00138